D0794085

DATE DUE

Tropes, Parables, Performatives
Essays on Twentieth-Century Literature

Tropes, Parables, Performatives
Essays on Twentieth-Century Literature

J. Hillis Miller

Duke University Press
Durham 1991

Published in 1991 in the United States
by Duke University Press

First published 1991 by
Harvester Wheatsheaf
66 Wood Lane End, Hemel Hempstead
Hertfordshire HP2 4RG
A division of
Simon & Schuster International Group

Printed and bound in Great Britain

Library of Congress Cataloging-in-Publication Data

Miller, J. Hillis (Joseph Hillis), 1928-
Tropes, parables, performatives : essays on twentieth-century
literature / J. Hillis Miller.
p. cm.
Includes index.
ISBN 0-8223-1111-9 (cloth)
1. English literature — 20th century — History and criticism.
2. American literature — 20th century — History and criticism.
I. Title
PR473.M55 1990
820.9 0091 — dc20   90-44886

Contents

Preface

If the preface as a genre is obliged to indicate some fundamental unity in the chapters that follow it, this is not a preface. Most of the essays gathered here are fairly recent, but the earliest goes back to 1952. They are brought together here by the accident that all are on twentieth-century works. Each essay is the result of a specific occasion in time and place, an occasion whose history could be recovered if there were reason to do so. Each essay entered history at a specific moment. Each is the memorial record of a discrete event of reading, not a stage in some predetermined itinerary fulfilling a single "research project." Gathered together they produce a strange topography of isolated local sites, with no clearly marked paths leading from one to the others. You can't get there from here. Each essay in its separation, disparity, or insularity seems for the moment to occupy the whole field of an intermittent but continuously renewed questioning of literature. Each goes as far as it can in that interrogation with its given work or works. The effort begins again from scratch in the next essay with new materials that seem for the moment to stretch out to the whole horizon all around, as if that one poem or story were all there were of literature.

Nevertheless, reviewing these old readings now, in a repetition that is more like new acts of reading than like distant memories of old ones, I can identify some features of the non-totalizable topography of this collection. One is indicated in what I have already said. An irresistible penchant for "close-reading" of individual texts has gone on winning out over any conscious commitment to seeking some pervasive unity of "consciousness" or theme in the whole work of an author or some spurious unity in the spirit of an age. Even the first essay here, though it addresses the whole work of Lawrence, centers on a reading of one story, "The Fox."

Appearances notwithstanding, I do not think this commitment to close reading is "an inheritance from the New Criticism." It springs rather from an initial and persistent fascination with local strangenesses in literary language. This fascination possessed me before I ever heard of the New Criticism, much less of Freud, Lacan, and Abraham and Torok. It was my motivation for turning from physics to literature in about 1946, and it has remained as strong as ever in all the years since. My conviction was then and remains now that it is only by noticing local oddnesses in language and following them as far as asking questions about them will take you that literature can be put to its best use – as a means of transportation or transport toward something glimpsed deep down or at the far horizon of each of those local spaces opened by a given work. The carrying on of this interrogation is another linguistic act – of teaching, writing, or lecturing. This new event of language has its modest chance to enter history on its own when it is published or uttered in public, thereby making the work effective once more, in the altered form of citation and "reading." These may be effective as a means of moving again toward that place behind or beyond all the places, that "center on the horizon"[1] toward which each work in its unique way beckons.

Rereading these essays I have noticed that in responding to the call to let reading carry me as far as it would go, I have kept coming back again and again, sometimes after long intervals, to the same authors: to Kafka, Stevens, Williams, and Conrad, especially to Hardy. Four of Hardy's poems are read here, after an initial general essay, in five pieces that go from 1967 to 1989. And those five essays are supplementary to a whole book on Hardy, as well as to two chapters on his novels in another book, and to a chapter on his poetry in yet another.[2] This compulsion to return to different works by the same author, or even, in the case of the recent essay here on Conrad's *Heart of Darkness*, to a work already read in an earlier essay,[3] seems driven by the categorical imperative that is the motive force of what I call the "ethics of reading." Such a demand to read testifies to two features of "close reading" as I have lived it as a vocation:

1. Close reading is the only way to get into any proximity to that "other" to which the works of any author seem to give access. Hardy's poems, for example, for me at least, yield their gnarled sweetness only when they are questioned one by one in detail. Each question leads to others, one behind the others, like those reflections of his ancestors the speaker in Hardy's "The Pedigree" sees in the mirror, "dwindling backward each past each . . . / Generation and generation of my mien, and build, and brow." The impossible ideal book on Hardy's poetry would consist of separate readings of all his lyrics, nearly a thousand in all.

2. The effort of reading must be constantly renewed because no one reading suffices. None ever gets the reader where he or she would like to go. Each new reading discounts and disqualifies all that preceded, but each fails to satisfy. As Stevens puts it, the search for what suffices never reaches its goal. "It can never be satisfied, the mind, never."[4] Neither poet nor critic ever reaches that palm at the end of the mind Stevens' last poem glimpses. The work of reading must always start again from the

beginning, even in a rereading of a work already read. Close reading reaches its limit in the constantly renewed experience of its failure to take you where you think you want to go and ought to go.

Rereading these essays I can see now that in spite of their insularity and difference, as each follows its own trajectory as far as it can, they are from early to late guided by a threefold presupposition about the right questions to ask. The formulation of these in their relation is only implicit at first but emerges with increasing clarity. This guiding intuition about literature may be framed by the three words I have used in my title: "trope," "parable," "performative."

Throughout all the essays there is attention to the tropological dimension of literary language, to the way figures of speech turn aside the telling of a story or the presentation of a lyrical theme. This was what initially fascinated me about literature, the way it does not straightforwardly say what it means, but always says it in terms of some other thing, often by way of what seem wildly ungrounded analogies.

The exploration of this turning gradually leads to the recognition that all works of literature are parabolic, "thrown beside" their real meaning. They tell one story but call forth something else. Two of the essays here are explicitly about parable, but other essays too recognize that the tropological dimension of literature is not local and intermittent, but pervasive. Each work is one long trope: an ironic catachresis invoking by indirection "something" that can be named in no literal way. "Parable" is one name for this large-scale indirection characteristic of literary language, indeed of language generally.

All parables, finally, are essentially performative, though I would initially have been able to identify this performative aspect only in terms of what Kenneth Burke calls "symbolic action." Parables do not merely name the "something" they point to by indirection or merely give the reader knowledge of it. They use words to try to make something happen in relation to the "other" that resonates in the work. They want to get the reader from here to there. They want to make the reader cross over into the "something" and dwell there. But the site to which parable would take the reader is something always other than itself, hence that experience of perpetual dissatisfaction. As Kafka puts this, "There is a goal but no way. What we call the way is only wandering." Nevertheless, this tropological, parabolic, performative dimension enables writing and reading to enter history and be effective there, for better or for worse. Each essay in this book attempts to formulate in its own terms what it is in a given case the reader might performatively enter by way of parabolic trope.

To think of literature as performative parable raises the question of whether a reading, as it works by citation and commentary, only describes the performative action of the work or whether the performative power of literature is carried over into criticism. To say, "The minister then says, 'I now pronounce you man and wife,'" does not marry anybody. And yet it may be that the performative aspect of literary works is effective in the absence of any freely willing "I," and without the dependence on proper context demanded by the classical theory of performatives. If so, citation and commentary in the work of reading may be another performative event. Much hangs on this possibility, not least the question of what function teaching literature has.

As the last essays here show, the figure of prosopopoeia is a gathering point for the performative working of parable. My three title motifs converge on prosopopoeia. The enigmatic and elusive "other" literature would reach is most often named as a face. Parable, like allegory, always embodies its riddling wisdom in some story that starts with an act of personification. To say that prosopopoeia is a speech act giving a name, a face, and a voice to the absent, the inanimate, or the dead is to confront an ultimate question. Is it the face of a pre-existent other we encounter through the transport of literature or is that face only invoked by the performative spell of the work, charmed into phantasmal existence by words? It seems the face is already there, but how would one know, for sure?

Parts of three essays here were incorporated in revised form in later books. I include them because each has its separate integrity of argumentation and analysis.

J. Hillis Miller
Irvine, California
January 27, 1990

Notes

1. Wallace Stevens, "A Primitive Like an Orb," l. 87.
2. In *Thomas Hardy: Distance and Desire* (1970), *Fiction and Repetition* (1982), and *The Linguistic Moment* (1985), respectively.
3. In *The Disappearance of God* (1963).
4. "The Well Dressed Man with a Beard," l. 17.

Acknowledgements

I am grateful to the publishers and editors for permission to reprint the following essays:

"D. H. Lawrence: The Fox and the Perspective Glass," *The Harvard Advocate*, CXXXVII (December 1952).

"Franz Kafka and the Metaphysics of Alienation," *The Tragic Vision and the Christian Faith*, N. A. Scott, Jr., ed. (Association Press, 1957).

"Wallace Stevens' Poetry of Being," *ELH*, XXXI (March 1964). Reprinted in *The Act of the Mind: Essays on the Poetry of Wallace Stevens*, Roy Harvey Pearce and J. Hillis Miller, eds (Baltimore, Md: Johns Hopkins Press, 1965). This essay was later incorporated in revised form as parts of the chapter on Stevens in *Poets of Reality* (Cambridge, Mass.: Harvard University Press, 1965).

"Introduction," *William Carlos Williams: A Collection of Critical Essays, Twentieth Century Views* series, J. Hillis Miller, ed. (Englewood Cliffs, NJ: Prentice-Hall, 1966). Material from this essay was later incorporated in revised form in the chapter on Williams in *The Linguistic Moment: From Wordsworth to Stevens*. Copyright © 1985 by Princeton University Press.

"Thomas Hardy: A Sketch for a Portrait," *De Ronsard à Breton: Hommages à Marcel Raymond* (Paris: Corti, 1967).

"Williams *Spring and All* and the Progress of Poetry." Reprinted by permission of *Dædalus*, Journal of the American Academy of Arts and Sciences, "Theory in Humanistic Studies." Spring 1970, Vol. 9, No. 2, Cambridge, Massachusetts. The part of this essay on *Spring and All* was later incorporated, in substantially revised form, in the chapter on Williams in *The Linguistic Moment: From Wordsworth to Stevens*. © 1985 by Princeton University Press.

"History as Repetition in Thomas Hardy's Poetry: The Example of 'Wessex Heights,'" *Victorian Poetry, Stratford-upon-Avon Studies*, M. Bradbury and D. Palmer, eds (England: Edward Arnold, 1972).

"Parable and Performative in the Gospels and in Modern Literature," *Humanizing America's Iconic Book*, Gene M. Tucker and Douglas A. Knight, eds (Chico, CA: Scholar's Press, 1982).

"Mr. Carmichael and Lily Briscoe: The Rhythm of Creativity in *To the*

Lighthouse," *Modernism Reconsidered,* Robert Kiely, ed. (Cambridge, Mass: Harvard University Press, 1983).

"Thomas Hardy, Jacques Derrida, and the 'Dislocation of Souls,'" *Taking Chances: Derrida, Psychoanalysis and Literature,* Joseph H. Smith and William Kerrigan, eds (Baltimore & London: The Johns Hopkins University Press, 1984). Copyright is held by the Forum on Psychiatry and the Humanities.

"Heart of Darkness Revisited," *Conrad Revisited: Essays for the Eighties,* Ross C. Murfin, ed. (University, Alabama: University of Alabama Press, 1985).

"Topography and Tropography in Thomas Hardy's *In Front of the Landscape,"* *Identity of the Literary Text,* Mario J. Valdés and Owen Miller, eds (Toronto, Buffalo, London: University of Toronto Press, 1985).

"Impossible Metaphor: Stevens's 'The Red Fern' as Example," *The Lesson of Paul de Man,* Peter Brooks, Shoshana Felman, and J. Hillis Miller, eds, *Yale French Studies,* 69 (1985).

"When Is a Primitive Like an Orb?," *Textual Analysis: Some Readers Reading,* Mary Ann Caws, ed. (New York: MLA, 1986).

"Prosopopoeia in Hardy and Stevens," *Alternative Hardy,* Lance St John Butler, ed. (London: Macmillan Press, 1989, USA: St. Martin's Press Inc., 1989).

"Not Ideas About the Thing but the Thing Itself," Copyright 1954 by Wallace Stevens. Reprinted from *The Collected Poems of Wallace Stevens,* by permission of Alfred A. Knopf Inc.

"The Red Fern" Copyright 1947 by Wallace Stevens. Reprinted from *The Collected Poems of Wallace Stevens,* by permission of Alfred A. Knopf Inc.

Thomas Hardy, "The Pedigree." Reprinted from *The Complete Poems* (London: Macmillan, 1976).

William Carlos Williams: "The Young Sycamore," *Collected Poems Volume I 1909–1939.* Copyright 1938 by New Directions Publishing Corporation. Reprinted by permission of New Directions Publishing Corporation (US and Canada). Reprinted by permission of Carcanet Press Ltd (UK and Commonwealth).

1

D. H. Lawrence

The Fox and the perspective glass

I

D. H. Lawrence has been dead now for over twenty years, but various impediments, his reputation for pornography and the unevenness of his work among them, have kept him from the serious reading he deserves. Even when his excellence has been praised he has often been misunderstood, and he has never been accorded his place as one of the masters of the short story and the novella. In addition, it has never been widely enough recognized that his work is one of the best keys to the central preoccupations of Western literature in our century so far. Motifs which lie more or less hidden behind much modern literature are overtly Lawrence's subject.

I shall begin with a somewhat detailed look at a single work and then go on to more macroscopic remarks about Lawrence's work. The essay will be like one of those road maps with an insert in one corner giving a much closer view of one part of the area.

Diana Trilling describes *The Fox* as "the most perfectly conceived and sustained of any of the novelettes." But it is more than that. Here the themes that most preoccupied Lawrence throughout his work received one of their most perfect expressions. The story was written in Lawrence's middle period (which came during and just after the first world war, and was the time of his best novels, *The Rainbow* and *Women in Love*). It is without the didacticism and mythologizing that mar later works like *The Plumed Serpent* or *The Man Who Died*. In *The Fox* there is a balance between the two extreme tendencies of Lawrence's fiction. At one extreme is the barely fictionalized autobiography of *Kangaroo* and *Aaron's Rod*, and at the other, symbolic or mythological fables, like *The Man Who Died*, in which the realistic first level tends to become wholly lost in the myth. The strength of the novel as a genre, even in "symbolic" works like *Heart of Darkness* or *Ulysses*, is always its

---

This essay was published in 1952. Lawrence died in 1930.

foundation in a story about believable people in a believable world. In Lawrence's best work the two extremes are avoided and the "meaning" rises naturally from the representation of some intense conflict in people we recognize as of our own earth.

The Fox is the story of two girls, Banford and March, both around thirty and seemingly destined to be old maids. They have taken a farm together, "intending to work it all by themselves." The story seems at first only a rather aimless description of the two girls and their failure to make the farm go. But in the midst of the seemingly naturalistic narrative there are details which later turn out to be of more significance. We learn that "Banford was a small, thin, delicate thing with spectacles," and that "March was more robust." "She would be the man about the place." This last sentence is the key to the relationship of Banford and March. For March has consciously dedicated herself to making Banford happy, as though she were Banford's husband.

Lawrence conveys this relationship and the resulting inner conflict in March (of which she herself is not really aware) by a subtle use of one of the best devices of his fiction: the naïve narrator. The teller of *The Fox* seems to know even less about the people than we can guess from what he says. He observes and wonders, but he draws no conclusions. He is curious, but detached. The words of this seeming innocent convey much that they do not directly state:

> March did most of the outdoor work. When she was out and about, in her puttees and breeches, her belted coat and her loose cap, she looked almost like some graceful, loose-balanced young man, for her shoulders were straight, and her movements easy and confident, even tinged with a little indifference, or irony. But her face was not a man's face, ever. The wisps of her crisp dark hair blew about her as she stooped, her eyes were big and wide and dark, when she looked up again, strange, startled, shy and sardonic at once. Her mouth, too, was almost pinched as if in pain and irony. There was something odd and unexplained about her.

Direct statements of the theme are masked as more or less irrelevant information about March's artistic talents:

> Both Banford and March disbelieved in living for work alone. They wanted to read or take a cycle-ride in the evening, or perhaps March wished to paint curvilinear swans on porcelain, with green background, or else make a marvellous firescreen by processes of elaborate cabinet work. For she was a creature of odd whims and unsatisfied tendencies.

The "curvilinear swans" act here as a symbol of that natural feminity which the "puttees and breeches" are keeping repressed in March. And the phrase about "odd whims and unsatisfied tendencies" states covertly the subject of the story. The description of the failure of March and Banford to make a go of the farm is really a description of the way they are destroying one another with their relationship:

> Although they were usually the best of friends, because Banford, though nervous and delicate, was a warm, generous soul, and March, though so odd and absent in herself, had a strange magnanimity, yet, in the long solitude, they were apt to become a little irritable with one another, tired of one another. March had four-fifths of the work to do, and though she did not mind, there seemed no relief, and it made her eyes flash curiously sometimes.

The Fox dramatizes the conflict within March in terms of a conflict between Banford and Henry, a young soldier who appears on the farm. Henry appears via the major symbol of the story, the fox. There is a real fox, the "evil . . . greater than any other" who carries off their hens. But the fox also becomes a symbol of that normal sexual life which March denies, a denial which reduces her often into an "odd, rapt state, her mouth rather screwed up." The symbolization is achieved by having March encounter the fox, alone:

> She lowered her eyes, and suddenly saw the fox. He was looking up at her. His chin was pressed down, and his eyes were looking up. They met her eyes. And he knew her. She was spellbound – she knew he knew her. So he looked into her eyes, and her soul failed her. He knew her, he was not daunted.

The equation between the fox and Henry is not very subtly made, but to miss it would be to miss the point of the story, so perhaps Lawrence intentionally made it hard to miss:

> . . . to March he was the fox. Whether it was the thrusting forward of his head, or the glisten of fine whitish hairs on the ruddy cheekbones, or the bright, keen eyes, that can never be said: but the boy was to her the fox, and she could not see him otherwise.

The equation is the crucial clue to Henry's nature and dramatic function. He is that recurrent figure in Lawrence's fiction, the man who has escaped the inhibitions imposed by civilization. This figure is often a soldier, and has often "come through" a nearly fatal illness into a new state of "resurrection." (*The Man Who Died* takes this as its central motif.) No such sickness is mentioned for Henry, but the connotations of the fox may be added to what we learn of his character. Like the fox he is the pariah, the banished one, somehow able to judge civilization and civilized morality because independent of them. He has a superior natural wisdom of his own. The dramatic function of this figure throughout Lawrence is to

awaken the sleeping sexuality of an over-civilized woman.
March is the sleeping beauty of *The Fox*. A dream she has will show
how Lawrence achieves "poetic" intensity and compression by expressing her awakening in terms of the fox–Henry equation:

> She dreamed she heard a singing outside which she could not understand,
> a singing that roamed round the house, in the fields, and in the darkness.
> It moved her so that she felt she must weep. She went out, and suddenly
> she knew it was the fox singing. He was very yellow and bright, like corn.
> She went nearer to him, but he ran away and ceased singing. He seemed
> near, and she wanted to touch him. She stretched out her hand, but
> suddenly he bit her wrist, and at the same instant, as she drew back, the
> fox, turning round to bound away, whisked his brush across her face, and
> it seemed his brush was on fire, for it seared and burned her mouth with a
> great pain. She awoke with the pain of it, and lay trembling as if she were
> really seared with a quick brushing kiss, that seemed to burn through her
> every fibre.

The rest of the story tells of the bitter conflict of Henry and Banford
for possession of March. Henry persuades March to promise to marry
him, but when he goes back to camp, Banford re-establishes her
domination over March and makes her break the engagement by letter.
Henry then comes in a black rage to the farm and the "idea" of the story
– that for March either Banford or Henry must cease to exist – is
dramatized in its most extreme terms. Henry finds March chopping
down a tree, while Banford watches. He offers to help, and calculates the
cutting so that the tree falls on Banford.

Once she is dead Henry and March are free to marry. This murder
dramatizes in shocking terms Lawrence's recurrent motif – the release of
a woman from repression. Banford, the "embodiment" of March's
repression, is judged and destroyed. Her death is an assertion that she
was already dead-in-life.

The Fox treats Lawrence's great theme, the conflict between a life
motivated by the mind and the will, and a life which attains what he
called "spontaneous creative fulness of being." For Lawrence the
outcome of commitment to the first way is death, the self-destruction
represented over and over again in his novels and stories. The outcome
of the other way is the best life possible for man. Lawrence saw
everywhere evidence that modern man is dominated by the first kind of
life and that our entire civilization is destroying itself.

II

If it is true, as William Empson says, that "original pieces of thinking
have . . . nearly always been started on metaphor," it could be said that

the originality of D. H. Lawrence lies in his exploration of the metaphor latent in the idea that "all man's vital experience is sexual." The metaphor says "human experience is sexual experience." Expanded, it says that everything important about human experience can be talked about in terms of sex.

There are two important notions behind the idea that original thinking is based on the exploration of a metaphor. One is that certain aspects of man's experience will be necessarily left out or distorted beyond recognition. This is the negative side. A metaphor is the assertion of a false identity. Man is not *simply* a sexual creature. Metaphor is thus an abstraction from the total reality (whatever that may be); it is characterized by what Whitehead calls "essential omission." However, there is a positive side too. The metaphor, if it is a good one, will imply, as the postulates of Euclidian geometry imply a whole system, important truths about man's nature and his relation to the universe. Metaphor is thus a means of knowledge; it offers a perspective on reality.

An obsolete meaning of "perspective" helps us here. In the seventeenth century "perspective" was the common name for a telescope or for any system of mirrors and lenses used to play tricks with light and apparent distance and shape. A metaphor works like a "perspective glass." It distorts and omits, but it reveals. If a "perspective," either metaphorical or actual, is luckily made, aspects of reality never before known will be revealed. We remember the telescope and the microscope, and the importance for Western thought of the metaphor that says a man is like a civilized society or like the universe (microcosm equals macrocosm).

To sum up, in a metaphor the "real" nature of an object is distorted or things are omitted from it, but our omission or distortion of them is what makes for the fecundity of implications about the object which may be evolved by developing the metaphor wholeheartedly. Poetry cannot lay claim to absolute truth, but any piece of thinking in poetry must be judged by how much experience it brings into consciousness or systematizes by means of its novel metaphor.

This may be a long preamble to my idea about Lawrence's contribution to literature. The idea is that Lawrence's work may be best understood as the exploration of a single key metaphor, an exploration which represents an important addition to our consciousness of ourselves and of the world we live in. Lawrence himself was not unaware of the contribution he had made. In a letter written near the end of his life he stated his credo:

I believe in the living extending consciousness of man. I believe the consciousness of man has now to embrace the emotions and passions of sex, and the deep effects of human physical contact. This is the glimmering edge of our awareness and our field of understanding, in the endless business of knowing ourselves.

Lawrence probably succeeded better in extending our consciousness in his earlier novels, *The Rainbow* and *Women in Love*, and in the admirable short stories than when it was so consciously his intention, as in *Lady Chatterly's Lover*. But his own formulation after the fact is a very good description of what his whole work succeeded in accomplishing.

Lawrence's accomplishment can perhaps best be shown by coming at it through a description of recurring motifs in his work. Taken altogether these suggest a single persistent "sense of the world," that is, a homogeneous body of experience from which his work springs or a single vision which his *oeuvre* expresses. A writer's "sense of the world" is something impossible to paraphrase, although sometimes a proposition, usually involving the writer's key metaphor, will seem adequately to sum it up.

If it is true that even the greatest writer repeats himself, and is in a way writing the same story over and over or giving a new treatment to the same inner conflict, the best way to understand the work of a writer is to isolate these obsessions, and describe whatever slow mutations they may have undergone. The obsessions may be located in repetitions of character, scene, and action or dramatic situation. All three in their interrelation tend to form what may be called a "myth" or myths. This myth postulates a certain nature and situation for man and certain possible outcomes for his actions. For example, for Lawrence there are two extreme outcomes which sum up the meaning of a character's life: (1) death, usually self-destruction and (2) a certain heightened state of existence, a fulfillment of the highest potentialities of human life. Paradoxically, these two extreme possibilities of the Lawrence world tend to overlap and merge, so that the highest fulfillment is, seen another way, death. The highest fulfillment is certainly isolation, isolation both from other people and from "normal" states of consciousness. In fact, it tends to abnegate consciousness. It was, again paradoxically, just this heightened state of *unconscious* knowledge (located, so Lawrence said, in the solar plexus) that Lawrence intended his work to bring to his reader's *consciousness*. At least so I understand the credo quoted above.

This likeness-in-unlikeness in the two extreme outcomes may be seen by comparing two stories written more or less consecutively, *The Woman Who Rode Away* and *Sun*. In the former an American woman in Mexico leaves her husband and an empty marriage and flees to an isolated Indian village deep in the mountains where she is eventually sacrificed in a tribal rite. In the rite she symbolically becomes the bride of the Indians' sun god. She has escaped a bourgeois "mental" marriage, but her sexual fulfillment is also death. Lawrence renders with great vividness his heroine's heightened state of consciousness as she is carried away to be sacrificed. Her death, like Gerald Crich's in *Women in Love*, is unconsciously wished for. In *Sun*, another lady, also victim of a sterile modern marriage, finds her fulfillment in lying naked in the Mediterranean sun. She repudiates her husband when he comes from New York in his grey business suit to take her back to a grey life in a New York apartment, and at the end of the story she is left presumably to lie naked forever communing with the sun who is her new husband. Her physical posture and her state of mind are oddly like that of the heroine of *The Woman Who Rode Away*, who is last seen lying on a stone altar in an ice cave, the priest's knife poised over her naked body, waiting for the setting sun to suffuse the cave with light.

Both stories use the motif of travel. Lawrence's own compulsive travels are similarly ambiguous, either escape from the deadness of England into the freedom of Australia or Mexico, or the carrying into reality of an impulse to wander to the Ultima Thule, to climb out of and beyond everything, which is a form of the impulse to self-destruction. The ambiguity makes an important assertion about the limitations of the human condition. It says that the attaining of wisdom or the bringing into being of a supremely good state of soul is also the attainment of an isolation from the unwise and not-good which is like death. *Women in Love*, probably the most perfect of Lawrence's novels, images this perfectly in the double ending: on the one hand the self-caused death of Gerald Crich in the blinding whiteness of a snow-covered alp, and on the other the marriage of Ursula and Birkin and their retreat from the conventional world into a world of "freedom together" travelling.

What is it that Lawrence's people are all so anxious to escape from? It is a state of bondage to another person, usually of the other sex, a state imaged in Lawrence's earliest important novel, *Sons and Lovers*, as bondage to the mother, and recurrently imaged either as this Oedipal fixation, or as love which is a transference of this fixation to another woman, as in Gerald's love for Gudrun Brangwen in *Women in Love* ("Mother and substance of all life she was. And he, child and man, received of her and was made whole . . . Like a child at the breast, he cleaved intensely to her, and she could not put him away"), or as a destructive homosexual relation (as in *The Prussian Officer*).

The problem which all of Lawrence's characters face is the problem of how to escape from the locked room of the mother fixation, from a love which inevitably destroys the lover. The escape into a relation between man and woman which avoids the destructiveness of transferred mother-love is to be attained only with the utmost difficulty. *Women in Love* is perhaps Lawrence's best novel because it dramatizes this escape believably in the relation of Ursula and Birkin. The recurrent image there for this "freedom together" is "star-equilibrium." The perfect marriage is a relation in which husband and wife are as free of one another and yet as related as two stars with their mutually dependent and stabilizing gravity systems. The escape into "equilibrium" also provides the special sort of knowledge which obsessed Lawrence, the dark knowledge of "mystic otherness." For example, this knowledge is attained by Birkin and Ursula when their relation finally reaches its climax:

> He knew her darkly, with fulness of dark knowledge. Now she would know him, and he too would be liberated. He would be night-free, like an Egyptian, steadfast in perfectly suspended equilibrium, pure mystic nodality of physical being. They would give each other this star-equilibrium which alone is freedom.

And then, after the physical consummation which has been so long held off until the "star-equilibrium" has been attained:

> She had her desire of him, she touched, she received the maximum of unspeakable communication in touch, dark, subtle, positively silent, a magnificent gift and give again, a perfect acceptance and yielding, a mystery, the reality of that which can never be known, mystic, sensual reality that can never be transmuted into mind content, but remains outside, living body of darkness and silence and subtlety, the mystic body of reality. She had her desire fulfilled. He had his desire fulfilled. For she was to him what he was to her, the immemorial magnificence of mystic, palpable, real otherness.

Perfect sexual experience is, then, the way to an especially profound sort of knowledge, deriving from "communication in touch." This passage, besides expressing one of Lawrence's central ideas, also exemplifies Lawrence's characteristic faults. It is over-written and therefore seems sentimental. It shows that lack of a sense of humor which T. S. Eliot isolated as one of Lawrence's chief faults. The faults are failures to get a meaning precisely and clearly stated. It would be difficult to say what Lawrence meant by "mystic," three times repeated in the paragraph. A sceptic might well ask if Lawrence's "communication in touch" is really anything more than an extension of the Biblical pun on "know": i.e. "He knew his wife, and she conceived." A good deal more can be said for it, though, as will be seen.

Lawrence's myth is the form of dramatization, recurring as sameness with difference, of his "sense of the world." It is also the dramatization of his key metaphor. The subject of the myth is man's sexual experience, conceiving "sexual experience" in an extended sense as the important relations of a man to his parents, to other men and women and to his wife.

All good fiction dramatizes transformations, either changes in an individual's personality or increases in knowledge, which come to much the same thing. Transformation in Lawrence's stories is imaged as change in the chief character following sexual experience or the refusal of sexual experience. The "situation" of man is the Oedipal situation, in which man is constantly threatened with destruction or nullity, death-in-life, through love either for the mother or for some woman imaged as the mother. On the other hand, refusal of sexual experience (which springs from the Oedipal block) is equally destructive, as is shown by the excellent story, *The Man Who Loved Islands*.

One of the frequent permutations of the myth is to change the sex of the protagonist. The problem then becomes how a woman can avoid destroying herself and her husband by treating him like her child, or how she can overcome the frigidity and repression which is bred into modern civilized women. The *deus ex machina* is the perfectly adjusted male, like Henry in *The Fox*, the man, usually from the lower class, who can awaken the lady's thwarted instincts, subdue her self-destructive will ("Will" is one of the hated words in Lawrence's vocabulary, like "Love," which means destructive "Oedipal" love) and give her that sort of fulfillment which is for Lawrence the highest value. This male paragon, who often is somehow in his occupation concerned with animals, appears even in Lawrence's early stories, but is of much more importance in the later ones. Each of them tells substantially the same story: an overcivilized Andromeda is freed from herself by a peasant Perseus, who is himself free from civilization because outside it. One may imagine, without too much malice, that this recurring character was Lawrence's idealized image of himself. This ideal man embodies perfectly "phallic consciousness," that awareness of nature and other people and oneself which replaces the sterile mental consciousness of modern civilized man with a capacity for vivid experience, experience in which the whole man, not just the mind, is involved. And Lawrence's ideal woman may be deduced from these stories to have been a sort of transformed Frieda (his wife), a woman who is able to escape from repression into a vital sexual relation with a man without trying to mother him. Both the perfect man and the perfect woman are required for any successful male–female relationship. Some men, like Gerald Crich in *Women in Love*, bring out the motherliness in women, and the relation is inevitably a failure. A man must be able to resist this, as Birkin did, must be able to keep his own separateness even in marriage. Birkin's famous stoning of the image of the moon in the water is a dramatic symbol of this resistance.

A man and a woman in their relationship, judged against the ideal of "star equilibrium," are the major figures of Lawrence's myth. There are also minor recurring figures: the older woman, a kind of mother-ogress, who destroys or tries to destroy her son or daughter, as the mother in *Mother and Daughter*, Hermione in *Women in Love*, the mother in *The Lovely Lady*, the grandmother in *The Virgin and the Gipsy*, and the mother of the Priestess of Isis in *The Man Who Died*. In these stories Lawrence has given us frightening representations of the power in a woman of "ghastly female will" to destroy her husband, her children, or even her grandchildren, by dominating them, keeping them children. Lawrence ought to have understood this character, as his mother was evidently just such a person. Another figure, the dominating father, appears less often, but he may be glimpsed in the Prussian officer and in the Australian fascist who gives *Kangaroo* its title. A Damon and Pythias relationship is also sometimes important in Lawrence, as in the relation of Gerald and Birkin in *Women in Love* or of Jack and Somers in *Kangaroo* or of Aaron and Lilly in *Aaron's Rod*. I believe it may be safely asserted that the dramatic roles of all the important characters in all of Lawrence's work may be understood in terms of these figures and the basic myth which they enact over and over again in different guises. It is just here, in his dependence, throughout his writing career, on stories about people caught in or escaping from situations much like his own, that Lawrence's chief limitation lies. All writers must work from their own experience, but some have "myths" which are capable of more permutations and developments than Lawrence's. After any extensive reading of Lawrence one becomes intensely aware of that "essential omission" which I spoke of as characteristic of the exploration of a single metaphor.

Lawrence's ideal relationship was marriage, a marriage which avoids the Scylla of sterility and repression on one side (like the relation of Lady Chatterly and her husband) and the Charybdis of a transferred mother-son relation on the other. This is clearly stated in *A Propos Lady Chatterly*:

> And the Church created marriage by making it a sacrament, a sacrament of man and woman united in the sex communion, and never to be separated, except by death . . . Marriage, making one complete body out of two incomplete ones, and providing for the complex development of the man's soul and the woman's soul in unison, throughout a life-time.

The fruit of such a perfect marriage is the most complete realization of valuable experience available to man: "While you *live* your life, you are in some way an organic whole with all life. But once you start the mental life you pluck the apple," says a character in *Lady Chatterly's Lover*. Sexual experience is the source of all real knowledge. "In him, she touched the centre of reality" says Lawrence of Will and Anna Brangwen in *The Rainbow*. And Mellors explains to Lady Chatterly: "Sex is really only touch, the closest of all touch. And it's touch we're afraid of. We're only half-conscious, and half alive. We've got to come alive and aware."

III

It has not, I think, often been recognized that Lawrence's work merely re-expressed the key romantic idea in terms of sexual experience. The romantic epistemology, as found, say, in Keats, Shelley or Wordsworth, depends on certain tricks played with the word or the idea of "sense" whereby "sense" as "sense experience" is asserted somehow to lead to "sense" as highest knowledge. (Notice how the phrase "sense of the world" depends on precisely this pun.) All the claims of the romantic poets for the value of poetry and its maker, the human imagination, also rest on this pun. Keats' "O for a Life of Sensations rather than of Thoughts" is echoed in Wordsworth's definition of a poet as "a man, who being possessed of more than usual organic sensibility, [has] also thought long and deeply," and in Shelley's definition of poets as "those of the most delicate sensibility and the most enlarged imaginations." And all three assert that the poet comes back from his journey into sensibility with new knowledge. Poetic language, said Shelley, "marks the before unapprehended relations of things and perpetuates their apprehension." Poetry "is at once the centre and circumference of knowledge; it is that which comprehends all science, and that to which all science must be referred." "What the Imagination seizes as Beauty must be Truth," said Keats, and by "Imagination" he meant the intense activity of the mind on the material of "Sensations." And an infrequently quoted passage from Wordsworth's preface to the second edition of *The Lyrical Ballads* puts the whole doctrine succinctly:

> Though the eyes and senses of man are, it is true, [the poet's] favourite guides, yet he will follow whersoever he can find an atmosphere of sensation in which to move his wings. Poetry is the first and last of all knowledge.

I am aware that this lumping blurs distinctions. To unblur them would take a book. But this tradition has dominated Western poetry theory since then. T. S. Eliot's praise of the Elizabethan period because then "the intellect was at the tips of the senses" would have seemed to Keats based on a valid criterion.

There is nothing at all unorthodox about Lawrence's key idea. It is precisely in keeping with that phase of thought which is often said to begin in poetry with the romantic movement (such things do not begin so abruptly, of course), and which still persists. In fact it might be said that the distinct contribution of twentieth-century literature to the romantic tradition has been to expound the two meanings of "sense" in terms of what is clearly one of the most intense forms of sense experience. And we must remember here how Lawrence broadened the definition of sexual experience. "Sex," he said, "to me, means the whole of the relationship between man and woman." This transformation of the basic romantic idea has the merit of bringing literature down from a subjective cloud where the poet, all sensibility, confronts the universe alone, to the realm of the personal relations of men and women. The romantic idea is thus transformed from lyric into dramatic.

The new statement of the romantic idea may be worked both ways. Either experience, which is actually larger than sexual, may be talked about in terms of sexual experience, as in Lawrence, or experience, which is basically sexual, may be dramatized as including something more, as in *The Lovesong of J. Alfred Prufrock*. Proust's work and much of Faulkner's, to name only two writers, represent explorations of the twentieth-century permutation of the key romantic idea. Lawrence's work is valuable partly because the metaphorical "perspective" which is used more covertly in other twentieth-century work appears so openly in Lawrence that it would be hard to miss it as his chief theme. Seen in this larger context, a context of which Lawrence himself was not wholly aware, his work seems clearly explicable as a continuation of that romantic "protest on behalf of the organic view of nature, and . . . against the exclusion of value from the essence of matter of fact" which Whitehead celebrated in *Science and the Modern World*. Like the work of Wordsworth and Shelley, Lawrence's writing may be taken as an assault on the "Fallacy of Misplaced Concreteness," the taking of mental abstractions as realities and the only realities. Whitehead's description of Wordsworth applies admirably to Lawrence. Like Wordsworth, Lawrence "opposes to the scientific abstractions his full concrete experience." Lawrence was violent in his denunciations of "mentality." "Man is great," he said, "according as his relation to the living universe is vast and vital." To "mentality" he opposes the fullest activity of all man's ways of getting in touch with the world outside himself.

Lawrence's cry for "More life! More *vivid* life!" finds its echo not only in Whitehead but in other exponents of this characteristic twentieth-century theory of value. Lawrence's explicit doctrine grew from his fiction and does not contradict its implications. Although Lawrence did not, so far as I know, read Whitehead, his theory was at times very close to Whitehead's notion that "value" resides in "events" (of greater or less complexity from stones on up to human beings) which "prehend" in themselves aspects of the whole universe, past, present and future:

The argument is, that between an individual and any external object with which he has an affective connection, there exists a definite vital flow, as definite and concrete as the electric current whose polarized circuit sets our tram-cars running and our lamps shining, or our Marconi wires vibrating. Whether this object be human, or animal, or plant, or quite inanimate, there is still a circuit. (*Fantasia of the Unconscious*)

And this, from a letter of June, 1914, to A. D. McLeod, which might stand as a summing up of what Lawrence had to say and what he "proved on our pulses" in his fiction:

I think the only re-sourcing of art, revivifying it, is to make it more the joint work of man and woman. I think *the* one thing to do, is for men to have courage to draw nearer to women, to expose themselves to them, and be altered by them: and for women to accept and admit men. That is the start – by bringing themselves together, men and women – revealing themselves each to the other, gaining great blind knowledge and suffering and joy, which it will take a big further lapse of civilization to exploit and work out. Because the source of all living is in the interchange and the meeting and mingling of these two: man-life and woman-life, man-knowledge and woman-knowledge, man-being and woman-being.

It is obvious, I think, what is wrong with Lawrence's doctrine, a wrongness that perhaps springs from the narrowness of the source of his creative inspiration of which I spoke above. Lawrence's personal and artistic preoccupation with the problems of sexual adjustment seems to have blinded him to another source of vital experience, which indeed operates to make sexual experience in man more than the coupling of beasts. For surely, even though it be admitted that "man's vital experience is sexual," in all Lawrence's rich meaning of sexual, there still remains another source both for value, "vivid life," and for man's worst evil, a source which interposes itself constantly to transform and combine elements of that rudimentary vital experience. The other source is simply the fact of mind or imagination in man, that mind which Lawrence so scorned. Whatever Lawrence may have desired, man cannot stop possessing mind. It is true, on one hand, to use Whitehead's words again, that "the growth of consciousness is the uprise of abstractions." (Cf. Lawrence, *Psychoanalysis and the Unconscious*:

Ideas are the dry, unliving, inscutient plumage which intervenes between us and the circumambient universe, forming at once an insulator and an instrument for the subduing of the universe. The mind is the instrument of instruments; it is not a creative reality. . . . The mind is the dead end of life.)

But it is also true, on the other hand, that the mind (in its ability to modify, transform, and interrelate the data of experience by means of its "coadunating imagination") is the source of man's most important enjoyment of "vivid life." Lawrence in his conscious theory never gave enough importance to the power of imagination so richly shown by his own best work. His successful stories are good not because of his theory or the evidence in them of his own intense experience. They are good because in them his imagination transformed his experience into unified symbolic representations of those conscious and unconscious preoccupations that made up his sense of the world.

2

Franz Kafka and the metaphysics of alienation

Had one to name the artist who comes nearest to bearing the same kind of relation to our age that Dante, Shakespeare and Goethe bore to theirs, Kafka is the first we would think of.

W. H. Auden

There is a goal, but no way; what we call the way is only wavering.

Kafka

Franz Kafka, from the very beginning of his life, was chained forever in the place of exile:

> It seems to me as if I had not come by myself but had been pushed here as a child and then chained to this spot; the consciousness of my misfortune only gradually dawned on me, my misfortune itself was already complete.[1]

Outside of the human world, outside of God's law, he felt condemned to wander forever in the wilderness outside of Canaan. This wandering is identical with being chained in one spot, for every place in the desert is identical with every other place, and they are all equally at an infinite distance from the goal:

> Why did I want to quit the world? Because "he" would not let me live in it, in his world. Though indeed I should not judge the matter so precisely, for I am now a citizen of this other world, whose relationship to the ordinary one is the relationship of the wilderness to cultivated land (I have been forty years wandering from Canaan). . . . It is indeed a kind of Wandering in the Wilderness in reverse that I am undergoing.[2]

Doubtless it is Kafka's acute consciousness of his irrevocable alienation, and the incomparably subtle analysis of it presented in his works, that earn him his place as the most representative figure in twentieth-century literature. For our time is, even more than the time of Hölderlin (it is only an extension of his), the time of distress, the time when the link

15

between God and man is broken, the time when God is no more present and is not yet again present, the time when He can only be experienced negatively, as a terrifying absence.

But the full consciousness of his plight only "gradually" dawns on the exiled one, and, besides, "the attraction of the human world is so immense, in an instant it can make one forget everything."[3] "I think," says Kafka, "that I am continually skirting the wilderness and am full of childish hopes . . . that 'perhaps I shall keep in Canaan after all.'"[4] Accordingly, the first act in the Kafkan drama is a frantic attempt to keep within the ordinary human world. At all costs he must believe that he is a perfectly normal person, that he is linked by a thousand ties to the tightly knit circle of the human community, that he has a justified and meaningful existence there, and that, above all, the established human world forms for him an avenue of approach to God. For is not the true way to God through the traditional institutions of the community? And if one does not belong to God, if one is not within the law, one does not exist, one is, literally, nothing: "The word 'sein' signifies in German both things: to be and to belong to Him."[5]

It is quite clear what Kafka meant by belonging to the human world. It meant, perhaps most of all in Kafka's Jewish tradition, being a good son, and, later, having a wife and children. Thus he writes in his journal: "The Talmud too says: A man without a woman is no person."[6] And he expresses again and again his horror of the bachelor's "ill-luck" and his painful longing for a wife and children. For children are a sign that one is in the right with God, that one has a meaningful part in history, in the temporal fulfillment of God's law on earth.

But belonging to the human world also meant for Kafka having a job and a profession. Only these would give one the strength to act decisively: "For without a center, without a profession, a love, a family, an income; i.e., without holding one's own against the world in the big things . . . one cannot protect oneself from losses that momentarily destroy one."[7] Thus the hero of *Amerika*, the shy and diffident Karl Rossmann, becomes aggressive and competent when he thinks he is established in the community, even at its lowest level:

> He marched up to the counter and rapped on it with his knuckles until someone came; . . . he shouted across high walls of human beings; he went up to people without hesitation. . . . He did all this not out of arrogance, nor from any lack of respect for difficulties, but because he felt himself in a secure position which gave him certain rights.[8]

To possess all these things – a family, a job, and a secured place in the general human family – would be, in other words, to enjoy the sense of wellbeing which K. in *The Castle* momentarily (and falsely) experiences.

And it would be to feel, as K. does, that his position allows him an avenue of approach to the divine power, here present in Klamm, the Castle official:

> Yet I have already a home, a position and real work to do, I have a promised wife who takes her share of my professional duties when I have other business, I'm going to marry her and become a member of the community, and besides my official connection I have also a personal connection with Klamm, although as yet I haven't been able to make use of it. That's surely quite a lot.[9]

So, then, a number of Kafka's stories, especially the early ones, can be interpreted as continuing that tradition which goes back through Dickens (whom he consciously imitated in *Amerika*) to the eighteenth-century novel. That is, they are stories about people who begin in estrangement from the human community, and who attempt through a series of adventures to find a stable place in society, and through that a meaningful identity. Kafka's most elaborate version of this traditional theme is *Amerika*: no other work expresses more clearly the opposition between the terrible freedom of having no connection with the human world and the longed-for security of a permanent place in the social order. But this same opposition between freedom and status is also central in other stories – in, for example, "A Report to an Academy," the disquieting story of an ape who, after being captured, escapes from his cage by finding "a special way" out, "the way of humanity":

> With an effort which up till now has never been repeated, [says the ape] I managed to reach the cultural level of an average European. . . . There is an excellent idiom: to fight one's way through the thick of things: that is what I have done, I have fought through the thick of things. There was nothing else for me to do, provided always that freedom was not to be my choice.[10]

It is a choice, then, between "dreadful freedom" outside the human world and meaningful existence within it. But in Kafka's later writings there is a strange transformation of the value of belonging to the human world. Now, instead of being identified with obedience to God's law, it is opposed to it. The choice now seems to be between fulfilling God's law in isolation and evading its imperatives through self-immersion in the human collective. Thus, in a bitterly ironic journal note of 1917, Kafka asserts that his real aim is not to obey God but to escape into the human world where he can sin with impunity:

> If I closely examine what is my ultimate aim, it turns out that I am not really striving to be good and to fulfill the demands of a Supreme Judgment, but rather very much the contrary: I strive to know the whole

human and animal community, to recognize their basic predilections, desires, moral ideals, to reduce these to simple rules and as quickly as possible to trim my behavior to these rules in order that I may find favor in the whole world's eyes; and, indeed (this is the inconsistency), so much favor that in the end I could openly perpetrate the iniquities within me without alienating the universal love in which I am held – the only sinner who won't be roasted.[11]

What has happened to bring about this reversal? The answer is that Kafka has come to recognize that everybody, without exception, is outside the law. The entire human community is in the desert, attempting to build an impious tower of Babel to scale heaven, but really cutting itself off more and more from God and creating a self-enclosed structure of purely human values and institutions. Kafka's judgment of our urban, technological, industrial, bureaucratic world is unequivocal. Once, long ago, as Kafka says in one of his very last stories, the Word was close to man, and interpenetrated his world, but now it has withdrawn altogether, and all mankind is lost:

> Even in those days wonders did not openly walk the streets for any one to seize; but all the same dogs [for "dogs" we are, of course, to understand: "men"] – I cannot put it in any other way – had not yet become so doggish as to-day, the edifice of dogdom was still loosely put together, the true Word could still have intervened, planning or replanning the structure, changing it at will, transforming it into its opposite; the Word was there, was very near at least, on the tip of everybody's tongue, any one might have hit upon it. And what has become of it to-day? To-day one may pluck out one's very heart and not find it.[12]

To live within the human community is no longer to live in a world which is transparent to God, but is to "hasten in almost guiltless silence towards death in a world *darkened by others.*"[13] In other words, the true reason Kafka is impelled to reject the way to God that lies through the human world, through a family or a profession or religious observances, is not, it seems, that he is exiled by that community, but that the community is itself no longer a way to God. One *is* lost, but then one *must* be lost. For the entire human community is lost, though this is not generally known. Each of us has taken a wrong turning, and we wander in endless aberration: "Every person is lost in himself beyond hope of rescue."[14] The only difference in Kafka's case is that he knows he is lost, and this is his chance. The discovery of alienation is, perhaps, the only remaining possibility of salvation. For the spiritual state of Kafka's heroes is not extraordinary. Rather it is the true state of us all, whether we know it or not. It is not only Kafka who wanders farther and farther into the desert, but all of us, together, and yet separated infinitely by our mutual silence:

When our first fathers strayed they had doubtless scarcely any notion that their aberration was to be an endless one, they could still literally see the cross-roads, it seemed an easy matter to turn back whenever they pleased, and if they hesitated to turn back it was merely because they wanted to enjoy a dog's life for a little while longer; it was not yet a genuine dog's life, and already it seemed intoxicatingly beautiful to them . . . and so they strayed farther.[15]

II

The Kafkan man, then, is in exile, and he must *wish* to be in exile, must constantly reaffirm and choose his exile as the only possibility left open to him. Kafka's stories and his personal writings, in spite of the recurrent "attraction of the human world," and in spite of his momentary feelings that the human world is good and that he belongs to it, are, for the most part, a long, patient, and exhaustive analysis of what it means to be outside of everything, even outside of oneself.

To be outside of everything means, first of all, to be unable to reach and touch anything outside of one's own narrow limits: "I am divided from all things by a hollow space,"[16] says Kafka, "I am too far away, am banished."[17] One remains *here*, and everyone and everything else is *out there*, seen coldly across a gap, as a mere phenomenal spectacle. Moreover, one is also separated from the past and from the future. A really meaningful human life, of course, possesses its past and its future, and they eventually form a full circle, a totality of homogeneous existence supporting one in a fullness of being:

We . . . are held in our past and future. . . . Whatever advantage the future has in size, the past compensates for in weight, and at the end the two are indeed no longer distinguishable, earliest youth later becomes distinct, as the future is, and the end of the future is really already experienced in all our sighs, and thus becomes the past. So this circle along whose rim we move almost closes.[18]

But the exiled one "has only the moment, the everlasting moment of torment which is followed by no glimpse of a moment of recovery."[19] Kafka's stories and journals are perfect expressions of this double isolation in the moment, isolation not only from all past and future moments, but also from what is seen and experienced in the moment itself. His heroes are, like Kafka himself, passive and cold, incapable of the least motion of human warmth which might extend outwards to embrace the world and other people: "A sad but calm astonishment at my lack of feeling often grips me"[20]; "It is as if I were made of stone,"[21] "I have become cold again, and insensible."[22] And the world seen from the point of view of cold, detached passivity is a long succession of disconnected appearances. One "isolated momentary observation"[23] follows another. Each appears suddenly before the field of vision, swells up to fill the whole, and is seen vividly in microscopic detail for a moment: "observations of the moment, mostly only indoors, where certain people suddenly and hugely bubble up before one's eyes."[24] Then, what had absorbed all of one's attention dissolves, disappears, to be forgotten and replaced by something else.

To begin to read one of Kafka's stories is to enter a space where one is always *indoors*, where there are always limits to one's vision. Even if one is in the midst of a trackless desert, one's vision is soon stopped by the indeterminate horizon of sand and sky, or by a thick murk of fog, or by the dazzling brilliance of sunlight itself. But most often one finds oneself in a dreamlike interior, a realm of theatrical hallucination. (Kafka was fascinated by the theater, and many of his own dreams took place in a theater.) There is nothing behind the insubstantial backdrops of these stage sets, solid though they seem – nothing but the discarded bric-à-brac of unused props and ropes, or, as it may be, simply another room just like the first. The world of Kafka's stories is a world without depth, a world of sheer surface, a world of continual movement, in which one is condemned to explore, one after another, indefinitely multiplied chambers which replace one another and which are all the equivalents of one another. The scene is always changing, but it never really changes. It is a universe of pure spectacle. And in such a universe all things are traps which fascinate our attention. The people are as depthless as the walls: we see their gestures and expressions with extraordinary distinctness, but the meaning of these gestures and these glances is precisely that they have no meaning. They are simply there before us. They connect with nothing before or after, and they contain no significance hidden in their depths: "Miserable observation," says Kafka, "which again is certainly the result of something artificially constructed whose lower end is swinging in emptiness somewhere."[25]

The world of *Amerika*, of *The Trial*, and *The Castle*, then, is a *labyrinth*. In this labyrinth, one moves constantly from place to place without ever getting anywhere, or reaching anything conclusive, or even knowing whether there is a goal to be reached:

> The truly terrible paths between freedom and slavery cross each other with no guide to the way ahead and accompanied by an immediate obliterating of the paths already traversed. There are a countless number of such paths, or only one, it cannot be determined, for there is no vantage ground from which to observe. There am I. I cannot leave.[26]

Thus, not one of Kafka's longer works is really finished. They could not, on principle, reach their end, since the very nature of the experience they describe is to be endless, or, rather, to be the "eternal recapitulation"[27] of the same experience. These novels, at best, can only jump over an infinite number of intermediate stages, and reach, as in the case of *The Trial*, their inevitable end. But, most often, that end is never reached: "A life like this could last forever and still be nothing but a moment. Moses fails to enter Canaan not because his life is too short but because it is a human life."[28]

In the end, however, Kafka's universe, for the very reason that it is so completely without depth, comes to seem very deep indeed. For the least gesture or glance from another person, the most insignificant detail observed in an inanimate object, precisely because they can be given no comforting human meaning, seem to put us in touch immediately with some unfathomable meaning from beyond the human world. They seem radiant with an ominous significance which transcends their immediate reality. The most we can hope is that this meaning has nothing directly to do with us: "The most appropriate situation for me: To listen to a conversation between two people who are discussing a matter that concerns them closely while I have only a remote interest in it which is in addition completely selfless."[29]

But, alas, such is not the case. The conversation *does* concern me. My guilt is being decided, and the moment of my execution set. All Kafka's stories about persons who wander within the labyrinth of the human world approach closer and closer to the same ending: the death of the hero, which is only the fulfillment of a spiritual death that precedes the beginning of the story. This is the central action of *The Trial*: Joseph K.'s slow recognition that he cannot ignore his trial, that he no longer belongs to the human world, that he is guilty, that his fate is to be executed. To yield onself to the human world, to leave one's safe enclosure, is to put oneself at the mercy of judges who are infinitely powerful and infinitely merciless, and whether one is "guilty" or "innocent" (that is, whether one knows or does not know that one is guilty), the end is the same: "Rossmann and K., the innocent and the guilty, both executed without distinction in the end, the guilty one with a gentler hand, more pushed aside than struck down."[30]

Only one escape seems to remain: to withdraw altogether from the human world, to surround oneself with impenetrable walls and to live safely in complete isolation within one's own private enclosure: "I'll shut myself off from everyone to the point of insensibility. Make an enemy of everyone, speak to no one."[31] "Two tasks on the threshold of life: To narrow your circle more and more, and constantly to make certain that you have not hidden yourself somewhere outside it."[32]

The quality of life within the pure circle of complete isolation is brilliantly dramatized in the story called "The Burrow." The interior world too, we discover, is a labyrinth, a labyrinth one has made for oneself. But this labyrinth does not even have the multiplicity and changefulness of the exterior one. Each chamber and each passageway is exactly like all the others, and reflects back only the absolute blandness and indeterminacy of one's own inner life. Where there is nothing but oneself, there is nothing. In isolation, there is a rapid exhaustion of one's forces, an evaporation of the self. In a moment, all thoughts, all emotions, all one's powers, are dissipated, and there is nothing left but a complete void. Kafka's diaries are full of descriptions of the absolute inner emptiness resulting from this disastrous withdrawal into one's own center: "My inner emptiness, an emptiness that replaces everything else is not even very great."[33] "Completely indifferent and apathetic. A well gone dry, water at an unattainable depth and no certainty it is there. Nothing, nothing."[34] It is as though one had, deliberately or by inadvertence, stepped off the rim of one's circle into a bottomless abyss:

> This circle indeed belongs to us, but belongs to us only so long as we keep to it, if we move to the side just once, in any chance forgetting of self, in some distraction, some fright, some astonishment, some fatigue, we have already lost it into space, until now we had our noses stuck into the tide of the times, now we step back, former swimmers, present walkers, and are lost.[35]

By enclosing oneself in a narrow circle of isolation, one has indeed stepped into a place of complete nullity. This nullity is not death, it is something worse, it is "the eternal torment of dying."[36] Gregor Samsa, for example, in "The Metamorphosis," after his horrible transformation into a cockroach, becomes more and more dry and empty within his carapace of solitude, but he is liberated, finally, by death. Gregor's end, however, like the death at the end of "The Judgment," or the execution at the end of *The Trial*, is as much wish-fulfillment as a possibility in which Kafka really believes. The true plight of Kafka's heroes is to be unable to die, to remain forever, like the hunter Gracchus, hovering between this world and the world of death, to remain in a prolonged emptiness which is neither death nor life:

> In a certain sense I am alive too. My death ship lost its way; a wrong turn of the wheel, a moment's absence of mind on the pilot's part. . . . I am forever . . . on the great stair that leads up to [the other world]. On that infinitely wide and spacious stair I clamber about, sometimes up, sometimes down, sometimes on the right, sometimes on the left, always in motion. . . . My ship has no rudder, and it is driven by the wind that blows in the undermost regions of death.[37]

The ultimate fate of Kafka's heroes, then, and of Kafka himself, is to reach a frightening state of being neither alive nor dead, in which one can only live by endlessly falling into the void. The Kafkan man is drawn relentlessly toward a supreme moment, a moment as long as eternity itself, a moment in which he is pure negative consciousness speeding with infinite acceleration toward an incomprehensible transcendent power which he can never reach or escape from, however far or fast he goes:

> To die would mean nothing else than to surrender a nothing to the nothing, but that would be impossible to conceive, for how could a person, even only as a nothing, consciously surrender himself to the nothing, and not merely to an empty nothing but rather to a roaring nothing whose nothingness consists only in its incomprehensibility.[38]

III

> Again encouragement. Again I catch hold of myself, as one catches hold of a ball in its fall. Tomorrow, today, I'll begin an extensive work. . . .[39]

Now one final possibility remains, and it is literature itself, the rescue of oneself through writing. Writing, it may be, is the one action which, depending on nothing outside the self, and deriving from a voluntary and autonomous exercise of the power to transform things into words, can stop the endless fall into the abyss. The self will seize the self, as one catches hold of a ball in mid-air, and give to itself an indestructible solidity. The crucial importance of Kafka for twentieth-century thought lies not only in his extreme experience of the loss of selfhood, but also in his deep exploration of the tangled relations between writing and salvation. For Kafka, as does the thought of our century in general, pursues to its end the attempt, begun by the Romantics, to find in literature itself a means of salvation. Abandoned to utter dereliction by the collapse of every other hope, Kafka turns to writing as the sole possibility remaining. And it was no light burden he put upon words: it was, indeed, a burden no less heavy than the weight of his entire life and destiny: "*I am more and more unable to think, to observe, to determine the truth of things, to remember, to speak, to share an experience; I am turning to stone, this is the truth. . . .* If I can't take refuge in some work, I am lost."[40] "But I will write in spite of everything, absolutely; it is my struggle for self-preservation."[41] "I am nothing but literature."[42]

Kafka's notion of the process by which literature would bring him salvation was precise and definite: the words would not merely be put down on the paper to exist independently of their creator. They would be a kind of magical incantation that would replace the inner emptiness with solidity and firmness: they would summon "life's splendour" which "forever lies in wait about each of us in all its fulness, but veiled

from view, deep down, invisible, far off."[42] "The firmness . . . which
the most insignificant writing brings about in me is beyond doubt and
wonderful."[44] "If you summon it by the right word, by its right name, it
will come. This is the essence of magic, which does not create but
summons."[45] "I have now . . . a great yearning to write all my anxiety
out of me, write it into the depths of the paper just as it comes out of the
depths of me, or write it down in such a way that I could draw what I
had written into me completely."[46]

But at first Kafka's relation to writing remains, precisely, a *striving*, a
yearning. The transformation of his inner life through writing is
something he believes in but has not experienced. For, though all his
inner forces rushed toward writing, Kafka was, for long months and
years, unable to achieve a definitive experience of the power of words.
What he lacked was time, for writing is "a task that can never succeed
except all at once."[47] His job, his family, all the connections he had with
the normal world, left him only the night for writing; and the night was
not long enough. Kafka's early diaries are full of laments over his lack of
time for writing, and full, too, of fragmentary stories, stories which start
off strongly, create their own world in a few powerful sentences, and
then suddenly and abruptly stop, like meteors which glow brightly in
rarefied air, but are burnt up in a moment by the lower atmosphere and
return to darkness. For Kafka cannot remain long enough in the upper
air. He must sink back to his quotidian indigence, and leave his story
behind to dissipate itself into the inarticulate chaos from which it came.
This chaos is within him, and yet painfully separated from him. Only a
complete story could bring the two together and give form and
expression simultaneously both to the chaos of inner forces and to his
consciousness itself: "I really don't have time for a story, time to expand
myself in every direction in the world, as I should have to do";[48]

> I have too little time to draw out of me all the possibilities of my talent.
> For that reason it is only disconnected starts that always make an
> appearance. . . . If I were ever able to write something large and whole,
> well-shaped from beginning to end, then in the end the story would never
> be able to detach itself from me and it would be possible for me calmly and
> with open eyes, as a blood relation of a healthy story, to hear it read, but as
> it is, every little piece of the story runs around homeless and drives me
> away from it in the opposite direction.[49]

Far from being able to escape out of his own inner emptiness into the
solidity and coherence of a story, Kafka is repulsed by the broken
fragments of incomplete ones, and kept outside in the void, hanging on,
as it were, with both hands. And, worse yet, within this void, he is
conscious of immense unused forces which circle in uncontrollable

violence, which permit him no rest or sleep, and, far from holding him together, tear him apart: "Then, already boiling, I went home, I couldn't withstand one of my ideas, disordered, pregnant, disheveled, swollen, amidst my furniture which was rolling about me; overwhelmed by my pains and worries, taking up as much space as possible."[50]

"The tremendous world I have in my head. But how to free myself and free it without being torn to pieces."[51] This is indeed the question: burnt up by "the unhappy sense of a consuming fire inside [him] that [is] not allowed to break out,"[52] tormented by "mysterious powers"[53] which have been unleashed within him and are tearing him to pieces, and prevented by external circumstances from directing them to a single continuous work, Kafka is driven toward a state even worse than those times when his mind is a "thoughtless vacuum." Indeed, he is driven, as he often feared, toward madness. In this dangerous condition, he is sustained only by an unproved conviction that this seeming chaos is really a harmony, a harmony which, if it were liberated, would not only fill up all the interior space of his consciousness, but would permit an expansion of that space toward unheard-of limits: "In the end this uproar is only a suppressed, restrained harmony, which, left free, would fill me completely, which would even widen me and yet still fill me."[54] "I have . . . experienced states (not many) . . . in which I completely dwelt in every idea, but also filled every idea, and in which I not only felt myself at my boundary, but at the boundary of the human in general."[55]

It is clear now what form Kafka's stories must take, if they are to be successful. They must be a perfect continuity, sweeping smoothly from beginning to end, with no scission or interstice, and they must be an expression, not of some limited action in the external world, but, precisely, of the *totality* of his inner world. In the words of the story, the emptiness of consciousness and the shapeless storms of unused forces must come together and fuse in the concrete particularity of narrative or image. We can see here why it is incorrect to speak of Kafka's stories as "symbolic," as if their mysterious images, descriptions, and actions *stood for* something other than themselves. They are not symbolic, but perfectly literal embodiments of his inner life. They are the very form his consciousness takes when it has any form at all, when it ceases to be a hollow shell filled with indeterminate energies careening in the void.

Kafka's definitive experience of the power of writing came on the night of September 22, 1912, when he wrote, in a single unbroken flow of inspiration, the short story called "The Judgment." That night he discovered that his literary powers were real, but he also discovered the true extent of those powers. He discovered that an authentic piece of writing would not simply give cohesion and firmness to his own narrow interior space, but would cause that interior space to expand and grow until it filled the entire universe. Or, rather, he discovered that the interior regions of his consciousness could, through the magic of words, become the entire universe turned inside out. Every person and thing, without exception, everything real or imaginable, could be transformed into words and placed there within himself in an immutable form. Literature was not simply the salvation of his own poor identity; it was also the salvation of the world itself. It was, necessarily, both at once, for so long as any particle or fragment of the world remained unchanged into words, into image, that fragment would remain other than the self and constitute a deadly threat to it. Writing, in other words, he discovered to be "'an assault, on the last earthly frontier,' an assault, moreover, launched from below, from mankind."[56]

> The strange, mysterious, perhaps dangerous, perhaps saving comfort that there is in writing: it is a leap out of murderer's row; it is a seeing of what is really taking place. This occurs by a higher type of observation, a higher, not a keener type, and the higher it is, and the less within reach of the "row," the more independent it becomes, the more obedient to its own laws of motion, the more incalculable, the more joyful, the more ascendant its course.[57]

Kafka, it seems, has escaped at last, though only by arrogating to himself almost divine powers. If narrowing oneself concentrically to even smaller and smaller dimensions provides no escape from the inexorable power of the world and of God, the other extreme alternative seems to work. By expanding his inner world ever further and further outwards until it includes in a new form everything that is, Kafka liberates himself at last from the annihilating pressures which initially surround him. He makes of his nothing, everything.

IV

But what is this "new form"? What are the characteristics of this realm in which Kafka places all his hopes? Slowly, bit by bit, in the form that his writings force themselves to take, and in the recognition of his own inner experiences while writing, Kafka comes to make the terrifying discovery that the space of literature is identical with the place of exile where he first began. At first, seemingly an infinitely complex assembly of integrated parts, like the machine of execution in the story called "In the Penal Colony," the world of words in Kafka undergoes a hideous process of disintegration in which piece after piece, driven by some irresistible internal compulsion, bursts out of its place, and rolls senselessly away, until finally the entire structure is reduced to dispersed and meaningless fragments.[58] This inexorable disaggregation of the literary construct is proof that, far from escaping the conditions of estrangement through writing, Kafka has merely reaffirmed them in exacerbated form. The central tragedy of his spiritual adventure is thus the collapse of the attempt to identify literature and salvation, and his lasting significance as a writer consists in large part in the example that his career provides of a writer who had the courage to explore that collapse to the bitter end.

Kafka learned by experience that writing is not a smooth continuous movement which changes the world altogether and flies off with it to the free upper air. His experiences within the literary space were exactly like those he had had in the desert of exile: an endless wavering which rose up only to fall back again, which never reached and possessed the goal. He found writing, like human life itself, to be an interminably prolonged death:

> What will be my fate as a writer is very simple. . . . I waver, continually fly to the summit of the mountain, but then fall back in a moment. Others waver too, but in lower regions, with greater strength; if they are in danger of falling, they are caught up by the kinsman who walks beside them for that very purpose. But I waver on the heights; it is not death, alas, but the eternal torments of dying.[59]

Kafka recognized in the end that the attempt to reach the goal through writing "is not a task at all, not even an impossible one, it is not even impossibility itself, it is nothing."[60] This task is even worse than impossible, because the space of literature is, *par excellence*, the place of separation. It is the place of separation, because it is the place where everything is transformed into image. To make an image of something makes that thing at once attainable and unattainable. An image makes what it represents simultaneously present and absent. It makes it available *as image*, therefore unavailable. When we reach out to touch it, it changes again, recedes, and hovers there before us just beyond our grasp. By the very fact that something is described, is turned into image, it becomes illusion, and therefore false, separated from the truth. It becomes the mediate symbol of the goal rather than the goal itself. Far from giving immutable truth to things, Kafka, this "man with the too great shadow,"[61] destroys all things he approaches. He destroys them by transforming them into the shadows of themselves, by transposing them from the tangibility and closeness of the physical world into the strange inner world where nothing can ever be possessed: "For all things outside the physical world language can be employed only as a sort of adumbration, but never with even approximate exactitude, since in accordance with the physical world it treats only of possession and its connotations."[62]

The realm of literature, then, delivers Kafka over to an endless sterile vacillation between the sin of *impatience* and the sin of *laziness*.[63] On the one hand, Kafka is driven by impatience, by the desire to reach the goal immediately. But to do this means to commit the fatal mistake of taking the mediate for the immediate, of confusing an image of the goal with the goal itself. No, one is condemned to play out the game to the end, without any premature renunciation of method, going with infinite slowness from one stage of the way to the next: "The road is endless, there is nothing that can be subtracted from it or added to it, and yet everyone insists on applying his own childish measuring yard. 'Yes, you will have to go the length of that measuring yard as well; it will not be forgiven you.'"[64] But, on the other hand, to become absorbed in the stages of the way is laziness, the negligence which ignores the goal for something less. For each stage is only a delusive mirroring of the goal. One must go directly toward the goal without intermediary. But this is impossible. Between these two requirements Kafka and all his heroes waver endlessly. He must continuously reject all immanence for the sake of a transcendence. But what is transcendent remains, by definition, out of reach, and Kafka's experience of immanence is not of possession or closeness, but of distance, lack. Belonging to society, an intimate relation to another person, writing, all these forms of life reduce themselves in the end to the same universal mode of existence, and we recognize at last that Kafka can, by no expedient, whether lawful or unlawful, escape from the realm of errancy to which he has been condemned.

The fullest expression of the movement by which every step toward the goal is a step away from it is, however, Kafka's masterpiece, *The Castle*. This novel is Kafka's fullest expression of his sense of human existence, and, at the same time, of his experience as a writer. The two are here identified as the same eternal wandering this side of the goal. K., the hero of *The Castle*, is the most conscious of all Kafka's heroes. True to the lot he has chosen, K. rejects every place or advantage he wins in the village beneath the Castle: Frieda, his room in the inn, his job in the school; and, when at last he has an interview with a secretary from the Castle, he falls asleep! He rejects all things he attains, because, by the very fact that he reaches them, they all become only images of his goal. K. is driven, always, to go beyond whatever he has, to go beyond even Klamm, who belongs to the Castle: "It was not Klamm's environment in itself that seemed to him worth striving for, but rather that he, K., he only and no one else, should attain to Klamm, and should attain to him not to rest with him, but to go on beyond him, farther yet, into the Castle."[65] One can see clearly that *The Castle*, like Kafka's other novels, was interminable, or could only end, as Max Brod has told us it was meant to end, with the death, by utter exhaustion, of the hero (though it is significant that Kafka never wrote the ending). The rejection of what one has reached for the sake of a goal which can never be reached can be repeated, must be repeated, again and again, forever.

Kafka remains, then, until the end, within an inner space which may expand indefinitely, or contract to nothing, but always remains the place of solitude, at the same distance from the unattainable paradise of possession. His plight is perpetual dying. It is exile in the desert, without the possibility of ever approaching closer to the goal. His fate might be defined as that of the Protestant who, having pushed to its extreme point the rejection of all mediation as idolatry, goes on to reject even the possibility of a Christ as Mediator: for Kafka believed that the coming of the Messiah would always remain an event to be expected in the future, that Christ would always come a day later than any day which might be named. "The Messiah will only come when he is no longer necessary, he will only come a day after his arrival, he won't come on the last day, but on the last day of all."[66]

Kafka could, in other words, never make the leap from tragic vision to Christian faith, or even to the point at which the possibility of Christian faith might be entertained. His closest approach to Christianity is probably to be found in an important chapter of *The Trial*, "In the Cathedral." In this chapter, a priest tells Joseph K. a parable about what is involved in reaching (or, perhaps, in never reaching) heaven, and this parable is the nearest thing to an explanation of his situation that Joseph K. ever receives. Earlier, he had seen on the cathedral wall a picture of Christ being lowered into the tomb, with a knight in attendance – that is, he had seen a representation of the most dreadful moment in the Christian story, the time when Christ, the God-Man, the Mediator, is dead, and the link between the fallen human world and the divine world is broken. This is the time which Hölderlin's poems describe, the hard time, when the gods are no longer present and are not yet again present to man. And this is Kafka's time too. For it is as though not only Joseph K. but all his characters had been condemned to endure permanently the terrible time between the death of Christ and his resurrection. This is the time when, as in the priest's parable to Joseph K., one stands forever at the door which is the beginning of the way to the Law, the promised land, and yet forever put off by the statement that this is indeed one's very own door, but that one may not yet enter it.

One may compare Kafka, then, with Pascal, for whom the mystery of the Incarnation, the joining of the two worlds through the God-Man, alone could provide an escape from the contradictions of the two. Only Christ, the *deus absconditus* made present and manifest, could, for Pascal, provide an avenue from the world of *divertissement* and ambiguity to the higher realm which is the simultaneous affirmation of the yes and the no. But for Kafka, obeying to the end the interdiction against idolatry, against the acceptance of any manifest Mediator, there was no way out of the world of endless wandering and contradiction. For Kafka there was a goal but no way, only endless wavering, and he chose to remain true to the wavering, to his "deeper, uneasier skepticism": with infinite patience, he pushed on, ever farther and farther into the desert with each work, until, paradoxically, his work became the falsehood which testifies to the truth, the wavering that reveals the goal, even though the goal is never reached. For Kafka God remained "*absconditus*," yet, in making this testimony, he did, in a way, testify to God's presence. And it is in this testimony to God in a time when he is absent that Kafka fulfills Auden's description of him as the most truly *exemplary* figure of our time.

Notes

1. Franz Kafka, *Diaries: 1914–1923*, Max Brod, ed., tr. Martin Greenberg and Hannah Arendt (New York, 1949), p. 211.
2. *ibid.*, p. 213.
3. *ibid.*, p. 215.
4. *ibid.*, p. 214.
5. Franz Kafka, *The Great Wall of China*, tr. Willa and Edwin Muir (New York, 1946), p. 288.
6. *Diaries: 1910–1913*, Max Brod, ed., tr. Joseph Kresh (New York, 1948), p. 162.
7. *ibid.*, p. 24.
8. *Amerika*, tr. Edwin Muir (New York, 1946), p.138.
9. *The Castle*, tr. Edwin and Willa Muir (New York, 1951), p. 256.
10. *Selected Short Stories*, tr. Willa and Edwin Muir (New York, 1952), p. 179.
11. *Dairies: 1914–1923*, pp. 187–8.
12. "Investigations of a Dog," *The Great Wall of China*, pp. 46–7.
13. *ibid.*, p. 47; my italics.
14. *Diaries: 1914–1923*, p. 10.
15. "Investigations of a Dog," *The Great Wall of China*, pp. 47–8.
16. *Diaries: 1914–1923*, p. 180.
17. *ibid.*, p. 215.
18. *Diaries: 1910–1913*, p. 27.
19. *ibid.*, p. 26.
20. *ibid.*, p. 180.
21. *ibid.*, p. 33.
22. *Diaries: 1914–1923*, p. 98.
23. *Diaries: 1910–1913*, p. 73.
24. *ibid.*, p. 69.
25. *ibid.*, p. 310.
26. *ibid.*, p. 324.
27. *The Great Wall of China*, p. 293.
28. *Diaries: 1914–1923*, p. 196.
29. *Diaries: 1910–1913*, p. 305.
30. *Diaries: 1914–1923*, p. 132.

31. *Diaries: 1910–1913*, p. 297.
32. *The Great Wall of China*, p. 302.
33. *Diaries: 1910–1913*, p. 323.
34. *Diaries: 1914–1923*, p. 126.
35. *Diaries: 1910–1913*, p. 27.
36. *Diaries: 1914–1923*, p. 77.
37. "The Hunter Gracchus," *The Great Wall of China*, pp. 210, 214.
38. *Diaries: 1910–1913*, p. 316.
39. *ibid.*, p. 254.
40. *Diaries: 1914–1923*, p. 68; italics in the original.
41. *ibid.*, p. 75.
42. *Diaries: 1910–1913*, p. 299.
43. *Diaries: 1914–1923*, p. 195.
44. *ibid.*, p. 314.
45. *ibid.*, p. 195.
46. *Diaries: 1910–1913*, p. 173.
47. *ibid.*, p. 248.
48. *ibid.*, p. 61.
49. *ibid.*, p. 134.
50. *ibid.*, p. 101.
51. *ibid.*, p. 288.
52. *Diaries: 1914–1923*, p. 142.
53. *Diaries: 1910–1913*, p. 76.
54. *ibid.*, p. 74–5.
55. *ibid.*, p. 58.
56. *Diaries: 1914–1923*, p. 202.
57. *ibid.*, p. 212.
58. See *Selected Stories*, p. 124.
59. *Diaries: 1914–1923*, p. 77.
60. *Diaries: 1910–1913*, p. 206.
61. *Diaries: 1914–1923*, p. 214.
62. *The Great Wall of China*, p. 292.
63. See *The Great Wall of China*, p. 278.
64. *ibid.*, p. 287.
65. *The Castle*, p. 146.
66. *Hochzeitsvorbereitungen auf dem Lande* (New York, 1953), p. 90; my translation.

3

Wallace Stevens' poetry of being

We were as Danes in Denmark all day long
And knew each other well, hale-hearted landsmen,
For whom the outlandish was another day

Of the week, queerer than Sunday. We thought alike
And that made brothers of us in a home
In which we fed on being brothers, fed

And fattened as on a decorous honeycomb.[1]

There was once a time when man lived in harmony with his fellows and his surroundings. This harmony was a unified culture, a single view of the world. All men thought alike and understood each other perfectly, like the most intimate of brothers. Since they all shared an interpretation of the world they did not think of it as one perspective among many possible ones. Any other interpretation was queer, outlandish, something wild, ignorant, barbarian. Each man felt at home. He was a Dane in Denmark, not a Dane in Greece or Patagonia. Just as he possessed his fellows in the brotherhood of a single culture, so he possessed nature through their collective interpretation of it. He was a landsman, an inlander, someone dwelling close to the earth. Since man, society, and environment made one inextricable unity, as of Danes in Denmark, no one was aware of himself as a separate mind. Each man was like the bee in the honeycomb, the dwelling-place which he has exuded from his own body, and which now forms his food. All self-consciousness was lost in this reflexive feeding and fattening, and man "lay sticky with sleep" (*CP*, 419).

So enduring and beneficent did this order seem that it was impossible to believe that man himself could have made it. Surely, we thought, our happy world must be the gift of some supernatural beings, and these gods must guarantee its rightness and permanence. They seemed outside of or beyond our world, "speechless, invisible" (*CP*, 262). They ruled us and sustained us "by / Our merest apprehension of their will" (*CP*, 262).

Our culture was revelation of the invisible and speech of the speechless gods.

Suddenly something catastrophic happened, and all our happy order was destroyed:

> A tempest cracked on the theatre. Quickly,
> The wind beat in the roof and half the walls.
> The ruin stood still in an external world.
>
> It had been real. It was not now. The rip
> Of the wind and the glittering were real now,
> In the spectacle of a new reality. (*CP*, 306)

Once the theater is destroyed it can never be rebuilt. The fact that it can be destroyed proves that even when it existed it was not what it seemed. It seemed a divine gift, something as solid as the earth itself. Now man discovers that all along it was a painted scene. The true reality has always been the wind and the indifferent glittering of an external world, a world in which man can never feel at home.

When the tempest cracks on the theater the whole thing disintegrates: "Exit the whole / Shebang" (*CP*, 37). Men are no longer brothers, but strange to one another. The land withdraws to a distance and comes to be seen as no longer included in man's interpretations of it. When nature becomes outlandish the gods disappear. They do not withdraw for a time to an unattainable distance, as they did for De Quincey or Matthew Arnold. They vanish altogether, leaving nothing behind. They reveal themselves to be fictions, aesthetic projections of man's gratuitous values. Having seen the gods of one culture disappear, man can never again believe in any god: "The death of one god is the death of all" (*CP*. 391).[2]

This evaporation of the gods, leaving a barren man in a barren land, is the basis of all Stevens' thought and poetry. The death of the gods coincides with a radical transformation in the way man sees the world. What had been a warm home takes on a look of hardness and emptiness, like the walls, floors, and banisters of a vacant house. Instead of being intimately possessed by man, things appear to close themselves within themselves. They become mute, static presences:

> To see the gods dispelled in mid-air and dissolve like clouds is one of the great human experiences. It is not as if they had gone over the horizon to disappear for a time; nor as if they had been overcome by other gods of greater power and profounder knowledge. It is simply that they came to nothing. Since we have always shared all things with them and have always had a part of their strength and, certainly, all of their knowledge, we shared likewise this experience of annihilation. It was their annihilation, not ours, and yet it left us feeling that in a measure, we, too, had been

annihilated. It left us feeling dispossessed and alone in a solitude, like children without parents, in a home that seemed deserted, in which the amical rooms and halls had taken on a look of hardness and emptiness. What was most extraordinary is that they left no mementoes behind, no thrones, no mystic rings, no texts either of the soil or of the soul. It was as if they had never inhabited the earth. There was no crying out for their return. (*OP*, 206, 207).

There was no crying out for their return because we knew they would never come back. They would never come back because they had never been there at all.

In this impoverishing of the world when the gods disappear man discovers himself, orphaned and dispossessed, a solitary consciousness. Then are we truly "natives of poverty, children of malheur" (*CP*, 322). The moment of self-awareness in Stevens coincides with the moment of the death of the gods. God is dead, therefore I am. But I am nothing. I am nothing because I have nothing, nothing but awareness of the barrenness within and without. When the gods dissolve like clouds they "come to nothing." When the gods come to nothing, man is "nothing himself," and, since this is so, he "beholds / Nothing that is not there and the nothing that is" (*CP*, 10).

After the death of the gods and the discovery of nothingness Stevens is left in a world made of two elements: subject and object, mind and matter, imagination and reality. Imagination is the inner nothingness, while reality is the barren external world with which imagination carries on its endless intercourse. Stevens' problem is to reconcile the two. But such a reconciliation turns out to be impossible. This way and that vibrates his thought, seeking to absorb imagination by reality, to engulf reality in imagination, or to marry them in metaphor. Nothing will suffice, and Stevens is driven to search on tirelessly for some escape from conflict. This endless seeking is the motive and life of his poetry. The human self, for him, is divided against itself. One part is committed to the brute substance of earth, things as they are, and the other just as tenaciously holds to its need for imaginative grandeur. Self-division, contradiction, perpetual oscillation of thought – these are the constants in Stevens' work. Is it possible, as some critics have thought, that he is just confused? Is it from mere absence of mind that he affirms on one page of his "Adagia" that reality is the only genius (*OP*, 177), only to reverse himself two pages later and declare just as categorically that imagination is the only genius (*OP*, 179)?

The critic can develop radically different notions of Stevens' aims as a poet, and for each of these it is easy to find apposite passages from the text. It can be shown that Stevens believes poetry is metaphor, and that he believes all metaphors are factitious. At times he is unequivocally committed to bare reality. At other times he repudiates reality and sings the praises of imagination. Nor is it just a question of contradictions in the logical statements of the prose which are reconciled in the poetry. For each position and for its antithesis there are fully elaborated poems or parts of poems. It is impossible to find a single one-dimensional theory of poetry and life in Stevens. His poetry defines a realm in which everything "is not what it is" (*OP*, 178). Such poetry is not dialectical, if that means a series of stages which build on one another, each transcending the last and moving on to a higher stage, in some version of the Hegelian sequence of thesis, antithesis, synthesis. At the beginning Stevens is already as far as he ever goes. After the disappearance of the gods the poet finds himself in a place where opposites are simultaneously true. It seems that this situation can be dealt with in poetry only by a succession of wild swings to one extreme or another, giving first one limit of the truth, then the other. To escape such oscillation Stevens must find a way to write poetry that will possess simultaneously both extremes.

The elaboration of such a mode of poetry is Stevens' chief contribution to literature. In the meditative poems of his later years he takes possession of a new domain. The finished unity of his early poems, which makes many of them seem like elaborately wrought pieces of jewelry, is gradually replaced by poems which are open-ended improvisations. Such poems are not a neat enclosure of words forming a complex organic unity. They begin in the middle of a thought, and their ending is arbitrary. "The Man with the Blue Guitar" has a special place in Stevens' canon. It marks his turning to the new style. The reader has the feeling that the poem has been going on for some time when he hears the first words, and the last verses are not really an ending. The twanging of the strings continues interminably. Such a poem could be endless, and indeed three more "Stanzas for 'The Man with the Blue Guitar'" are given in *Opus Posthumous* (72, 73). The man with the guitar is described in "An Ordinary Evening in New Haven" as a permanent presence, someone always there in the mind's eye, watching the poet, and reminding him of his obligation to a faithful thinking of things as they are (*CP*, 483).

Life, for Stevens, is a series of states of consciousness with neither start nor finish. If the poem is to be true to life it must be a constant flowing of images which come as they come, and are not distorted by the logical mind in its eagerness for order. "One's grand flights," says Stevens, "one's Sunday baths, / One's tootings at the weddings of the soul / Occur as they occur" (*CP*, 222). Just as "The Man with the Blue Guitar" refuses to round itself off formally with beginning, middle, and end, so the parts which are given do not organize themselves into a whole, or even into part of a whole. There is no coherent pattern of symbols and metaphors, each one referring to all the others. One metaphor or symbol is introduced, developed for a while, then dropped. Another motif appears, is developed in its turn, disappears, is replaced by another which has no connection with the other two, and so on. "The Man with the Blue Guitar" proceeds in a series of disconnected short flights, each persisting for only a brief span of time. Each short flight, while it lasts, is like a "half-arc hanging in mid-air / Composed, appropriate to the incomplete" (*CP*, 309).

The same thing is true of Stevens' other long poems, "Esthetique du Mal," or "Notes toward a Supreme Fiction," or "An Ordinary Evening in New Haven." These poems keep close to the quality of life as it is. Such poems, like life, proceed in a series of momentary crystallizations or globulations of thought, followed by dissolution, and then re-conglomeration in another form. "Thought," says Stevens, "tends to collect in pools" (*OP*, 170). A man's mental energy tends to organize itself momentarily in a certain shape, but life flows on, and a new pattern is called for. The mind has a powerful resistance to doing the same thing twice, and "originality is an escape from repetition" (*OP*, 177). "As a man becomes familiar with his own poetry," says Stevens, "it becomes as obsolete for himself as for anyone else. From this it follows that one of the motives in writing is renewal" (*OP*, 220). Stevens always emphasizes the evanescence of poetry. Poetry is like a snowflake fluttering through the air and dissolving in the sea. It is radically bound to a time experienced as a sequence of present moments, each real and valid only so long as it is present. "Poetry," says Stevens, "is a finikin thing of air / That lives uncertainly and not for long" (*CP*, 155). In the "Adagia," "Poetry is a pheasant disappearing in the brush" (*OP*, 173). Most succinctly: "A poem is a meteor" (*OP*, 158).

This fragmentary quality is evident in Stevens' titles, both those for individual poems and those for books. Each poem by itself, like the whole mass of them together, is a hesitant and uncertain movement toward a goal which is never reached. He calls a poem "Prelude to Objects," or "Asides on the Oboe," or "Extracts from Addresses to the Academy of Fine Ideas," or "Debris of Life and Mind," or "Notes toward a Supreme Fiction," or "Prologues to What is Possible," in each case emphasizing the broken, partial nature of the poem, the way it is a piece of something larger, or is only an indirect and incomplete movement toward its object, something preliminary and unfinished. The titles of his books of poetry suggest the same qualities. The harmonium is a small key-board organ used in the home. The book of poems called *Harmonium* seems to be a series of improvisations on this amateur's instrument. But Stevens wanted to call his first book "The Grand Poem: Preliminary

Minutiae."[3] This title would have been a perfect expression of the nature of all his poems. "Harmonium" too suggests something of this notion of tentative fragments. Stevens may have been remembering this, as well as trying to affirm the unity of his work, when he wanted to call his collected poems *The Whole of Harmonium* (*OP*, xiv). The titles of his other books are just as tentative: *Ideas of Order, Parts of a World, Transport to Summer* (in which one side of the pun gives the idea of motion in the direction of summer), and *The Auroras of Autumn* (an apt phrase to describe poems which are a flickering continuum of light). Only *The Rock* suggests something final and stable, but that title was affixed after Stevens had attained the ultimate immobility of death. All his poems taken together form a single poem. This poem is a long series of provisional pools of imagery, each drawn toward a goal which can never be named directly or embodied in any poem. Man can never live again in a unified homeland. "We live in a constellation / Of patches and of pitches, / Not in a single world," and we are therefore always "Thinkers without final thoughts / In an always incipient cosmos" (*OP*, 114, 115).

Within the "endlessly elaborating poem" (*CP*, 486) which is life, the same sequence of events is constantly happening over and over again. First something happens which "decreates," which destroys an earlier imagination of the world. Then man is left face to face with the bare rock of reality. This happens every year in autumn. When the leaves have all fallen, "we return / To a plain sense of things," and "it is as if / We had come to an end of the imagination" (*CP*, 502). This clearing away is experienced not as a loss but as a gain. What is removed was a fictive covering of the rock, and what is exposed is the real in all its clarity:

> The barrenness that appears is an exposing.
> It is not part of what is absent, a halt
> For farewells, a sad hanging on for remembrances.
>
> It is a coming on and a coming forth.
> The pines that were fans and fragrances emerge,
> Staked solidly in a gusty grappling with rocks. (*CP*, 487)

The autumnal experience of decreation, as of leaves turning brown and falling, gives man a sense of "cold and earliness and bright origin" (*CP*, 481). It is as if the poet were like the first man facing an "uncreated" world, with everything still to be imagined.

This experience of coldness and earliness is only the start. The poet is not satisfied to confront a bare and unimagined world. He wants to possess it, and it can only be possessed by being imagined well. Man is inhabited by a "will to change" (*CP*, 397) which is just as unappeasable as his will to see the rock of reality exposed in all its bareness. The experience of decreation is followed by the reconstruction of a new imagination of the world. Spring follows winter, the rock is covered with leaves which are the icon of the poem, and what had been the simplicity of beginning becomes the ornate complexity of the end. The poet moves from "naked Alpha," "the infant A standing on infant legs" to "hierophant Omega," "twisted, stooping, polymathic Z" (*CP*, 469). If the beginning is bare and simple, the end is multiple and encrusted with color, like an illuminated manuscript, or like a splendid robe of state, "adorned with cryptic stones and sliding shines, . . . / With the whole spirit sparkling in its cloth, / Generations of the imagination piled / In the manner of its stitchings, of its thread" (*CP*, 434).

No sooner has the mind created a new fictive world than this "recent imagining of reality" (*CP*, 465) becomes obsolete in its turn, and must be rejected. This rejection is the act of decreation, and returns man once more to unadorned reality. The cycle then begins again: imagining followed by decreation followed by imagining and so on for as long as life lasts. In this rhythmic alternation lies our only hope to possess reality. Each moment is born in newness and freedom, with no connections to the past. Man must match the ever-renewed freedom of time with an equally radical freedom on his own part, a willed disencumbering of himself of all the corpses of the past. This is the sense in which "all men are murderers" (*OP*, 168), for "Freedom is like a man who kills himself / Each night, an incessant butcher, whose knife / Grows sharp in blood" (*CP*, 292), and "All things destroy themselves or are destroyed" (*OP*, 46). So Stevens cries: "what good were yesterday's devotions?" (*CP*, 264). This refusal of the past gives him a possession of the present moment in all its instantaneous vitality: "I affirm and then at midnight the great cat / Leaps quickly from the fireside and is gone" (*CP*, 264).

The present is the great cat who leaps from the fireside and is gone. It can never be seized or held and it lasts only for the blink of an eye. But if life is a series of such moments, how is it possible to justify even the cycle of decreation followed by a re-imagining of reality? This cycle seems to move with a slow and stately turning, like the sequence of the seasons that is so often its image. If the poet pauses long enough to write the poem of winter it will already be part of the dead past long before he has finished it, and so for the poems of the other seasons. It seems that the poet will make sterile vibrations back and forth between one spiritual season and the other, always a little behind the perpetual flowing of reality.

There is one way to escape this impasse, and the discovery of this way gives its special character to all Stevens' later poetry. He can move so fast from one season to another that all the extreme postures of the spirit are present in a single moment. If he can do this he will never pause long enough at any extreme for it to freeze into dead fixity, and he will appease at last his longing to have both imagination and reality at once. An oscillation rapid enough becomes a blur in which opposites are touched simultaneously, as alternating current produces a steady beam of light, and the cycle of decreation and imagining, hopelessly false if the poet goes through it at leisure, becomes true at last to things as they are if he moves through it fast enough. Each tick of the clock is "the starting point of the human and the end" (*CP*, 528). In "this present" there is a "dazzle-dazzle of being new / And of becoming," "an air of freshness, clearness, greenness, blueness, / That which is always beginning because it is part / Of that which is always beginning, over and over" (*CP*, 530). The present is always beginning over and over because it has no sooner begun than it has gone all the way to the end, and has moved so rapidly that "this end and this beginning are one" (*CP*, 506). All the possible elements of experience are always present in every instant of time, and in every season or weather of the mind: consciousness in its emptiness detached from reality and seeking it in bare impoverishment, the imagination covering the rock with leaves, flowers, and fruit, the drying and falling of the leaves in autumn.

Stevens' *Collected Poems* moves in a stately round through the whole cycle of the seasons, from the gaudy, spring-like poems of *Harmonium*, like new buds on the rock, through *Transport to Summer* and *The Auroras of Autumn*, and then back again to winter's bareness with *The Rock*. Every authentic image, from one end of his poetry to the other, recapitulates this sequence in a breath. In "Notes toward a Supreme Fiction" Stevens says that a true poem allows the reader to share, for a moment, the "first idea." This means having a vision of things in the radiance of their presence, without any intervening film between man and the pure sensation of things as they are. To do this, Stevens says, is to see things in "living changingness" (*CP*, 380), to go in a moment from the white candor of the beginning in its original freshness to the white candor of the end in its multiplicity of imaginative enhancements. "We move between these points: / From that ever-early candor to its late plural" (*CP*, 382).

In "The Owl in the Sarcophagus" (*CP*, 431–6) Stevens gives his fullest dramatization of the way time moves from beginning to end in a moment. The poem is about "the forms of thought," that is, about the universal limits between which human thought moves, and in terms of which man lives, for "we live in the mind." If man lives in the mind he dies there too:

It is a child that sings itself to sleep,
The mind, among the creatures that it makes,
The people, those by which it lives and dies. (*CP*, 436)

Man dies in the mind because the mind too is bound by time. This means that it is defined by the fact that it will one day die. Life dwells within death, is constantly coming from and returning to death, as its origin, home, and end. The owl, Minerva, the mind, lives in a sarcophagus, and the poem describes "the mythology of modern death" (*CP*, 435). It embodies the forces which determine the mind's activity, "the creatures that it makes." These forces are "death's own supremest images, / The pure perfections of parental space, / The children of a desire that is the will, / Even of death, the beings of the mind / In the light-bound space of the mind, the floreate flare . . ." (*CP*, 436).

Since the figures of the poem live in the perpetual present of mental space, they live "in an element not the heaviness of time" (*CP*, 432), that is, in "a time / That of itself [stands] still, perennial" (*CP*, 432). The moment is "less time than place" (*CP*, 433) because it is outside of time, though it is the only living part of time.

The figures of the mythology of modern death are three: sleep, peace, and "she that says / Good-by in the darkness" (*CP*, 431). Sleep is the beginning, the radiant candor of pure mind without any content, mind as it is when it faces a bare unimagined reality, or mind as it is when it has completed the work of decreation, and is ready "in an ever-changing, calmest unity" (*CP*, 433) to begin imagining again: "Sleep realized / Was the whiteness that is the ultimate intellect, / A diamond jubilance beyond the fire" (*CP*, 433).

If sleep is the beginning, peace is the end, "the brother of sleep," "the prince of shither-shade and tinsel lights" (*CP*, 434). "Peace after death" is the end in the sense that it represents a fulfillment of imagination. Sleep is prior to life, since ultimate intellect cannot even be called consciousness, or is consciousness with no content. Peace is the death at the end of life, the death of a consummation of the imagination. Peace, like sleep, is that death man touches in every moment as he moves all the way from the immaculate beginning to its late plural. Peace is "that figure stationed at our end, / Always, in brilliance, fatal, final, formed / Out of our lives to keep us in our death" (*CP*, 434).

What of the third figure, "she that says good-by," who is she? She broods over the moment of life, the infinitesimally brief flash between start and finish which is living reality, surrounded on all sides by death. She dwells in what Stevens calls in another poem "the mobile and immobile flickering / In the area between is and was" (*CP*, 474). This moment, evanescent as it is, is the only reality, and it is only in the moment, a moment that changes and evaporates with the utmost rapidity, that man can glimpse things as they are. Things exist only in the time they are moving from is to was, and the third figure is the embodiment of this presence of the present, a presence which is like that of a glow in molten iron, such a glow as fades even as we watch it.

How is it possible to write poetry which will match the mobility of the moment? It would seem that any image or form of words would be too fixed to move with a time which changes so instantaneously. A poem of any length would be far too long to be a meteor. It would transform the living flow of reality into a clumsy machine wholly unable to keep up with time. Such a poem would be a dead relic of the past long before the reader had reached the last line.

Stevens gradually develops, as his poetry progresses, a way of matching the fluidity of time. He comes to write a poetry of flickering mobility, a poetry in which each phrase moves so rapidly it has beginning and ending at once. Instead of being fixed and unyielding, a solid piece of language interacting with other words, each image recapitulates within itself the coming into being of the moment and its disappearance. The fluctuation between beginning and ending has become so rapid that it takes place in a single phrase, or in a "syllable between life / And death" (*CP*, 432). Each image in a poem of such phrases is a meteor. "An Ordinary Evening in New Haven," for example, constantly generates itself out of its own annihilation, ending and beginning again indefatigably. It expresses, in its "flickings from finikin to fine finikin," "the edgings and inchings of final form, / The swarming activities of the formulae / Of statement, directly and indirectly getting at" (*CP*, 488).

At first, after the dissolution of the gods, it seemed that Stevens was left, like post-Cartesian man in general, in a world riven in two, split irreparably into subject and object, imagination and reality. All his work seems based on this dualism. Any attempt to escape it by affirming the priority of one or the other power leads to falsehood. But as his work progresses, Stevens comes more and more to discover that there is after all only one realm, always and everywhere the realm of some new conjunction of imagination and reality. Imagination is still present in the most absolute commitment of the mind to reality, and reality is still there in the wildest imaginary fiction. The later Stevens is beyond metaphysical dualism, and beyond representational thinking. In his late poems it is no longer a question of some reality which already exists out there in the world, and of which the poet then makes an image. The image is inextricably part of the thing, and the most extreme imaginative "distortion" is still based on reality. There is only one ever-present existence: consciousness *of* some reality. Imagination is reality, or, as Stevens says: "poetry and reality are one."[4] In another formulation: "the structure of poetry and the structure of reality are one" (*NA*, 81). If this is the case, then there is no real thing which is transformed into various imaginary aspects. The real thing is already imagined, and "imaginative transcripts" are as much a part of reality as anything else is. "What our eyes behold," says Stevens, "may well be the text of life but one's meditations on the text and the disclosures of these meditations are no less a part of the structure of reality" (*NA*, 76). As he puts it in the title of a very late poem: "Reality is an activity of the most august imagination" (*OP*, 110).

This discovery of the identity of all the elements of life means a redefinition of poetry. Words are not pictures of reality. They are part of the thing, tangled inextricably with the event they describe. "The poem is the cry of its occasion, / Part of the res itself and not about it" (*CP*, 473), and therefore "description is revelation" (*CP*, 344). Words are the vortex of the whirlpool, where imagination and reality merge, for "words of the world are the life of the world" (*CP*, 474).

This seems to be Stevens' ultimate position: a resolution of imagination and reality in a theory of the identity of poetry and life, and the development of a poetry of flickering mobility to sustain this identity. But there is one more aspect of his thought, and this is the most difficult to see or to say.

It begins with an increasing movement toward nothingness in Stevens' later poetry. Along with the phrases expressing the swarming plenitude of the moment there is something different. At the same time as its tensions are resolved, Stevens' poetry gets more and more disembodied, more and more a matter of "the spirit's alchemicana," and less and less a matter of the solid and tangible, the pears on their dish, the round peaches with their fuzz and juice. It seems as if the poetry becomes more and more intangible as the oscillations between imagination and reality get more and more rapid, until, at the limit, the poem evaporates altogether. At the extreme of speed all solidity disappears. It is as if the same speed which allows beginning and ending to merge also releases something else: a glimpse of the nothingness that underlies all existence.

The word or the idea of nothingness comes back more and more often. Nothingness appears as early as *Harmonium*, but there it is associated with the bareness of winter. Only the snow man, the man who is "nothing himself," is free of imagination's fictions and can behold "nothing that is not there and the nothing that is." Stevens' later poetry is continuous with this early intuition of nothing, but the theme of nothingness gradually becomes more dominant. In the later poetry nothingness appears to be the source and end of everything, and to underlie everything as its present reality. Imagination is nothing. Reality is nothing. The mind is nothing. Words are nothing. God is nothing. Perhaps it is the fact that all these things are equivalent to nothing which makes them all equivalents of one another. All things come together in the nothing. Stevens speaks of "the priest of nothingness who intones" on the rock of reality (*OP*, 88). In another poem the wind "intones its single emptiness" (*CP*, 294). He tells of a room "emptier than nothingness" (*CP*, 286), or of a moon which is "a lustred nothingness" (*CP*, 320). He asks for a "god in the house" who will be so insubstantial that he will be "a coolness, / A vermilioned nothingness" (*CP*, 328), and speaks of metaphysical presences which are like "beasts that one never sees, / Moving so that the foot-falls are slight and almost nothing" (*CP*, 337). Again and again he says that all things, "seen and unseen," are "created from nothingness" (*CP*, 486; *OP*, 100), or "forced up from nothing" (*CP*, 363). The growth of leaves on the rock of reality comes from nothing, "as if," says Stevens, "nothingness contained a métier" (*CP*, 526). In another poem, the first breath of spring "creates a fresh universe out of nothingness" (*CP*, 517).

The rock of reality seems not to be a substantial reality, material and present before the poet's eyes. It seems to have come from nothingness. If it has come from nothingness, its source still defines it, and all things dwell in the "stale grandeur of annihilation" (*CP*, 505). As Stevens says in a striking phrase: "Reality is a vacuum" (*OP*, 168).

A number of his poems attempt to express the way reality is a vacuum. In such poems "we breathe / An odor evoking nothing, absolute" (*CP*, 394, 395). "A Clear Day and No Memories" (*OP*, 113) describes a weather in which "the air is clear of everything," "has no knowledge except of nothingness," and "flows over us without meanings" in an "invisible activity." "Chocorua to Its Neighbor" (*CP*, 296–302) is an extraordinarily disembodied poem, the subject of which is a strange shadow, "an eminence, / But of nothing" (*CP*, 300). In "The Auroras of Autumn" a serpent is present everywhere in the landscape, and yet present as form disappearing into formlessness:

> This is where the serpent lives, the bodiless.
> His head is air. . . .

> This is where the serpent lives. This is his nest,
> These fields, these hills, these tinted distances,
> And the pines above and along and beside the sea.

> This is form gulping after formlessness,
> Skin flashing to wished-for disappearances
> And the serpent body flashing without the skin. (*CP*, 411)

Such poems accomplish a hollowing out or subtilizing of reality. They give the reader the feeling of what it is like to see reality not as a solid substance, but as something less tangible than the finest mist. They attempt to make visible something which is "always too heavy for the sense / To seize, the obscurest as, the distant was" (*CP*, 441). They are based on the presupposition that the center of reality is a nothingness which is "a nakedness, a point, / Beyond which fact could not progress as fact / . . . Beyond which thought could not progress as thought" (*CP*, 402, 403). If it is true that the underlying substance of reality is a vacuum, "the dominant blank, the unapproachable" (*CP*, 477), then we must give up the idea that reality is a solid rock, and see it as a nameless, evanescent flowing, something hovering on the edge of oblivion. "It is not in the premise that reality / Is a solid," says Stevens in the last words of "An Ordinary Evening in New Haven." "It may be a shade that traverses / A dust, a force that traverses a shade" (*CP*, 489).

If reality is a vacuum, imagination is no less empty. It is the "nothing" of "Imago" (*CP*, 439), which lifts all things. Man in a world where reality is nonentity "has his poverty and nothing more" (*CP*, 427). Such a man is defined as "desire," and is "always in emptiness that would be filled" (*CP*, 467).

It seemed that Stevens was moving closer and closer to a full possession of the plenitude of things, but as the tension between imagination and reality diminishes there is an unperceived emptying out of both, until, at the moment they touch, in the brevity of a poem which includes beginning and ending in a breath, the poet finds himself face to face with a universal nothing.

Nevertheless, this apparent defeat is the supreme victory, for the nothing is not nothing. It is. It is being. Being is the universal power, visible nowhere in itself, and yet visible everywhere in all things. It is what all things share through the fact that they are. Being is not a thing like other things, and therefore can appear to man only as nothing, yet it is what all things participate in if they are to exist at all. All Stevens' later poetry has as its goal the releasing of the evanescent glimpse of being which is as close as man can come to a possession of the ground of things. The paradoxical appearance to man of being in the form of nothing is the true cause of the ambiguity of his poetry. Man's inability to see being as being causes the poet to say of it: "It is and it / Is not and, therefore, is" (*CP*, 440), and yet in the supreme moments of insight he can speak directly of it, in lines which are a cry of ecstatic discovery:

> It is like a thing of ether that exists
> Almost as predicate. But it exists,
> It exists, it is visible, it is, it is. (*CP*, 418)

The nothing is, but it is not merely the nothingness of consciousness.

Human nature participates in being, but so do all other existences. Wherever the poet thinks to catch it, it disappears, melting into the landscape and leaving just the pines and rock and water which are there, or being absorbed into the mind and taking the mind's own shape: "If in the mind, he vanished, taking there / The mind's own limits, like a tragic thing / Without existence, existing everywhere" (*CP*, 298). Being is released in the flash of time from is to was, just as it is released in the expansion of perception to occupy space. Being is the presentness of things present, the radiance of things as they are, and is therefore "physical if the eye is quick enough" (*CP*, 301).

In two late poems, "Metaphor as Degeneration" (*CP*, 444) and "The River of Rivers in Connecticut" (*CP*, 533) Stevens sees being as a river, hidden behind all the appearances that tell of it, and yet flowing everywhere, through all space and time, and through all the contents of space and time. In these two poems he gives his most succinct expression of his apprehension of being:

> It is certain that the river
>
> Is not Swatara. The swarthy water
> That flows round the earth and through the skies,
> Twisting among the universal spaces,
>
> Is not Swatara. It is being. (*CP*, 444)

> It is not to be seen beneath the appearances
> That tell of it. The steeple at Farmington
> Stands glistening and Haddam shines and sways.
>
> It is the third commonness with light and air,
> A curriculum, a vigor, a local abstraction . . .
> Call it, once more, a river, an unnamed flowing,
>
> Spaced-filled, reflecting the seasons, the folk-lore
> Of each of the senses; call it, again and again,
> The river that flows nowhere, like a sea. (*CP*, 533)

At the heart of Stevens' poetry there is a precise metaphysical experience. Or, rather, this experience is beyond metaphysics, since the tradition of metaphysics is based on a dualism putting ultimate being in some transcendent realm, above and beyond what man can see. Being, for Stevens, is within things as they are, here and now, revealed in the glistening of the steeple at Farmington, in the flowing of time, in the presentness of things present, in the interior fons of man.

Stevens' experience of being is "a difficult apperception," "disposed and re-disposed / By such slight genii in such pale air" (*CP*, 440). To speak directly of this apperception, to analyze it, is almost inevitably to falsify it, to fix it in some abstraction, and therefore to kill it. Though man participates in being, he does not confront it directly. It is the center of which each man is an eccentric particle, for he is always "helplessly at the edge" (*CP*, 430). When he tries to grasp it, it disappears. Man can never possess "the bouquet of being" (*OP*, 109), that fugitive aroma. The best we can do is "to realize / That the sense of being changes as we talk" (*OP*, 109), and go on talking in the hope that if we are careful to see that "nothing [is] fixed by a single word" (*OP*, 114), nothing will be, in another sense, fixed momentarily in a word, and we shall have another evanescent insight into being.

The only passage in Stevens' prose which speaks directly of his perception of being, "that nobility which is our spiritual height and depth" (*NA*, 33, 34), is curiously evasive. It is evasive because its subject is evasive. There is *something* there, Stevens says, but it can only be described negatively, for to define it is to fix it, and it must not be fixed:

> I mean that nobility which is our spiritual height and depth; and while I know how difficult it is to express it, nevertheless I am bound to give a sense of it. Nothing could be more evasive and inaccessible. Nothing distorts itself and seeks disguise more quickly. There is a shame of disclosing it and in its definite presentations a horror of it. But there it is. The fact that it is there is what makes it possible to invite to the reading and writing of poetry men of intelligence and desire for life. I am not thinking of the ethical or the sonorous or at all of the manner of it. The manner of it is, in fact, its difficulty, which each man must feel each day differently, for himself. I am not thinking of the solemn, the portentous or demoded. On the other hand, I am evading a definition. If it is defined, it will be fixed and it must not be fixed. And in the case of an external thing, nobility resolves itself into an enormous number of vibrations, movements, changes. To fix it is to put an end to it. (*NA*, 33, 34)

To fix it is to put an end to it, but in poetry it can be caught unfixed. The mobile, flickering poetry of Stevens' later style, poetry which fears stillness beyond anything, is more than a revelation of the impossibility of escaping the war of the mind and sky. It is a revelation of being. The poem names being, the human-like figure which the mind is always confronting at every extreme, but which it is never able to catch and immobilize in words. The nothing which makes it impossible ever to rest, which makes nonsense of any attempt to express things rationally, and which always drives the poet on to another effort to seize the nothing by marrying imagination and reality – this nothing turns out to be being. The poetry of flittering metamorphosis is the only poetry that is simultaneously true to both imagination and reality, and it is the only poetry that will catch being. Being is "the dominant blank, the unapproachable," but it is nevertheless the source of everything, all man sees and all he is. The ultimate tragedy is that being is transformed instantaneously into nothing, and therefore though the poet has it he has it as an absence. Only a poetry of iridescent frettings will remain in touch with it, for "life / Itself is like a poverty in the space of life, / So that the flapping of the wind . . . / Is something in tatters that [man] cannot hold" (*CP*, 298, 299). Being is inherent in human nature, but it is inherent as a center which can never be embraced. In the process of going in a moment through the whole cycle from A to Z something is released, glimpsed, and annihilated, like those atomic particles which live only a millionth of a second. This something is being. As soon as it is named, it disappears, takes the limits of the mind, or melts into the limited existence of the object. But for a moment it is seen. "It is and it / Is not and, therefore, is."

The motive for rapid motion in Stevens' poetry is not only that speed reconciles imagination and reality. Speed also makes possible a vision of being – in the moment of its disappearance. After reading one of Stevens' poems the reader has the feeling that, after all, nothing has happened, no change of the world such as science or technology can perform: "And yet nothing has been changed except what is / Unreal, as if nothing had been changed at all" (*OP*, 117). At the end it *was* there. It is already part of the past. Poetry is a pheasant disappearing in the brush. So Santayana, in "To an Old Philosopher in Rome," lives "on the threshold of heaven," and sees things double, things and the presence of being in things, "The extreme of the known in the presence of the extreme / Of the unknown" (*CP*, 508). To see things transfigured in this way is still to see them just as they are, in all their barrenness and poverty. This world and the other are "two alike in the make of the mind" (*CP*, 508), and the old philosopher's ultimate insight, like Stevens' own, is not at all a vision of things beyond this world:

> It is a kind of total grandeur at the end,
> With every visible thing enlarged and yet
> No more than a bed, a chair and moving nuns,
> The immensest theatre, the pillared porch,
> The book and candle in your ambered room . . . (*CP*, 510)

But merely to see being in things is not enough. Being must be spoken. The speaking of poetry liberates being in the presence of things. Through words man participates in being, for words of the world are the life of the world, and "the word is the making of the world, / The buzzing world and lisping firmament" (*CP*, 345). Poetry does not name something which has already been perceived, or put in words a pre-existent mental conception. The act of naming brings things together, gathers them into one, and makes present the things which are present. Speaking belongs to being, and in naming things in their presence poetry releases a glimpse of being.

From De Quincey through Arnold and Browning to Hopkins, Yeats, and Stevens the absence of God is starting point and basis. Various poets, Browning or Yeats for example, beginning in this situation are able to make a recovery of immanence. Perhaps it is Stevens' way, the movement from the dissolution of the gods to the difficult apperception of being, that represents the next step forward in the spiritual history of man. Stevens may be in the vanguard of a movement "toward the end of ontology," as Jean Wahl calls it.[5] Central in this movement is the idea that all our spiritual height and depth is available here and now or nowhere. The last stanza of "A Primitive like an Orb" is one of Stevens' most eloquent statements of his belief that all the words and all the experiences of man are part of being, eccentric particles of the giant "at the center on the horizon," the giant who can never be fully possessed or spoken in any words, but who is shared by all. If this is the case, then the simplest phrase, in all its limitation, is indeed "the human end in the spirit's greatest reach" (*CP*, 508):

> That's it. The lover writes, the believer hears,
> The poet mumbles and the painter sees,
> Each one, his fated eccentricity,
> As a part, but part, but tenacious particle,
> Of the skeleton of the ether, the total
> Of letters, prophecies, perceptions, clods
> Of color, the giant of nothingness, each one
> And the giant ever changing, living in change. (*CP*, 443)

Notes

1. *The Collected Poems of Wallace Stevens* (New York, 1954), p. 419. This volume will hereafter be cited as *CP*.
2. See also Wallace Stevens, *Opus Posthumous* (New York, 1957), p. 165. This volume will hereafter be cited as *OP*.
3. *Poems by Wallace Stevens*, selected, and with an Introduction, by Samuel French Morse (New York, 1961), p. viii.
4. Wallace Stevens, *The Necessary Angel: Essays on Reality and the Imagination* (New York, 1951), p. 81. This volume will hereafter be cited as *NA*.
5. See *Vers la fin de l'ontologie* (Paris, 1956).

4

Williams' poetry of resignation

William Carlos Williams was born in Rutherford, New Jersey, in 1883. After medical training at the University of Pennsylvania, he spent the rest of his life, until his retirement in 1951, practicing medicine in Rutherford. He met Ezra Pound at the University of Pennsylvania, and later came to know Marianne Moore, Wallace Stevens, Louis Zukofsky, and other poets and artists. During a long lifetime he published several dozen books – poems, plays, stories, novels, essays, a book about American history, an autobiography. The complete body of his published poetry, with a few unimportant omissions, may be read in four volumes: *The Collected Earlier Poems, The Collected Later Poems, Paterson,* and *Pictures from Brueghel.* He died in 1963 at the age of seventy-nine.[1]

Though Williams' work received considerable attention during his lifetime, he has only gradually come to be recognized as one of the most important of twentieth-century American poets, one deserving a place beside Pound, Eliot, Frost, and Stevens. His work registers a change in sensibility that puts him, along with other writers in America and abroad, beyond the characteristic assumptions of romanticism. Since these assumptions have for the most part been dominant in Western literature since the late eighteenth century, full understanding of Williams' work has been slow to develop. Though there is a recognizable kinship between that work and the work of certain other poets, artists, and philosophers of the twentieth century, Williams' presuppositions about poetry and human existence are his own. They are a unique version of a new tradition. What they are and the way they are implicit in each of his poems can only be discovered by that immersion in his writing which must precede interpretation of any part of it.

The difficulties of such interpretation may be suggested by consideration of the ways Williams' work fails to provide the reader habituated to romantic or symbolist poetry with the qualities he expects. Like a late eighteenth-century reader encountering the *Lyrical Ballads,* many present-day readers of Williams "will look round for poetry, and will be induced to inquire by what species of courtesy these attempts can be permitted to assume that title."[2] Here is a characteristic text from "Collected Poems 1934":

Young Sycamore

I must tell you
this young tree
whose round and firm trunk
between the wet

pavement and the gutter
(where water
is trickling) rises
bodily

into the air with
one undulant
thrust half its height –
and then

dividing and waning
sending out
young branches on
all sides –

hung with cocoons
it thins
till nothing is left of it
but two

eccentric knotted
twigs
bending forward
hornlike at the top[3]

Such a poem seems recalcitrant to analysis. The sycamore is not a symbol. "No symbolism is acceptable," says the poet (*SE*, 213). The tree does not stand for anything, or point to anything beyond itself. Like the red wheelbarrow, or the sea-trout and butterfish, or the flowering chicory in other poems by Williams, the young sycamore is itself, means itself. It is an object in space, separated from other objects in space, with its own sharp edges, its own innate particularity. The tree stands "between" the pavement and the gutter, but there is no assertion of an interchange between the three objects, no flow of an ubiquitous nature-spirit binding all things together. Things for Williams exist side by side in the world, and the poet here locates the sycamore by reference to the things closest to it.

The avoidance of symbolism in Williams' poetry is related to the absence of another quality – the dimension of depth. In romantic poetry, space frequently leads out to a "behind" or "beyond" which the poet may reach through objects, or which objects signify at a distance. In the Christian and Platonic traditions, things of this world in one way or another stand for things of the other world. Romantic poets inherit or extend this tradition, as in the thoughts too deep for tears which for Wordsworth are given by the meanest flower that blows, or as in the attraction of the "Far–far–away" for Tennyson, or as in Yeats' reaffirmation of the hermetic tradition in "Ribh Denounces Patrick": "For things below are copies, the Great Smaragdine Tablet said." In Williams' poetry this kind of depth has disappeared and with it the symbolism appropriate to it. Objects for him exist within a shallow space, like that created on the canvases of the American abstract expressionists. "Anywhere is everywhere" (*P*, 273), and there is no lure of distances which stretch out beyond what can be immediately seen. Nothing exists but what stands just before the poet's wide-awake senses, and "Heaven seems frankly impossible" (*SL*, 147).

For this reason there is no need to go anywhere or do anything to possess the plenitude of existence. Each of Williams' poems, to borrow the title of one of them, is "the world contracted to a recognizable image" (*PB*, 42). The poet has that power of "seeing the thing itself without forethought or afterthought but with great intensity of perception" which he praises in his mother (*SE*, 5), and all his poems have the quality which he claims for "Chicory and Daisies": "A poet witnessing the chicory flower and realizing its virtues of form and color so constructs his praise of it as to borrow no particle from right or left. He gives his poem over to the flower and its plant themselves" (*SE*, 17). While a poem lasts nothing exists beyond it – nothing but the chicory, in one poem, or bits of broken glass on cinders, in another, or the young sycamore between pavement and gutter in another. Immediacy in space, and also immediacy in time. The present alone is, and the aim of a poem must therefore be "to refine, to clarify, to intensify that eternal moment in which we alone live" (*SA*, 3). "Young Sycamore" is written in the present tense. It records the instant of Williams' confrontation of the tree.

There can also be for Williams little figurative language, little of that creation of a "pattern of imagery" which often unifies poems written in older traditions. Metaphors compare one thing to another and so blur the individuality of those things. For Williams the uniqueness of each thing is more important than any horizontal resonances it may have with other things:

> Although it is a quality of the imagination that it seeks to place together those things which have a common relationship, yet the coining of similes

is a pastime of very low order, depending as it does upon a nearly
vegetable coincidence. Much more keen is that power which discovers in
things those inimitable particles of dissimilarity to all other things which
are the peculiar perfections of the thing in question. (*SE*, 16)

"Young Sycamore" contains a single figurative word, "hornlike," and
though this word is of great importance in the poem, spreading its
implications backward to pick up the overtones of words like "bodily"
or "thrust" and suggesting that the sycamore has an animal-like volition
and power (or perhaps, as Wallace Stevens has said, the lithe sinuosity of
a snake), nevertheless the personification is attenuated. The poem is
made chiefly of a long clause which in straightforward language
describes the tree from trunk to topmost twig.

Such poetry provides problems not only for the analytical critic, but
also for a reader concerned about the uses of poetry. Poetry of the
romantic and symbolist traditions is usually dramatic or dialectical in
structure. It often presupposes a double division of existence. The objects
of this world are separated from the supernatural realities they signify,
and the consciousness of the poet is separated both from objects and from
their celestial models. A poetry based on such assumptions will be a
verbal act bringing about a change in man's relation to the world. In
uniting subject and object it will give the poet momentary possession of
that distant reality the object symbolizes. Such a poetry is the enactment
of a journey which may take the poet and his reader to the very bourne of
heaven. Mallarmé's work provides a symbolist version of this poetry of
dramatic action. He must avoid at any cost that direct description
Williams so willingly accepts, and write a poetry of indirection in which
the covert naming of things is the annihilation of those things so that
they may be replaced, beyond negation, by an essence which is purely
notional, an aroma "absent from all bouquets."

Nothing of this sort happens in Williams' poetry. "Young Sycamore"
does not go anywhere or accomplish any new possession of the tree.
There is no gradual approach of subject and object which leads to their
merger in an ecstatic union. The reader at the end is where he was at the
beginning – standing in imagination before the tree. The sycamore and
the poem about the sycamore are separate things, side by side in the
world in the same way that the tree stands between the pavement and the
gutter without participating in either. Romantic and symbolist poetry is
usually an art of willed transformation. In this it is, like science or
technology, an example of that changing of things into artifacts which
assimilates them into the human world. Williams' poetry, on the other
hand, is content to let things be. A good poet, he says, "doesn't *select* his
material. What is there to select? It *is*."[4]

No symbolism, no depth, no reference to a world beyond the world, no pattern of imagery, no dialectical structure, no interaction of subject and object – just description. How can the critic "analyze" such a poem? What does it mean? Of what use is it? How can the poet justify the urgency of his first line: "I must tell you"? If the poem does not make anything happen, or give the reader something he did not have before, it seems of no more use than a photograph of the tree.

The answers to these questions can be given only if the reader places himself within the context of the assumptions which underlie the poem. Anywhere is everywhere for Williams not because all places are indifferent, so that one place is as good as another, each one confessing the same failure of mind, objects, and their meanings to become one. Quite the opposite is the case. His poetry can give itself to calm description because all objects are already possessed from the beginning, in what he calls an "approximate co-extension with the universe" (*SA*, 27). The co-extension need be only approximate because that concentration on a single object or group of objects so habitual to Williams confirms his identification with all things. In order to attain that concentration, other things, for the moment, must be set aside; but they are no less there, no less latently present in the realm of co-extension the poet has entered. A primordial union of subject and object is the basic presupposition of Williams' poetry.

In assuming such a union his work joins in that return to the facts of immediate experience which is a widespread tendency in twentieth-century thought and art. This tendency may be identified in painters from Cézanne through cubism to abstract expressionism. It may be seen in poets like René Char, Jorge Guillén, Charles Olson, and Robert Creeley. It is visible in that transformation of fiction which has, most recently, generated the French "new novel," the *romans blancs* of Alain Robbe-Grillet or Nathalie Sarraute. It may be found in the linguistic philosophy of Wittgenstein in the *Philosophical Investigations*, and in the tradition of phenomenology from Husserl through Heidegger and Merleau-Ponty. Williams' poetry has its own unique structure and assumptions, but if any milieu is needed for it, this new tradition is the proper one. Though he understood the connection between his work and modern painting, and though he admired, for example, the poetry of Char, the similarities between his writing and other work should not be thought of in terms of "influences." The similarities are rather a matter of independent responses to a new experience of life.

Williams differs from other recent English and American poets in the timing of his acceptance of the new relation to the world. Yeats, Eliot, and Stevens, for example, also move beyond dualism, but this movement fills the whole course of their lives. It is accomplished only in their last work – in the explosive poetry of the moment in Yeats' "High Talk" or "News for the Delphic Oracle," or in the poetry of Incarnation in Eliot's *Four Quartets*, or in the fluid improvisations, joining imagination and reality, of Stevens' "An Ordinary Evening in New Haven." Williams, however, begins his career with the abandonment of his separate ego. Only in the unfinished narrative poem written during his medical studies[5] and in his first published volume, the *Poems* of 1909, does he remain within the romantic tradition. Themes of spatial distance and of the isolation of the self are dominant there. With his next long poem, "The Wanderer," Williams takes the step beyond romanticism. The poem ends with the protagonist's plunge into the "filthy Passaic." He is swallowed up by "the utter depth of its rottenness" until his separate existence is lost, and he can say, "I knew all – it became me" (*CEP*, 12). This "interpenetration, both ways" (*P*, 12) is assumed in all Williams' later poetry. His situation may be defined as "the mind turned inside out" into the world (*KH*, 72), or, alternatively, as the world turned inside out into the mind, for in the union of poet and river both his separate ego and the objective world disappear. An important letter to Marianne Moore describes this union of inner and outer and the "security" which resulted from it. It is, he says,

> something which occurred once when I was about twenty, a sudden resignation to existence, a despair – if you wish to call it that, but a despair which made everything a unit and at the same time a part of myself. I suppose it might be called a sort of nameless religious experience. I resigned, I gave up. (*SL*, 147)

"Young Sycamore," like the rest of Williams' mature poetry, is written on the basis of this act of resignation. In the poem there is neither subject nor object, but a single realm in which all things are both subjective and objective at once: the tree, the pavement, the gutter, the poem, the poet. The reader is included too, the "you" of the first line. The poet's address to the reader assimilates him into the realm of interpenetration in what Williams calls "a fraternal embrace, the classic caress of author and reader" (*SA*, 3). In Williams' poetry there is no description of private inner experience. There is also no description of objects which are external to the poet's mind. Nothing is external to his mind. His mind overlaps with things; things overlap with his mind. For this reason "Young Sycamore" is without dramatic action and can limit itself to an itemizing of the parts of the tree. There is no need to do anything to possess the tree because it is already possessed from the beginning.

The imaginary space generated by the words of "Young Sycamore" is not that space of separation, primarily optical, which the reader enters, for example, in the poetry of Matthew Arnold. The poem creates a space appropriate to the more intimate senses whereby the body internalizes the world. Such a space is characterized by intimacy and participation. It denies the laws of geometrical space, in which each thing is in one place and is limited by its surfaces. So Williams describes, for example, that aural space in which each sound permeates the whole world, like the pervasive tone in "The Desert Music" which is everywhere at once, "as when Casals struck / and held a deep cello tone" (*PB*, 119). Or in "Queen-Ann's-Lace" he experiences a woman and a field of the white flower not as metaphors of one another, but as interpenetrating realities. The poet's body, for Williams, is the place where subject and object are joined, and so, in "Young Sycamore," the tree is described as though its life were taking place inside his own life. The poem is a characteristic example of Williams' minimizing of eyesight and his emphasis on the more intimate senses, hearing, tasting, smelling, and above all touch, that *tactus eruditus* (CEP, 63) which it is proper for a physician to have. The assimilation of the world by the senses makes of the body a kinesthetic pantomime of the activity of nature. "A thing known," says Williams, "passes out of the mind into the muscles" (*KH*, 71). "Young Sycamore" affirms this possession not only in the tactile imagery of "round and firm trunk" and "bodily," but also in the pattern of verbs or verbals which makes up the framework of the poem: "rises," "undulant/ thrust," "dividing and waning," "sending out," "hung," "thins," "knotted," "bending." These words articulate the way the poet lives the life of the tree.

The sequence of verbal forms also expresses the special way in which "Young Sycamore" takes place in a single moment. The instant for Williams is a field of forces in tension. In one sense his poetry is static and spatial. The red wheelbarrow, the locust tree in flower, the young sycamore, even all the things named in long poems like *Paterson* or "Asphodel, That Greeny Flower," stand fixed in the span of an instant. It is therefore appropriate that Book Five of *Paterson*, for example, should be organized according to the spatial image of a tapestry. Nevertheless, there is in every moment a dynamic motion. "Young Sycamore" exemplifies one of the most important modes of this in Williams' poetry: flowering or growth. According to the cosmology of three elements which underlies Williams' poetry,[6] things rise from the "unfathomable ground / where we walk daily" (*CLP*, 23), take form in the open, and in that openness uncover a glimpse of the "hidden flame" (*IAG*, 204), the universal beauty each formed thing both reveals and hides. This revelation takes place only in the process of growing, not in the thing full grown. For Williams the momentary existence even of a static thing like a wheelbarrow contains future and past as horizons of the present. In its reaching out toward them it reveals the presence of things present, that "strange phosphorus of the life" (*IAG*, [vii]). His poetry is not primarily spatial. Time, for him, is the fundamental dimension of existence. The dynamic motion of the present creates space, unfolding it in the energy which brings form out of the ground so that it may, for the moment, reveal the "radiant gist" (*P*, 133). Though the young sycamore is all there in the instant, from trunk to topmost twig, the poet experiences this stasis as a growth within the moment. It is an "undulant thrust" taking the tree up out of the dark ground as a bodily presence which pushes on into the air, "dividing and waning," until it thins out in the last two eccentric knotted twigs bending forward with the aggressive force of horns.

A grammatical peculiarity of the poem may be noted here as a stroke of genius which makes the poem a perfect imitation of the activity of nature. When the undulant thrust from trunk to twigs has been followed to its end the sycamore seems to stand fixed, its energy exhausted, the vitality which urged it into the air now too far from its source in the dark earth. But this is not really true. The inexhaustible force of the temporal thrust of the tree is expressed not only in the cocoons which promise a renewal of the cycle of growth, but also in the fact that there is no main verb in the second clause of the long sentence which makes up the poem. The poem contains so much verbal action that this may not be noticed, but all these verbs are part of a subordinate clause following "whose." Their subject is "trunk" not "tree," and "trunk" is also the apparent referent of "it" in line eighteen. All the movement in the poem takes place within the confines of the subordinate clause. The second line, "this young tree," still hovers incomplete at the end of the poem, reaching out toward the verb which will complement its substantiality with an appropriate action. If the subordinate clause is omitted the poem says: "I must tell you / this young tree" – and then stops. This is undoubtedly the way the poet wanted it. It makes the poem hold permanently open that beauty which is revealed in the tree, just as, in one of Williams' last poems, "Asphodel, That Greeny Flower," the moment of the poem is the endless space of time between a flash of lightning and the sound of thunder:

> The light
>   for all time shall outspeed
>   the thunder crack. (*PB*, 181)

"Young Sycamore" too prolongs indefinitely the moment between beginning and ending, birth and death. There is, however, a contradiction in what I have said so far about the poem. To say the poem "expresses" Williams' experience of the temporality of objects is more or less the same thing as to say it "pictures" or "represents" or "describes" this. Such a notion presupposes a quadruple division of existence. The poet is in one place and looks at a tree which is outside himself. On the basis of his experience of the tree he makes a poem which mirrors in language his experience. The reader re-creates the experience through the mediation of the poem. This is precisely the theory of poetry which Williams emphatically denies. Again and again he dismisses the representational theory of art. Like Charles Olson, he avoids all "pictorial effects" (*ML*, 9), all that " 'evocation' of the 'image' which served us for a time" (*SA*, 20). Poetry, for him, is "not a mirror up to nature" (*SA*, 91), "not a matter of 'representation' " (*SA*, 45), "nor is it description nor an evocation of objects or situations" (*SA*, 91). The poet must deny such notions of poetry if his writing is to be true to that union of subject and object he gains with his plunge into the Passaic. But if the sycamore is already possessed in the perception of it, of what use is the poem? And yet Williams says that the aim of poetry is "to repair, to rescue, to complete" (*SL*, 147). What can this mean? The answer is suggested by another passage from the letters: "To copy nature is a spineless activity; it gives us a sense of our mere existence but hardly more than that. But to imitate nature involves the verb: we then ourselves become nature, and so invent an object which is an extension of the process" (*SL*, 297). "Young Sycamore" is an object, like the tree itself, and it grows out of the poet's identification with nature. Like the tree again, the poem exists as an activity, not as a passive substance. For this reason it must be a dynamic thing, primarily verbal.

What it means to think of a poem as a thing rather than as a picture of something is revealed not only by Williams' constant poetic practice, but, most explicitly, in the important prose sections of *Spring and All* now available in *Imaginations*. Words are for Williams part of the already existing furniture of the world. They are objects, just as the red wheelbarrow, the bits of green glass, and the sycamore tree are objects. As a painting is made of paint, or music of sounds, so a poem is "a small (or large) machine made of words" (*SE*, 256). Words differ from bits of green glass or a sycamore not because meanings are inherent in one case and ascribed in the other. Both a word and a tree have their meanings as inextricable parts of their substances. But the meaning which is intrinsic to a word is its power of referring to something beyond itself. Williams has no fear of the referential power of words. It is an integral part of his theory of imagination. On the one hand he rejects those poets who "use unoriented sounds in place of conventional words" (*SA*, 92). On the other hand he also rejects the notion that things depend on words. The thing "needs no personal support but exists free from human action" (*SA*, 91). To think of words as too close to the objects they name would be a return to that kind of description in which "words adhere to certain objects, and have the effect on the sense of oysters, or barnacles" (*SA*, 90). A further sentence from the prose of *Spring and All* expresses in admirably exact language Williams' way of avoiding these extremes:

> The word is not liberated, therefore able to communicate release from the fixities which destroy it until it is accurately tuned to the fact which giving it reality, by its own reality establishes its own freedom from the necessity of a word, thus freeing it and dynamizing it at the same time. (*SA*, 93)

Here is a concept of poetry which differs both from the classical theory of art as a mirror up to nature and from the romantic theory of art as a lamp radiating unifying light. The word is given reality by the fact it names, but the independence of the fact from the word frees the word to be a fact in its own right and at the same time "dynamizes" it with meaning. The word can then carry the facts named in a new form into the realm of imagination. In this sense poetry rescues and completes. It lifts things up. "Words occur in liberation by virtue of its processes" (*SA*, 90), but as the words are liberated, so also are the facts they name: "the same things exist, but in a different condition when energized by the imagination" (*SA*, 75). The words of a poem and the facts they name exist in a tension of attraction and repulsion, of incarnation and transcendence, which is like the relation of dancer and dance. So John of Gaunt's speech in *Richard II* is "a dance over the body of his condition accurately accompanying it" (*SA*, 91). The poem about the sycamore creates a new object, something "transfused with the same forces which transfuse the earth" (*SA*, 50). In doing this it affirms its own reality, and it also affirms the independent reality of the tree. The tree is free of the poem, but not free of the poet, for both poem and tree exist with other things in the space of inwardness entered by the poet in his dive into the Passaic. This notion of a free play of words above things, different from them but not detached from them, is expressed concisely in another sentence from *Spring and All*: "As birds' wings beat the solid air without which none could fly so words freed by the imagination affirm reality by their flight" (*SA*, 91). Bird and air are both real, both equally real, but the bird cannot fly without the air whose solidity it reveals in its flight. So the poem about the sycamore both depends on the tree and is free of it. In its freedom it allows the tree to be itself, at the same time as it confirms its own independent existence.

Now it is possible to see why Williams makes verbs and verb forms the axis of "Young Sycamore." The poem is not a picture of the tree. It is an object which has the same kind of life as the tree. It is an extension of nature's process. In order to be such an object it must have "an intrinsic movement of its own to verify its authenticity" (*SE*, 257). The pattern of verbs creates this movement. "The poem is made of things – on a field" (*A*, 333), but words, like other things, exist primarily as energies, directed forces. Words are nodes of linguistic power. This power is their potentiality for combining with other words to form grammatical structures. When words are placed side by side against the white field of the page they interact with one another to create a space occupied by energies in mobile tension.

All Williams' ways with language go to make words act in this way: his rhythmical delicacy, that modulation of words according to the natural measure of breathing which culminates in his development in his last years of the "variable foot"; the separation of words from "greasy contexts" so that, as in the poetry of Marianne Moore, each word stands, "crystal clear with no attachments" (*SE*, 128); the short lines which slow the pace, break grammatical units, and place ordinarily unnoticed words in positions of prominence so that their qualities as centers of linguistic energy may stand out (as in the seventh line of "Young Sycamore," three verbs or verb forms in a row: "is trickling) rises"); the emphasis on the syntax of simple sentences, the "grammatical play" of words which Williams praises in the work of Gertrude Stein (*SE*, 115). In "Young Sycamore," as in Williams' other poems, each word stands by itself, but is held within the space of the poem by the tension which relates it in undulant motion to the other words. As in the writing of Stein and Laurence Sterne, "The feeling is of words themselves, a curious immediate quality quite apart from their meaning, much as in music different notes are dropped, so to speak, into repeated chords one at a time, one after the other – for themselves alone" (*SE*, 114). The musical metaphor is important here. The space of the poem is generated by the temporal design of the words. In the time structure of the poem as it is read, as in the tense life of the tree thrusting from trunk to twigs, future and past are held out as horizons of the present in its disclosure.

Poems are more, however, than objects added to the store of objects already existing in nature. The words of a poem "affirm reality by their flight." Language is so natural to man and so taken for granted as part of his being that it is difficult to imagine what the world would be like without it. Though man is not human if he is completely bereft of speech, his language may become soiled or corrupted. Then it will no longer affirm reality, but hide it. It will become part of the "constant barrier between the reader and his consciousness of immediate contact with the world" (*SA*, 1). The theme of the degradation of language runs all through Williams' writing, from the prose of *Spring and All* and *The Great American Novel* through the analysis of American civilization in *In the American Grain* to the passages on the speech of urban man in *Paterson*: "The language, the language / fails them" (*P*, 20). Even though man's language is corrupt, the sycamore will still be there and will still be a revelation of beauty. The failure of language, however, means necessarily a failure of man's power to perceive the tree and share its life. The loss of a proper language accompanies man's detachment from the world and from other people. Authentic speech sustains man's openness to the world. It is this sense that "we smell, hear and see with words and words alone, and . . . with a new language we smell, hear and see afresh" (*SE*, 266). As Williams puts it in a phrase, the poem alone "focuses the world" (*SE*, 242).

Language is the unique power man has to bring beauty out of hiding and in so doing to lift up, to repair, to rescue, to complete: "Only the made poem, the verb calls it / into being" (*PB*, 110). The radiant gist is present in the young sycamore, not projected there by the poet, but it is hidden from most people, for the language fails them. The poet's language brings into the open the revelation which is going on secretly everywhere. It uncovers the presence of things present. This presence inheres in things and in other people, and it also inheres in our speech:

> It is actually there, in the life before us, every minute that we are listening, a rarest element – not in our imaginations but there, there in fact. It is that essence which is hidden in the very words which are going in at our ears and from which we must recover underlying meaning as realistically as we recover metal out of ore. (*A*, 362).

These sentences define exactly Williams' aim as a poet: the attempt through a purification and renewal of language to uncover that rarest element which dwells obscured in the life before us. This notion of the function of poetry justifies the urgency of the first line of "Young Sycamore": "I must tell you." Only in proper language does man's interpenetration with the world exist, and therefore the poet *must* speak. The poem does not make anything happen or transform things in any way. When it is over the tree still stands tranquilly between the wet pavement and the gutter. But in letting the sycamore be, the poem brings it into existence for the reader, through the words, in that caress of intimacy which the first line affirms.

Notes

1. Since 1966, when this essay was published, some work by Williams referred to in this essay has been made available in new editions, in particular *Imaginations* (New York: New Directions, 1970). The latter reprints both *Kora in Hell* (1920) and the original version of *Spring and All* (1923), in which the poems are interspersed with prose of great importance for understanding Williams' theory of the poetic act. Material from this essay was later

incorporated in revised form in the chapter on Williams in my *The Linguistic Moment* (Princeton, New Jersey, 1985).

2. Wordsworth's phrasing, in the preface to *Lyrical Ballads* (*The Poetical Works of William Wordsworth*, E. de Selincourt, ed., II [London: Oxford University Press, 1952], p. 386).

3. The following texts of Williams' work have been used in this essay. Each is accompanied by the abbreviation which will hereafter be employed in citations. *KH – Kora in Hell: Improvisations* (San Francisco, 1957); *SA – Spring and All* (Dijon, 1923); *IAG – In the American Grain* (New York, 1956); *CEP – The Collected Earlier Poems* (New York, 1951); *A – The Autobiography of William Carlos Williams* (New York, 1951); *SE – Selected Essays* (New York, 1954); *SL – Selected Letters*, John C. Thirlwall, ed. (New York, 1957); *ML – Many Loves and Other Plays* (New York, 1961); *PB – Pictures from Brueghel and Other Poems* (New York, 1962); *CLP – The Collected Later Poems* (New York, 1963); *P – Paterson* (New York, 1963). "Young Sycamore" is from *CEP.*, p. 332.

4. Introduction to Byron Vazakas, *Transfigured Night* (New York, 1946), p. xi.

5. See the *Autobiography*, pp. 59, 60, for his description of this poem.

6. For a description of this elemental cosmology see pp. 328–36 of my essay on Williams in *Poets of Reality: Six Twentieth-Century Writers* (Cambridge, Mass., 1965).

5

Thomas Hardy

A sketch for a portrait

Nowhere in Hardy's writings is there a description of an originating act of the mind in which consciousness separates itself from everything but itself. The self-consciousness of Hardy and his characters is always inextricably involved in their awareness of the world. Their minds are turned habitually outward, and almost every sentence Hardy ever wrote, whether in his fiction, in his poetry, or in his more private writings, is objective in the sense that it names something or someone outside consciousness of which that consciousness is aware. A passage in Florence Emily Hardy's *Life*, however, takes the reader as close to the intrinsic quality of Hardy's mind as any words he wrote. This text, like the rest of the *Life*, was probably written by Hardy himself, or least had his approval:

> One event of this date or a little later [when Hardy was about six] stood out, he used to say, more distinctly than any [other]. He was lying on his back in the sun, thinking how useless he was, and covered his face with his straw hat. The sun's rays streamed through the interstices of the straw, the lining having disappeared. Reflecting on his experiences of the world so far as he had got, he came to the conclusion that he did not wish to grow up. Other boys were always talking of when they would be men; he did not want at all to be a man, or to possess things, but to remain as he was, in the same spot, and to know no more people than he already knew (about half a dozen[1].)

Though this passage is near Hardy's "point de départ," it does not coincide with the genetic moment. Two events have preceded this scene and are reflected in it. The first is certain "experiences of the world." The nature of Hardy's experience of life is suggested by a passage at the opening of *Jude the Obscure* which so closely resembles the text in the *Life* that it may be called an anticipatory commentary on it. Hardy, like the

---

The reading of Hardy sketched out in this essay was later elaborated in *Thomas Hardy: Distance and Desire* (Cambridge, Mass., 1970).

young Jude, has learned that a man is not born free, but is ushered into the world in a certain spot in space and time. He has certain ancestors, and finds himself with a certain role to play in his family, in his community, in his social class, in his nation, even on the stage of world history. Hardy has a strong sense of each man's limitations by physical and social forces he has not created or chosen. Like the young Jude, who is shown in the middle of a "vast concave" corn-field which goes "right up towards the sky all round, where it [is] lost by degrees in the mist that shut[s] out the actual verge and accentuate[s] the solitude,"[2] each man finds himself at the center of an indefinitely receding series of concentric circles which locate him and define him. This imprisonment is all the more painful for being so intangible and for being not incompatible with a sense of isolation. Jude stands alone and in the open, but he is nonetheless bound by the situation he has inherited. Like the young Pip in Dickens' *Great Expectations*, he is an orphan and has been told by his foster-mother that he is "useless" and would be better dead.[3] Like so many other heroes of nineteenth-century novels, Hardy's protagonists find themselves "living in a world which [does] not want them."[4] Though Hardy was not an orphan and seems to have had a fairly happy childhood, he too, in the passage quoted above, broods over how "useless" he is. The conventional motifs of the orphan-hero and the indifferent foster-parent express Hardy's sense of the way a man's situation is not of his making and fits him ill.

Hardy's response to this experience of life is so instinctive that it is never recorded, but always precedes any record, though it is repeated again and again in his own life and in that of his characters. This response is a movement of passive withdrawal. Like a snail crawling into its shell, or like a furtive animal creeping into its burrow, Hardy pulls his hat over his face and looks quietly at what he can see through the interstices of the straw. Though he has separated himself from the world, he does not turn away from it to investigate the realms of interior space. Hardy and his characters are distinguished by the shallowness of their minds. They have no profound inner depths leading down to the "real self" or to God. They remain even in detachment oriented toward the outside world and reflecting it, mirror-like. But though Hardy remains turned toward the exterior, looking at it or thinking about it, nevertheless his movement of retraction separates him from blind engagement and turns everything he sees into something viewed from the outside. Like Herman Melville's Bartleby, Hardy decides he "would prefer not to" – prefer not to grow up, prefer not to take responsibility, prefer not to move out of his own narrow circle, prefer not to possess things, prefer not to know more people. The young Jude expresses a similar desire to remain on the periphery of life. He too pulls his hat over his eyes and lies "vaguely reflecting." "As you got older," he thinks, "and felt yourself to be at the centre of your time, and not at a point in its circumference, as you had felt when you were little, you were seized with a sort of shuddering, he perceived. All around you there seemed to be something glaring, garish, rattling, and the noises and glares hit upon the little cell called your life, and shook it, and warped it. If he could only prevent himself growing up! He did not want to be a man."[5] In the same way the speaker in a late poem by Hardy remembers as a child crouching safely in a thicket of ferns and asking himself: "Why should I have to grow to man's estate, / And this afar-noised World perambulate."[6] At the origin of Hardy's view of things is a decisive act of will, the will not to seek the kinds of ownership and fulfillment of desire on which others spend their lives, the will not to engage himself in the world, the will not to become an expanding center which moves out from its own vantage point to dominate an ever-widening expanse. Hardy's fundamental spiritual movement is the exact opposite of Nietzsche's will to power. It is the will not to will, the will to remain quietly watching on the sidelines.[7]

Having given up the virile goals which motivate most men, Hardy can turn back on the world and watch it from a safe distance, see it clearly with a "full look at the Worst,"[8] and judge it. This way of being related to the world is the origin of his art. Such an attitude determines the habitual stance of his narrators: that detachment which sees events from above them or from a time long after they have happened. Or it might be better to say that these spatial and temporal distances objectify a separation which is outside of time and space altogether. So the speaker in "Wessex Heights" says he seems "where I was before my birth, and after death may be."[9] The tone of voice natural to a spectator who sees things from such a position imparts its slightly acerb flavor throughout Hardy's work as a compound of irony, cold detachment, musing reminiscent bitterness, an odd kind of sympathy which might be called "pity at distance," and, mixed with these, a curious joy, a grim satis-faction that things have, as was foreseen, come out for the worst in this worst of all possible worlds. Such a perspective is also possessed by many of the protagonists in Hardy's novels, those watchers from a distance like Gabriel Oak in *Far from the Madding Crowd*, Christopher Julian in *The Hand of Ethelberta*, Diggory Venn in *The Return of the Native*, Elizabeth-Jane Henchard in *The Mayor of Casterbridge*, or Giles Winterborne in *The Woodlanders*. The detachment of such characters is expressed in the recurrent motif of spying in the fiction. Hardy frequently presents a scene in which one character sees another without being seen, watches from an upper window or a hill, peeks in a window from outside at night, or studies covertly a reflection in a mirror. In the lyric poetry such standing back is habitual. The speaker of the poems is

"The Dead Man Walking," to borrow the title of one of them.[10] He is withdrawn from the present, "with no listing or longing to join,"[11] and concentrates his attention on the ghosts of the past. He sees things from the perspective of death, and as a consequence is so quiet a watcher, so effaced, that birds, animals, and forlorn strangers pay no attention to him, knowing that his vision is as distant as the stars.[12] This detachment is most elaborately dramatized in the choruses of spirits in *The Dynasts*. These spirits, says Hardy, "are not supposed to be more than the best human intelligence of their time in a sort of quintessential form." From this generalization he excludes the Chorus of Pities. They are "merely Humanity, with all its weaknesses."[13] The careful attention to details of optical placement in *The Dynasts*, which John Wain, quite rightly, has associated with cinematic technique,[14] is more than a matter of vivid presentation. It is an extension of the implicit point of view in the novels and in the lyric poems. It has a thematic as well as technical meaning. The Choruses in *The Dynasts* are able to see the whole expanse of history at a glance. When they focus on a particular event they see it in the context of this all-encompassing panoramic vision:

> We'll close up Time, as a bird its van,
> We'll traverse Space, as spirits can,
> Link pulses severed by leagues and years,
> Bring cradles into touch with biers;
> So that the far-off Consequence appears
> Prompt at the heel of foregone Cause.[15]

From the point of view of such separation the world is no longer so close that one can only be aware of its dangerous energy, its glare and garish rattling. A man who is engaged in life is blind to all but what lies immediately before his eyes. Only the man who is disengaged can see the whole. In *Desperate Remedies*, Aeneas Manston, himself caught up in a crucial moment of decision, obtains, as a reflex of his absorption, its reverse. It is one of those times, so important in Hardy's fiction, when the perspective of the character approaches, if only for an instant, the perspective of the narrator:

> There exists, as it were, an outer chamber to the mind, in which, when a man is occupied centrally with the most momentous question of his life, casual and trifling thoughts are just allowed to wander softly for an interval, before being banished altogether. Thus, amid his concentration did Manston receive perceptions of the individuals about him in the lively thoroughfare of the Strand; tall men looking insignificant; little men looking great and profound; lost women of miserable repute looking as happy as the days are long; wives, happy by assumption, looking careworn and miserable. Each and all were alike in this one respect, that

they followed a solitary trail like the inwoven threads which form a banner, and all were equally unconscious of the significant whole they collectively showed forth.[16]

What Manston has for an instant, Hardy has as a permanent possession. He sees each individual life in the context of the whole cloth of which it is part. This superimposition of the engaged view and the detached, wide view pervades his writing, and is the source of its characteristic ironies. If much of the texture of his work is made up of careful notation of immediate particulars: the weather, the landscape, a house or a room, the colors of things, apparently irrelevant details, what the characters say, think, or do as they seek satisfaction of their desires, the narrative perspective on these particulars, present in the steady and cold tone of the language, is a vision so wide that it reduces any particular to utter insignificance. Such a view reveals the fact that "winning, equally with losing," in any of the games of life, is "below the zero of the true philosopher's concern."[17]

The nature of the universe seen from this distance is expressed figuratively in the key images of *The Dynasts*. The motif of the single thread in a cloth reappears there when the Spirit of the Years says that the story of the Napoleonic wars is "but one flimsy riband" of the "web Enorm" woven by the Immanent Will through "ceaseless artistries in Circumstance / Of curious stuff and braid."[18] Along with this image goes another, that of a monstrous mass in senseless motion. The writhing of the whole includes in its random movement all men and women driven by their desires and intentions. *Desperate Remedies* anticipates this motif too. In one scene Aeneas Manston looks into a rain-water-butt and watches as

> hundreds of thousands of minute living creatures sported and tumbled in its depth with every contortion that gaiety could suggest; perfectly happy, though consisting only of a head, or a tail, or at most a head and a tail, and all doomed to die within the twenty-four hours.[19]

Perfect image of man's life as Hardy sees it! In *The Dynasts*, published over thirty years after *Desperate Remedies*, the same image reappears in Hardy's picture of the peoples of the earth, "distressed by events which they did not cause," "writhing, crawling, heaving, and vibrating in their various cities and nationalities,"[20] or "busying themselves like cheese-mites," or advancing with a "motion . . . peristaltic and vermicular," like a monstrous caterpillar,[21] or "like slowworms through grass."[22] The actions of man are controlled by the unconscious motion of the universe, "a brain-like network of currents and ejections, twitching, interpenetrating, entangling, and thrusting hither and thither the human forms."[23]

Hardy's conception of human life presupposes a paradoxical form of dualism. There is only one realm, that of matter in motion, but out of this "unweeting"[24] movement human consciousness has arisen, accidentally, from the play of physical causes. Though the detached clarity of vision which is possible to the human mind has come from physical nature, it is radically different from its source. It sees nature for the first time as it is, has for the first time pity for animal and human suffering, and brings into the universe a desire that events should be logical or reasonable, a desire that people should get what they deserve. But of course the world does not correspond to this desire. This is seen as soon as the desire appears. Knowledge of the injustice woven into the texture of things does not require extensive experience. The young Jude musing under his hat perceives already the clash of man's logic and nature's: "Events did not rhyme quite as he had thought. Nature's logic was too horrid for him to care for. That mercy towards one set of creatures was cruelty towards another sickened his sense of harmony."[25] Like little Father Time in *Jude the Obscure*, Hardy is already as old as the hills when he is born, foresees the vanity of every wish, and knows that death is the end of life. To see life clearly is already to be detached from it.

In Hardy's world there is no supernatural hierarchy of ideals or commandments, nor is there any law inherent in the physical world which says it is right to do one thing, wrong to do another, or establishes any relative worth among things or people. Events happen as they happen, and have neither value in themselves nor value in relation to any end beyond them. Worse yet, suffering is certain for man. In place of God there is the Immanent Will, and this unthinking force is sure to inflict pain on a man until he is lucky enough to die. Birth itself is "an ordeal of degrading personal compulsion, whose gratuitousness nothing in the result seemed to justify."[26] Best of all would be not to be born at all, as Hardy affirms poignantly in "To an Unborn Pauper Child."[27]

Both halves of the term "Immanent Will" are important. The supreme power is immanent rather than transcendent. It does not come from outside the world, but is an energy within nature, part of its substance. It is identical with the inherent energy of the physical world as seen by nineteenth-century science: an unconscious force working by regular laws of matter in motion. Though what happens is ordained by no divine lawgiver, nevertheless the state of the universe at any one moment leads inevitably to its state at the next moment. Existence is made up of an enormous number of simultaneous energies each doing its little bit to make the whole mechanism move. If a man has enough knowledge he can predict exactly what will be the state of the universe ten years from now or ten thousand. All things have been fated from all time.

The term "Will" is equally important. Hardy's use of this word supports Martin Heidegger's claim that a dualistic metaphysics leads to the establishment of volition as the supreme category of being.[28] Hardy recognizes that his nomenclature may seem odd, since what he has in mind is not conscious willing. Nevertheless he defends "will" in a letter to Edward Clodd as the most exact word for his meaning: "What you say about the 'Will' is true enough, if you take the word in its ordinary sense. But in the lack of another word to express precisely what is meant a secondary sense has gradually arisen, that of effort exercised in a reflex or unconscious manner. Another word would have been better if one could have had it, though 'Power' would not do, as power can be suspended or withheld, and the forces of nature cannot."[29] Though the Immanent Will is not conscious, it is still will, a blind force sweeping through the universe, urging things to happen as they do happen, weaving the web of circumstances, shaping things in patterns determined by its irresistible energy.

Hardy's vision of things is not too different from Nietzsche's, but his response to this vision is radically different. Nietzsche defines man as the will to power, tells him that in a world of amoral determinism he should take matters into his own hands, become a center of force organizing the world in patterns of value. The man of will can turn his life from fated repetition into willed repetition and so escape into a paradoxical freedom. Hardy, on the other hand, is more passive and despairing. Like so many of his countrymen, Dickens for example, he fears the guilt involved in becoming the autonomous center of his world. Willing means for Hardy yielding to those emotions which orient a man toward other people. The longing for power and ownership involves a man in the swarming activity of the Immanent Will, and so alienates him from himself, as Napoleon in *The Dynasts*, surely a man of will, is an instrument of impersonal forces working through him. His victory is in the fact that he comes to see this. The more powerfully a man wills, the more surely he becomes the puppet of an all-shaping energy, and the quicker he encompasses his own destruction. As soon as he engages himself in life he becomes part of a vast streaming movement urging him on toward death and the failure of his desires.

Safety therefore lies in passivity, in secrecy, effacement, reticence, in the refusal of emotions and their temptations to involvement. Many of Hardy's characters have some inkling of the way they become victims of an alienating force as soon as they yield to desire. This is suggested by their extreme fear of engaging themselves in life. They have a "field-mouse fear of the coulter of destiny despite fair promise,"[30] and rightly, for only when the world becomes "a mere painted scene"[31] to them, as it does for Henchard at the end of *The Mayor of Casterbridge*, will they be free of the dominion of the Immanent Will. The characteristic action of

Hardy's novels is a gradual approach of the protagonist's attitude toward that of the narrator, and his work as a whole might therefore be defined as an attempt to vindicate the attitude of passive, watching detachment. This justification of withdrawal can only be accomplished by showing the folly of its opposite. Hardy is fascinated by the theme of fascination, and novel after novel tells the story of someone who falls in love and then concentrates his life on attaining possession of the "well-beloved."[32] The detached looking or spying which so often constitutes the drama of Hardy's scenes makes many of his characters like the narrator himself, but there is an all-important difference. Hardy's watchers at a distance, Gabriel Oak, or Giles Winterborne, or Elizabeth-Jane Henchard, are usually infatuated with another person. Their watching has a focus. The person they love has become a center of power, organizing the world and polarizing circumambient objects through his or her presence. A constant theme of Hardy's writing is the way a place, a scene, most often a house, becomes imbued with a personality and inseparable from it. In *Tess of the d'Urbervilles*, to give one example, it seems to Angel Clare that the dairy-house and its surroundings are permeated with Tess's presence:

> The aged and lichened brick gables breathed forth "Stay!" The windows smiled, the door coaxed and beckoned, the creeper blushed confederacy. A personality within it was so far-reaching in her influence as to spread into and make the bricks, mortar, and whole overhanging sky throb with a burning sensibility.[33]

There is, however, a deeper reason why Hardy is so interested in the theme of fascination. Love at first seems to offer the only guiltless escape from the poverty of detachment. If a man becomes his own source of order, imposing himself on other people, creating patterns, and establishing relative values, he is implicitly recognizing that the world as it is has no given order or value. Hardy seems condemned to this form of nihilism. He has faith neither in a benign nature spirit, nor in society as the expression of a Providential power, nor in a transcendent God manipulating the lives of his people for good ends. If he is to avoid the bad alternatives of either having no order or making one for himself, he can do so only by finding a source of order in the one place it may remain: in another person. This is precisely what love means for Hardy. It means finding someone who appears to radiate life and energy around her, establishing a measure of the worth of all things. If I can possess the person I love, then I can, without guilt, escape the world of flat desolation in which I began. But I must not take possession through an act of wilful appropriation. I must wait passively, watching and loving at a distance, as Gabriel Oak does or as Diggory Venn does, until the loved one willingly returns my love, closing the distance between us.

This strategy can never work. Like Marcel Proust, whom he influenced and whom he resembles in more ways than one, Hardy is much interested in the process of falling out of love. The only happy relationships, for him, are those that for one reason or another prolong indefinitely the time of approach, the time before possession. This is implied, for example, in an odd story called "The Waiting Supper," and is argued more openly in "The Minute Before Meeting." In that poem he asks to "live in close expectance never closed / In change for far expectance closed at last."[34] This may seem an echo of Robert Browning's "The Last Ride Together," but in fact it is radically different. Browning wants to prolong forever the last time of a kind of possession; Hardy wants to prolong forever the moment before possession. He knows that as the interval between himself and the woman he loves gradually closes, he will find himself with nothing. "Loves lives on propinquity, but dies of contact"[35] – this is the law of love for Hardy. As soon as I possess the person I love, all the magic which she has radiated on the world disappears, and I find myself back again in a universe infinitely wide in space and time, a universe which no field of force orients as to high and low, great or small, good or bad. The word "blank" or "blankness" echoes through the poems as a term for this "vision appalling"[36]:

> . . . it cannot be
> That the prize I drew
> Is a blank to me![37]

> There shall remain no trace
> Of what so closely tied us,
> And blank as ere love eyed us
> Will be our meeting-place.[38]

> Till in darkening dankness
> The yawning blankness
> Of the perspective sickens me![39]

When I win the woman I have loved from a distance I discover that she is a human being like myself, and that as such she has no more right than I do to be the center of the world. Worse yet, when I win her my perspective coincides with hers, and I discover that her extraordinary power comes only from me and has existed only in my own eyes. I am the source of her power and endow her with the divine aura she seems to have. Her seeming "glory"[40] has come only from myself. To fall out of love is to be doubly disillusioned: it means finding that there is, after all, no exterior source of value, and it means finding that I have been unwittingly the origin of what seemed to be an objective structuring of the world. But this is just the situation I have been trying to avoid, and so I am returned, at "the end of the episode," back to a world moved only by the incessant impulsions of the Immanent Will.

This sequence is the characteristic dialectic of Hardy's writing. It is succinctly expressed in a late poem called "I Was the Midmost."[41] The first stanza recalls the text from the *Life* discussed earlier and affirms that when the speaker was a child he was the "midmost" of his world, though only a few people "gleamed" within its "circuit." The second stanza describes his infatuation with a lady who becomes a new center, the axis around which everything else revolves:

> She was the midmost of my world
> When I went further forth,
> And hence it was that, whether I turned
> To south, east, west, or north,
> Beams of an all-day Polestar burned
> From that new axe of earth.

The final stanza moves to the stage of disillusionment. The speaker discovers that there is in fact no center of the world, only a confused babble of voices soliciting his attention from every direction:

> No midmost shows it here, or there,
> When wistful voices call
> "We are fain! We are fain!" from everywhere
> On Earth's bewildering ball!

In such a world there is nothing to do but to await death, or perhaps even to seek it. Hardy's most powerful novels end with the deaths of their protagonists, a death now fiercely desired as the only appropriate end of such a life. So die Aeneas Manston, Giles Winterborne, Eustacia Vye, Henchard, Tess, and Jude.

But Hardy did not choose death. He chose to be a writer instead, and lived out a long life writing indefatigably to the end. If his characters have sought happiness, lost it, and in the end die cursing their lives with a certain masochistic joy, Hardy himself, from the perspective of that detachment which foresees the end of every involvement, turns back on the lives of his people after they are dead and broods over them with absorbed attention. The great outpouring of poems about his first wife and about their early days of love came after her death, as a magical release of feeling and power of speech which was possible only when she had died. Life must pass through death before it can be rescued in art. The theme of the revivification of the past which runs all through Hardy's poems may be seen as a commentary on the fact that the use of the past tense in his fiction is more than a mere convention. He is the man who sees ghosts and remembers what everyone else has forgotten. From a time far after the events he turns back with "long vision"[42] not only to watch and remember, but to record what has happened in a poem or story. This record gives the dead a permanent existence in an art which is memory embodied. Such an art matches reality at a distance, like the hymn by Watts, "And now another day is gone," which Hardy as a child used to sing before a certain red wall at sunset, "not for any religious reason, but from a sense that the scene suited the lines."[43]

Such a taking stock of reality and its injustice is man's contribution, beyond the uncomprehending power of immediate suffering, to the universe. It is possible only to human consciousness and only to a consciousness which, like the Spirit of the Years in *The Dynasts*, has been clarified of all the obscurities of emotional attachment. This patient registering of the facts is a defiance in the sense that it says how things are, but in its proof that things do always turn out for the worst, Hardy's art is, paradoxically, a happy one. It demonstrates the eternal fitness of things. Each man gets what the prescient expect, and even what the knowing want, as victim desires the knife. Moreover, Hardy's recording of the fated course of a life, his following of one strand in the web through to its happily unhappy end turns numb suffering into the symmetry of art, that high form of art which is objective recording of the way things are. Singing "And now another day is gone" in the face of the red wall, like writing *Tess of the d'Urbervilles* or *The Mayor of Casterbridge*, transforms the fated into art, and therefore transcends the power of the Immanent Will.

This art finds value and meaning in a world previously without them. In his own oblique way Hardy accepts the will to power after all, for, as he says repeatedly in his poems, the pattern of a life is hidden from the person who is living it from day to day. It exists only in a retrospective view which turns back on the past from enough distance to put the moments together in a way which reveals their hidden pattern. This pattern exists objectively, but it can only be seen by someone with the remembering clarity of the artist. The pattern is uncovered through art, and art is therefore a victory of consciousness over suffering. It is a sly and evasive victory, surely, for Hardy only stands back and watches, recording what he sees from his separateness, but it is an authentic victory nevertheless. Only from such a distance is the pattern visible, and this discovery of pattern, even if it is achieved on the basis of self-effacing objectivity, is that version of the will to power which is the creation of a work of art, transforming events into a verbal form which brings their secret significance into the open. Just as Hardy in his poems sustains in being the ghosts of the past, playing in this a role traditionally assigned to

God, so in his function as artist-preserver he is the closest thing to a deity his universe has. Without his clear registering of what he sees, events would happen and then pass away forever. Hardy's writing, to give it a final definition, is a resurrection and safeguarding of the dead.

Notes

1. Florence Emily Hardy, *The Life of Thomas Hardy: 1840–1928* (London, New York, 1962), pp. 15–16.
2. *Jude the Obscure*, vol. III of the Anniversary Edition of *The Writings of Thomas Hardy in Prose and Verse* (New York and London, 1920), pp. 9–10. Further references to Hardy's writings will be to this edition, except in those cases where other editions are identified. The Anniversary Edition is based on the standard "Wessex Edition."
3. *Jude the Obscure*, p. 8.
4. *ibid.*, p. 11.
5. *ibid.*, p. 15.
6. "Childhood Among the Ferns," *The Collected Poems of Thomas Hardy* (London, 1952), p. 825.
7. It is therefore not surprising that Hardy should have spoken of Nietzsche with abhorrence as "a megalomaniac and not truly a philosopher at all" (*Life and Art*, Ernest Brennecke, Jr., ed. [New York, 1925], pp. 137, 138).
8. "In Tenebris, II," *Collected Poems*, p. 154.
9. *Collected Poems*, p. 300.
10. *ibid.*, pp. 202–3.
11. "In Tenebris, III," *Collected Poems*, p. 155.
12. "I Am the One," *Collected Poems*, p. 799.
13. *Notes on "The Dynasts" in Four Letters to Edward Clodd*, Edinburgh (Printed [for Thomas J. Wise] for Private Circulation Only by the Dunedin Press, Limited, 1929), p. 8.
14. See his "Introduction" to *The Dynasts: An Epic-Drama of the War with Napoleon* (London, New York, 1965), pp. ix–xix. Quotations from *The Dynasts* in this essay are from this edition.
15. *The Dynasts*, p. 7.
16. *Desperate Remedies*, p. 354.
17. *The Hand of Ethelberta*, p. 257.
18. *The Dynasts*, pp. 521, 522.
19. *Desperate Remedies*, p. 245.
20. *The Dynasts*, p. 6.
21. *ibid.*, p. 290.
22. *ibid.*, p. 454.
23. *ibid.*, p. 118.
24. *ibid.*, p. 99.
25. *Jude the Obscure*, p. 15.
26. *Tess of the d'Urbervilles*, p. 455.
27. *Collected Poems*, pp. 116–17.
28. For example, in "Nietzsches Wort 'Gott ist tot,'" *Holzwege* (Frankfurt am Main, 1950).
29. *Notes on "The Dynasts,"* p. 8.
30. *The Mayor of Casterbridge*, p. 100.

31. *ibid.*, p. 369.
32. *The Well-Beloved* is of course the title of one of Hardy's novels.
33. *Tess of the d'Urbervilles*, p. 198.
34. *Collected Poems*, p. 219.
35. Quoted from a notebook in *"Dearest Emmie": Thomas Hardy's Letters to His First Wife*, Carl J. Weber, ed. (London, 1963), p. 25.
36. "At Waking", *Collected Poems*, p. 209.
37. *ibid.*
38. "The End of the Episode," *Collected Poems*, p. 211.
39. "The Going," *Collected Poems*, p. 318.
40. "Quid Hic Agis," *Collected Poems*, p. 415.
41. *Collected Poems*, p. 630.
42. "Wessex Heights," *Collected Poems*, p. 301.
43. Florence Emily Hardy, *The Life of Thomas Hardy: 1840–1928*, p. 15.

6

Williams' *Spring and All* and the progress of poetry

To discuss progress in the humanities is like picking up the loose end of a tangled ball of yarn: The first thread leads immediately to another with which it is inextricably entwined. In no time there comes to hand a host of themes in a crisscross of lines involving fundamental questions about the arts, interpretation, and history. In my discussion of these, for the most part I shall use literature and literary criticism, which, for my purposes, may conveniently stand by synecdoche for all the humanities.

Progress in the humanities, one instinctively assumes, must have occurred, as there has been progress in the other areas of culture, most spectacularly in science. The nearly commensurate effort in the humanities – all the books, editions, scholarly journals, research grants, institutes, and symposia – must have accomplished something. This raises immediately the question of what might be meant by progress in the humanities. Presumably the humanities are not .the arts themselves but the study of them, the establishment of texts and facts and the interpretation of the monuments of the past and the present. Even so, it is impossible to make the same distinction between humanistic study and its subject-matter that can be made more or less unequivocally between nature and the sciences investigating it. The arts and their interpretation have been inextricably connected throughout history. This symbiosis has meant that important "advances" in techniques of interpretation have usually coincided with periods of notable flowering in the arts, as in the case of Aristotle and Greek tragedy, Romantic criticism and Romantic literature, or the criticism and art of our own day. Moreover, the same people or those in closely related fields have often been responsible for "progress" both in the arts and in their interpretation – for example, Coleridge, Matthew Arnold, Baudelaire, Henry James, T. S. Eliot, and Russian formalists in association with Futurists. In spite of Darwin, it obviously would not make sense to speak of a progress in nature accompanying the striking progress in scientific methodology accomplished during the last four centuries. Progress in the humanistic studies, on the other hand, cannot be dissociated from progress in the arts themselves.

If this is so, the problem of a definition of progress in humanistic studies cannot be separated from a similar problem in the arts themselves. How would we recognize an example of such progress? By what yardstick or according to what scale would we measure it? What fixed external point of reference could we use? Does progress in the arts increase power to imitate what is already known to be there as the real and the true; or to bring into the open what is already there but has been hidden; or to create only out of signs ever more subtle and complex forms, imposed on chaos to order it and make it habitable? *Mimesis, aletheia*, independent creation – these three theories of art in their conflict and interdependence have dominated Western thought since before Plato. To each corresponds a different set of theories of interpretation, that is, theories of the humanistic studies. The conscious or unconscious assumption that one of the three is exclusively valid tends to determine not only procedures of interpretation, but also criteria by which progress in the humanities might be identified and measured.

Two contradictory notions about progress in the arts and the corresponding progress in interpretation have governed the habitual thought of Western man. On the one hand, there is an almost irresistible tendency to think of literary history and the history of the arts as a progressive refinement in sophistication and subtlety. The "history of the English novel," for example, is often thought to begin with the rude forms of the late sixteenth century, develop complex narrative techniques in the eighteenth and nineteenth centuries, and culminate in the refinement of James, Conrad, Joyce, and Woolf. Henry James is seen as more "complex," more "advanced," and more "profound" than Jane Austen. This progress in the novel, it is assumed, has accompanied a commensurate improvement in the tools available for interpreting fiction, James's own celebrated prefaces being among the most powerful.

There are many versions of this paradigm of progress. Scientists, for the most part, do not need a library with all the technical books and papers going back to the origins of modern science. They require only the journals of the last five years or so and would be willing to have the earlier scientific material stored, buried, or perhaps even burnt. There is a continual self-destruction involved in scientific progress; progress in the humanities is sometimes considered analogous. Each new generation of scholars, it seems, has more facts, better texts, and more powerful tools of interpretation than the last. Earlier editions and critical interpretations are continually being rendered obsolete. Of what use are nineteenth-century texts of Shakespeare or of other Renaissance writers, now that the science of textual criticism has advanced to such a peak of perfection? Each scholar is only one of a long line of tillers of the soil; he justifies himself by destroying the scholars who preceded him. The publication of his findings is suicidal in the sense that he is offering himself up to be destroyed in his turn by the next scholar. As Arthur Rimbaud, that great explorer of the myths of progress, puts it, "[T]here will come other horrible workers: they will begin at the horizons where he has succumbed."[1]

This picture of progress in the humanities is related to the beguiling dream of a final, perfect, full interpretation of a given text. The day will come when the last word will have been said about *Hamlet*, the "Ode to a Nightingale," or *Bleak House*. Some great critic will write a definitive critical essay, and then nothing more will remain to be said about *Paradise Lost*. Sometimes, as a nightmare sprung from his "professional deformation," the scholar may be seized by a vision of the gradual self-destruction of his enterprise. As one by one all the texts are exhausted and definitive editions and interpretations are established, his reason for existing will fade and ultimately vanish. The teacher of the humanities seems destined to be replaced by the tape-recorder – thousands of classrooms simultaneously playing the same superlative lecture on *Hamlet*, perhaps to a lecture hall empty of all save recorders taking down the absent professor's lecture on behalf of the absent students, all of whom are presumably busy somewhere else. It is only a step from this to another fantasy, also not my invention. This is the dream of a periodical destruction of all the texts, critical books, and scholarly journals, perhaps a destruction, too, of the scholars with their elephantine memories; then the job of interpretation could start in happy ignorance again from the beginning. Once more all the interesting projects would remain to be done – anything to prevent the humanistic scholars from becoming victims of their own success, sufferers from a new kind of technological unemployment. This fantasy has its parallel in the arts, for example, in an idea important to Ezra Pound and T. S. Eliot. Since all literature of Western Europe forms a whole, once a certain thing has been done in language – *La divina commedia, Madame Bovary*, or whatever – it never has to be done again. In fact, it cannot be repeated, so that poets by their accomplishments are gradually putting themselves out of business.

Alongside this *idée reçue* of progress in the humanities, with its many versions, shadings, and comical extravagances, goes a diametrically opposed notion, a notion no less widespread and no less (for the most part) an unexamined prejudice. This is the idea that the progress of civilization is incompatible with the progress of poetry. The more refined our culture becomes, the more difficult it is to write authentic poetry. In a perfected civilization poetry would disappear. Poetry is destroyed by the self-consciousness, the consciousness of the past, the distance from nature, and the loss of natural spontaneity characteristic of man in a highly cultivated state of society. The first poems and paintings were the best. Since those primitive geniuses produced their masterpieces, the history of the arts has been one of progressive degeneration and thinning out. This conception is related in a subtle way to that myth of modernity which Paul de Man has discussed so perceptively in "Literary History and Literary Modernity". Authenticity in poetry lies in unself-conscious spontaneity. True poetry must have no history; it must rise immediately from the moment of perception. The increasing weight of history on the mind of civilized man makes this naked confrontation with the immediate sources of poetry more and more difficult.

There are many variations of this myth of decline. To mention several of the more recent, it is a fundamental aspect of the thought of Jean-Jacques Rousseau; and it is present in Hegel's notion of a withering away of poetry as the absolute Spirit gradually perfects itself, or in Thomas Love Peacock's *Four Ages of Poetry*, with its picture of a golden civilization producing poets of brass. More influential than Peacock's shrewdly ironic challenge to the idea of progress is Matthew Arnold's anti-modernism. For Arnold, Homer was the best of poets. Poetry, he thought, has gone downhill ever since. The Romantic poets were unable to write the same kind of poetry as Shakespeare because they lived in a different age of the world. "The *what you have to say* depends on your age."[2] The efforts of the Romantic poets were meretricious because they tried to write a kind of poetry possible only in a different time. As Arnold says:

> More and more I feel that the difference between a mature and a youthful age of the world compels the poetry of the former to use great plainness of speech as compared with that of the latter: and that Keats and Shelley were on a false track when they set themselves to reproduce the exuberance of expression, the charm, the richness of images, and the felicity, of the Elizabethan poets.[3]

Poor Arnold was born in a bad time, a time when the springs of poetry had gone dry. He had to lay his weary bones among the dry rocks of the nineteenth-century wasteland. He lamented the loss in his too-mature time of the world of the "admirable Homeric qualities" of "out-of-doors freshness, life, naturalness, buoyant rapidity."[4] For him, the first writers, like Homer, were closer to the sources of poetry than we are.

This gives rise to a curious paradox of degradation in Arnold's thought: Because the first poets had less to say, they could say it with greater richness and exuberance. We latecomers have inherited the past experience of the world and have added new experience of our own. The result is that we must concentrate what we have to say in a great barrenness of style.

> [H]ad Shakespeare and Milton lived in the atmosphere of modern feeling, had they had the multitude of new thoughts and feelings to deal with a

modern has, I think it likely the style of each would have been far less *curious* and exquisite. . . . In the 17th century it was *a smaller harvest than now*, and sooner to be reaped: and therefore to its reaper was left time to stow it more finely and curiously. Still more was this the case in the ancient world. The poet's matter being *the hitherto experience of the world, and his own*, increases with every century.[5]

Try as he may to simplify his style in order to encompass the matter he has to say, the modern poet finds himself overwhelmed with material, much of it inherited from the past. The result is that decadence in poetry happens according to an inevitable historical law. Decadence is defined as a copying of the style and matter of previous masters as opposed to the return to the fecund soil from which poetry has flowered as a fresh and immediate growth. Again, to quote Arnold:

> One does not always remember that one of the signs of the Decadence of a literature, one of the factors of its decadent condition indeed, is this – that new authors attach themselves to the poetic expression the founders of a literature have flowered into, which may be *learned* by a sensitive person, to the neglect of an inward poetic life.[6]

In "The English Poet and the Burden of the Past, 1660–1820,"[7] Walter Jackson Bate has investigated with admirable learning and verve one permutation of this myth. Bate's essay establishes the tradition within which Arnold's pessimism may be understood. A "comprehensive way of taking up the whole of English poetry from the middle seventeenth century down to the present," suggests Bate, would be by exploring the "accumulating anxiety" of the burden of the past which presents to each new generation with increasing urgency the question, "What is there left to do?"[8]

> [T]his remorseless deepening of self-consciousness, before the rich and intimidating legacy of the past, becomes the greatest single problem that modern art (art, that is to say, since the close of the seventeenth century) has had to face, and . . . it will become so increasingly in the future.[9]

Taking examples from a wide range of writers in the eighteenth century and in the Romantic period, Bate shows a developing polarity between the virtue of continuity with the past and the virtue of originality. Though his sympathies are for an art that follows with some conscious piety in the line of its ancestors, nevertheless he sees the value of the "never before." There is obviously more than historical objectivity in the intensity with which, at the end of his essay, he describes the plight of the poet who must obey simultaneously two contradictory demands. This was the "fearful legacy" inherited by the great Romantics: "To begin with, you were exhorted to be 'original' at all costs, and yet reminded that you could not be 'original' about the most important things."[10] Being original meant going directly to nature. The opposing virtue was emulation of the great models of the past. Bate sees this opposition as the source of the difficulties and, if one may read between his lines, the decadence of the poetry of the nineteeth and twentieth centuries:

> In no other case are you simultaneously enjoined to admire and at the same time to try, at all costs, *not* to follow closely what you admire, not merely in any of the details but in over-all procedure, in general object, in any of the broader conventions of mode, vocabulary, or idiom. Yet here, in the arts this split is widening with every generation, and not only widening but dramatized, with a helpless and blind militancy on each side. . . . The arts stutter, stagger, pull back into paralysis and indecision before such a conflict of demand.[11]

Torn to pieces by the contrary pulls toward novelty and toward tradition, toward a poetry produced from original soil and "a poetry produced largely from the soil of past poetry,"[12] literature is gradually destroyed by its own success. Ultimately the "burden of the past" becomes impossible to bear. The answer to the question, "What is there left to do?" becomes "Nothing at all," and the poets lapse into impotent silence.

Beside this dark version of the myth of decline may be set that conception of the "progress of poetry" which Geoffrey Hartman is following with such penetrating subtlety from the late sixteenth century down to our own day.[13] As in the case of Bate's essay, Hartman's point of focus is the eighteenth century and the period of Romanticism. Beginning with Milton and a look backward at Spenser, he shows the ramifications through Gray, Collins, and others down to Blake, Wordsworth, and Coleridge of a concept of poetry as the purification, rationalizing, or enlightening of a dark, daemonic ground. This notion of poetry as the demystifying of superstitious Romance, "*psyche* emerg[ing] from the spooky larvae of masques and moralities like a free-ranging butterfly,"[14] is to be associated with the widespread Enlightenment topos of the progress of poetry as a "stepping westward" of the poetic spirit from country to country of Europe until finally it must be naturalized on England's shores, there to be "grounded in the reasonableness of a specific national temperament."[15]

The idea of poetry Hartman finds in his authors presupposes the existence of a sub-world of multiple chthonic spirits, a super-nature at the base of nature which the poets must both encounter and tame, "the enlightened mind . . . emerging, and even constructing itself, out of its involvement with Romance."[16]

With Milton, the Spirit of Romance begins to simplify itself. It becomes the creative spirit, and frees itself from the great mass of medieval and post-medieval romances in the same way as the Spirit of Protestantism from the formalism of temples.[17]

L'Allegro and *Il Penseroso* have special importance for Hartman as a turning point in this development. "They show a mind moving from one position to another and projecting an image of its freedom against a darker, daemonic ground. Poetry, like religion, purifies that ground: it cannot leave it."[18] Poems as late as Wordsworth's *The White Doe of Rylstone*, however, still have the same structure, "that of the reflective encirclement and progressive purification of symbols from Romance."[19] In Hartman's view, in fact, this is the permanent structure of all authentic poetry:

> If Romance is an eternal rather than archaic portion of the human mind, and poetry its purification, then every poem will be an act of resistance, of negative creation – a flight from one enchantment into another. The farewell to the impure gods becomes part of a nativity ode welcoming the new god.[20]

The question posed by this conception of poetry is "whether poetry can survive its own 'enlightenment,' 'civilization,' or 'self-consciousness.'"[21] This is a version of the image of progressive degeneration proposed by W. J. Bate. As the daemonic ground that is the source of poetry is gradually brought into the light and subjected to the control of a human mind no longer the helpless victim of supernatural energies, poetry may get more and more fragile and superficial, mere *vers de société*. In this process of deterioration,

> Romance loses its shadow, its genuine darkness: nothing remains of the drama of liberation whereby ingenium is born from Genius, psyche from persona, and the spirit of poetry from the grave-clothes of Romance.[22]

Since some form of mythological machinery is necessary to all true poetry, another way to ask this question is to wonder whether demystification also means, inevitably, demythologizing.[23] Only if poetry can be enlightened without losing its contact with myth and with the archaic forces that are its origin can the progress of poetry be other than an effacement of poetry.

A final form of this notion will return to the question of progress in humanistic studies. If the enlightenment of the poets will perhaps make poetry impossible, the development of sophisticated techniques of interpretation may also hasten the destruction of poetry. An age of criticism and an age of abundant creativity cannot occur simultaneously, Matthew Arnold believed. The assumption that a proliferation of elaborate methods of analysis – rationalizing poetry, dissecting it, and finding out its secret – makes it less and less possible for the poets to write poetry is widespread in our own century. "Fruitless for the academic tapeworm to hoard its excrementa in books," says William Carlos Williams in *Spring and All*.[24] This assumption is also present in the modesty of those critics who freely admit that their work has only a negative relation to the creation of poetry. Literary criticism is a part of science that happens to take poems as its objects of study rather than stars or atoms. If authenticity in poetry arises from unthinking spontaneity in its creation, the study of poetry is its bringing to consciousness, its interpretation, and therefore its destruction. Criticism is the act whereby the critic puts an end to the objects that are his *raison d'être*. This version of the myth of decline reminds one of those delicate cave or tomb paintings that vanish when they are exposed to light and air. The critic is a graverobber who destroys what he means to steal. He leaves only bare walls where once were masterpieces of primitive and unsophisticated creativity.

Meanwhile the poems remain, in the undiminished splendor of their presence. Far from being the epoch of the vanishing of poetry, the twentieth century has witnessed a remarkable flourishing of all the arts. We have had poets, painters, composers, and playwrights able to hold their own against any in history. At the same time the various modes of interpretation have been impressively practiced. There must be something wrong with these prophecies of doom for poetry. Moreover, it does not take much wit to see that the two myths, that of progress and that of decline, have homologous structures. They are, in fact, mirror images of one another, or they are like the "two" sides of a Moebius strip which returns to itself from the other side if it is followed to its limit. This further suggests that something is amiss, since poetry can hardly progress and decline at the same time.

My examples of the myths of progress and of decline are structured around a fundamental polarity. In both, the undivided presence of the mind to itself is opposed to the split in the mind when it becomes conscious of itself. A sophisticated self-consciousness in the poet inhibits his creativity. Self-consciousness in the critic, an objective holding at arm's length of the poem, a peeping and botanizing at the flowers of poetry, destroys what it would understand. The presence to nature of an unreflective mind in the immediate moment of direct experience, in the presence of the present or the nick of time, is opposed to any mediate relation to nature by way of cultural forms inherited from the past. These are seen as forming an increasingly opaque screen cutting the mind off from nature and from its own depths. Whether the springs of poetry are thought of as outside, in the perennial freshness of nature, or as within, in the interior regions of the mind, where no artificial forms can come, the category of immediacy, of presence, of proximity to the origin, is the basic test of validity. True poetry must rise spontaneously, as a spring bubbles from a cleft in the rocks or as a wild flower lifts itself from the primeval earth. Once this criterion of authenticity is assumed, there appears inevitably the paradox of a progress of poetry that is at the same time an exhaustion of poetry. Poetry itself comes to stand as an implacable barrier between man and what makes poetry possible. Man must then live encapsulated in a culture which is factitious in the sense that it has been detached from its roots. A finished civilization is like a bunch of cut flowers in a vase. Though there might be "progress in the humanities" in such a culture, an increasing perfection in the establishing of texts, facts, and explications, this is an increasing perfection in the embalming of dead forms, forms with less and less function or relevance.

Against this unhappy prospect stands the fact that the arts and their interpretation have neither declined nor progressed, but exist more or less as they always have, just as the poems of the past remain available to those who would read them. One begins to suspect that the myths of progress and decline must be based on false ideas of culture, of history, of human temporality, of consciousness, of poetic language, and of interpretation.

A clue to the way this is so is given in W. J. Bate's healthy distaste for the Hegelian *Zeitgeist*, for the concept of periodization in the arts when it implies that there is a climate of ideas and forms irresistibly limiting what can be thought or created in a given age.[25] A further clue is Bate's recognition that the great artists have always built on their predecessors. Their works do not spring full-blown from the immediate moment, but are always products of emulation or even of plagiarism. Each great poem incorporates some reference to anterior works to which it is related in a complex combination of sameness and difference. In Bate's words:

> It is like that habit of Keats of beginning each large new effort by rereading *Lear* and of keeping always close at hand that engraving of Shakespeare which he found in the lodging house in the Isle of Wight when he went off to begin *Endymion*; in a sense, what this typifies was true of them all: true at least of the greatest artists (Wordsworth, looking constantly back as he did to Milton; Beethoven, who in his last days kept rereading the scores of Handel; Goethe, who constantly returned to the Greeks or to Shakespeare).[26]

Another hint is given by a tension or fold in the thought of Geoffrey Hartman's essays. On the one hand, there is the idea of a slow purification of the dark sources of poetry until finally, one may imagine, all the darkness will be light. On the other hand stands Hartman's affirmation that there is no progress, only an eternal re-enactment of the same dangerous encounter, since poetry must always return to its daemonic ground. "This romantic purification of Romance," says Hartman, "is endless; it is the true and unceasing spiritual combat."[27] In one case, poetry is seen as the progressive victory of light over darkness, as a secularizing, humanizing force. In the other case, poetry must constantly renew itself in the darkness if it is to remain authentic. There is no progress of poetry, no one-way development of literary history through various periods which build on one another, each new one leaving the other behind forever. There is only a perpetual replaying of the same drama in different forms. In one case, Orpheus wants to make Eurydice over into a white bride fit to live all the year in the sunlight. In the other, Orpheus' impossible and perpetually renewed task is to bring Eurydice into the light with all her rich darkness still clinging to her.

To follow these clues out of the labyrinth of a situation in which our habits of thought lead us by serpentine windings until we find ourselves face to face with a paradoxical conclusion in obvious contradiction with the facts, it may be useful to investigate a single text. In such a text my tangle of themes may be present not haphazardly, as they have appeared dispersed in a multitude of writers old and new, but articulated in the more closely-knit web of a single work. William Carlos Williams' *Spring and All* is an admirable work of this sort.

Spring and All was printed at Dijon in 1923 and published by the Contact Publishing Company, one of Williams' joint enterprises with Robert McAlmon. It is a handsome little book bound in blue paper covers, dedicated to Williams' friend, the painter Charles Demuth. *Spring and All* has never been republished in its entirety, though in its integral form it is perhaps the most important single work by Williams. "Nobody ever saw it," he says, " – it had no circulation at all – but I had a lot of fun with it."[28] It contains two of Williams' most famous lyrics, "By the road to the contagious hospital" and "The Red Wheelbarrow," along with twenty-five others. The poems are dispersed among passages of prose, some of which are prose poems in the manner of Williams' earlier *Kora in Hell* (1920) or of Rimbaud's *Illuminations*, and some of which are Williams' fullest statements of his theory of poetry.

One aspect of *Spring and All* will make it possible to follow somewhat further one of the clues out of the labyrinth cited above from W. J. Bate. In spite of the absolute value Williams here and elsewhere puts on making it new in America, *Spring and All* is self-consciously imitative of Rimbaud and the Surrealists. "Thank you," says Williams at one particularly Rimbaudian moment, "I know well what I am plagiarising."[29] Moreover, the book doubles back on itself and contains its own interpretation. Just as *Kora in Hell* is made up of prose poems and "interpretations" of them written later,[30] so in *Spring and All* the prose passages present the theory of imaginative action exemplified in the poems. These are strewn throughout the prose like gemstones in clay. "Who am I," asks Williams, "but my own critic?" (*SA*, 36). The poems sometimes come with fine dramatic suddenness. This is seen most strikingly when a discussion in the prose of what would make the complete novelty of spring possible is followed immediately by the celebrated enactment of spring burgeoning in "By the road to the contagious hospital." Such dramatic interaction between the prose and the poetry is lost in the publication of the poems alone in *The Collected Earlier Poems*. If *Spring and All* has its pre-texts, it is also divided within itself between text and interpretation. The critic adds his interpretation to the text as one more link in a chain. Far from springing without a past from the immediate moment of experience, *Spring and All* is interpretation of previous texts and even interpretation of interpretation. It is caught already in the serpent spirals of the hermeneutical circle. The critic's commentary engages itself in the circle and adds one more twist to the screw.

This structure of self-interpretation is characteristic in one way or another of all literature and of all art. Every poem has other poems anterior to it to which it refers in one way or another. It also contains linguistic elements which are self-referential or "metapoetical." Some language in the poem is about the poem itself. The combination of overt critical discussion and poetry in *Spring and All* is only an unusually visible example of this, not something rare in literature. Critical discourse is language about language which is already about its own language. The language of the poem in its turn is about other poems which precede it and to which it is "allegorically" related.[31] These earlier poems also have anterior texts to which they refer in an endless sequence, each item referring back to earlier ones or ahead to the ones not yet written in a movement of meaning without origin or end. If this is so, the critic of *Spring and All* need not fear that the text is a fragile tissue he will destroy by interpreting. His reading inserts itself in the texture of words which is already there and follows one thread or another in the weaving as it tries to identify a fundamental pattern. In this case the background design is a network of contradictions and tensions in aesthetic theory as old as Plato and Aristotle. Apparently without full awareness of its lineage, Williams has knitted this pattern into his text. The poems that matter and the interpretations that matter are not the ones that "dissolve" such contradictions, for they cannot be unravelled, but those that "elucidate" them, to use one of the key words of *Spring and All*.

The verbal tissue of *Spring and All* is made up of the repetition, modulation, and connection of such key words as they weave in and out of the text creating various patterns and combinations. Among them, along with "elucidate," are "spring," "beginning," "new," "allevi-ation," "enlargement," "imagination," "force," "life," "sympathy," "composition," "design," "dynamize," "reality," "nature," "the moment," "transcription," "fixation," "value," "truth," "invention," "name," "experience," "repetition," "representation," "imitation," "copy," "plagiarism," "illusion," and "symbolism." These words arrange themselves in two groups, the larger related to "spring," immediacy, "life", and newness; the smaller polarized around the notions of "repetition" and "imitation."

In perfect consonance with the tradition explored earlier in this essay, *Spring and All* is based on an affirmation of the supreme value of presence and of the present, and on a repudiation of all that is derived, repetitive, and copied. This opposition is initially given an overtly temporal expression. Authentic life exists only in the present moment of immediate experience, but most people live detached from that moment. They remain lost in memory of the no longer real past, or in anticipation of the not yet existing future, or in thoughts about some distant place. They are unable to concentrate on what is here and now, before the senses. According to Williams:

> There is a constant barrier between the reader and his consciousness of immediate contact with the world. . . . [T]he whole world is between: Yesterday, tomorrow, Europe, Asia, Africa, – all things removed and impossible, the tower of the church at Seville, the Parthenon. . . . The reader knows himself as he was twenty years ago and he has also in mind a vision of what he would be, some day. Oh, some day! But the thing he never knows and never dares to know is what he is at the exact moment that he is. And this moment is the only thing in which I am at all interested. (1, 2, 3)

Among the most impenetrable substances standing as a screen between man and the present moment is traditional art, the art of "illusion," "representation," and the "copy after nature." "[N]early all writing, up to the present," says Williams, "if not all art, has been especially designed to keep up the barrier between sense and the vaporous fringe which distracts the attention from its agonized approaches to the moment. It has been always a search for 'the beautiful illusion'" (3). Art adds itself in "layers of demoded words and shapes" (19) to the vaporous fringe of the past, the future, and the distant to double the barrier between consciousness and the luminous center of the moment. Art is, like past and future, like all things removed and distant, a form of the mediate, the secondary. The most resolute repudiation ever expressed of the tradition of mimetic art runs as a continuous filament through *Spring and All*. Representational artists are "the traditionalists of plagiarism" (10, 15). They commit themselves to "the falseness of attempting to 'copy' nature" (30). Such copying is the "crude symbolism" of "strained associations" (22). It is "plagiarism after nature" (35):

> I suppose Shakespeare's familiar aphorism about holding the mirror up to nature has done more harm in stabilizing the copyist tendency of the arts among us than – [sic] the mistake in it . . . is to have believed that the reflection of nature is nature. It is not. It is only a sham nature, a 'lie.'" (50, 51)

Williams glimpses the indissoluble connection of the art of *mimesis* with symbolism, with subjectivism, and with the notion that the center or origin of the objective world, of man's subjectivity, and of artistic forms is located in another world. What Williams rejects as "crude symbolism" is the traditional universe of hierarchical levels in participation, whereby things of the outer world are properly symbols of qualities in man's subjective world. This correspondence is validated by the resonance of both with the supernatural center that is their source. "Crude symbolism," says Williams, "is to associate emotions with natural phenomena such as anger with lightning, flowers with love. . . . Such work is empty" (20). Elsewhere, speaking of the way the paintings of Juan Gris detach the things of everyday experience and present them in unfamiliar juxtapositions, making it impossible for the onlooker to think of the canvas as a photographic representation of reality, Williams brings to the surface the association of representational art with subjectivism and with belief in an extraterrestrial center:

> This [the "distortion" of Juan Gris] was not necessary where the subject of art was not "reality" but related to the "gods" – by force or otherwise. There was no need of the "illusion" in such a case since there was none possible where a picture or a work represented simply the imaginative reality which existed in the mind of the onlooker. (35)

In rejecting the art of imitation, Williams wants also to reject those other elements – symbolism, subjectivism, and supernaturalism – with which it is systematically connected. All these aspects of art stand between man and the living moment. The whole fabric must go. "Exit the whole shebang."[32]

The project of *Spring and All* is a version of that "deconstruction of metaphysics" that has been a recurrent theme in Western thought and that is particularly to be associated in its modern form with Friedrich Neitzsche. What, for Williams, will be the instrument of this prodigious act of demolition? What power in man can blow up all the barriers and return man to the moment? The answer is unequivocal: "To refine, to clarify, to intensify that eternal moment in which we alone live there is but a single force – the imagination. This is its book" (3). The prose of *Spring and All* centers on a definition or redefinition of this traditional romantic term. The imagination is the only power that can reach through all obstacles to the reality of the present moment. Williams uses language drawn from physics to describe how this happens:

> [T]the imagination is an actual force comparable to electricity or steam, it is not a plaything but a power that has been used from the first to raise the understanding of – [Here as often Williams leaves the reader to fill in the missing words, in this case, I suppose, "life," "nature," "reality," "the moment."] . . . [T]he work of the imagination [is] not "like" anything but [is] transfused with the same forces which transfuse the earth – at least one small part of them. (49, 50)

The imagination is that energy in man through which flows the same force as that outside man, creating weeds, stones, trees, and white chickens. The imagination is part of nature. By its means the poet can cast out all the past, all inherited and demoded forms. He can then turn directly to nature as it is now present before the senses, activating his liaison with it.

Turn to nature in what way? What, in fact, is the work of the imagination? Here Williams' thought turns curiously back on itself and then even redoubles that doubling. The imagination is, in one sense, a creative force linking man to nature. The poems and paintings produced by the imagination grow from nature and remain rooted in it. The compositions of great writers like Homer, says Williams, "have as their excellence an identity with life since they are as actual, as sappy as the leaf of the tree which never moves from one spot" (22). (Here is Williams' version of Matthew Arnold's admiration for the immediacy and freshness of Homer.) In another sense, however, the imagination is a destructive force, perhaps the most powerful explosive of all. It has power to annihilate everything. Though it is part of nature, its essential function is to destroy nature. The opening pages of *Spring and All* express a joyous dedication to the destruction of the world. The instrument of this annihilation is the imagination:

> The imagination intoxicated by prohibitions, rises to drunken heights to destroy the world. Let it rage, let it kill. The imagination is supreme. . . . To it now we come to dedicate our secret project: The annihilation of every human creature on the face of the earth. . . . None to remain; nothing but the lower vertebrates, the mollusks, insects and plants. Then at last will the world be made anew. (5, 6)

It is easy to see the rigorous logic according to which the imagination must be destructive as well as creative. As Williams says in the fifteenth poem of *Spring and All*, "destruction and creation / are simultaneous" (59). If dead forms of language stand between man and the novelty of the moment, so also do those objects in nature already there a moment or a decade ago. The first movement of the imagination must, therefore, be violently anarchistic, the "destruction of what is," to borrow the slogan of the Professor in Joseph Conrad's *The Secret Agent*. The pre-text here is again Rimbaud's *Illuminations*. In "Conte," for example, a bored prince dedicates himself to sadistic cruelty:

> All the women who had known him were assassinated; what havoc in the garden of beauty! . . . He amused himself cutting the throats of rare animals. He set palaces on fire. He would rush upon people and hack them to pieces.[33]

Like Rimbaud, Williams must break down all cultural and natural forms, kill everyone, and destroy everything in order to return things to the primal chaos from which a reality without any antecedents may spring.

As in the case of Conrad's Professor, Williams' destructive rage must be directed especially against mankind. Human beings most remember the past or anticipate the future and therefore are the least real. "I love my fellow creature," says Williams. "Jesus, how I love him: endways, sideways, frontways and all the other ways – but he doesn't exist! Neither does she. I do, in a bastardly sort of way" (3). Since the subjectivity of ordinary humankind is perhaps the most recalcitrant way in which the unreal corrupts the real, it must be the special target of imaginative action. It can be erased first by being merged in the imagination of the poet-protagonist. He does exist, in a bastardly sort of way, because he lives in the imagination: "In the imagination, we are from henceforth (so long as you read) locked in a fraternal embrace, the classic caress of author and reader. We are one" (3, 4). Williams' readers must abandon their separate selves and lose themselves in the imagi-nation of the poet, sharing with him there in the action whereby every man, woman, and child on the face of the earth is annihilated. In this annihilation all the separate unreal minds are merged in a single real soul:

> This final and self inflicted holocaust has been all for love, for sweetest love, that together the human race, yellow, black, brown, red and white, agglutinated into one enormous soul may be gratified with the sight. . . . (6)

Once this monstrous act of demolition has been satisfactorily completed, the world will be new, and the imagination can turn from acts of destruction to acts of authentic creation. Here, however, Williams turns back on himself unexpectedly a second time. The world after its destruction is not new at all. It repeats itself exactly again from the beginning, down to the last detail. If an art of *mimesis* is bad because it is sterile copying, there is in nature a similar tendency toward plagiarism. Williams' hyperbolic act of destruction leads him only to witness the comedy of a nature which, destroyed so that spring may begin, repeats itself exactly as it was, as if it had not wit or energy enough to be different:

> It is spring! but miracle of miracles a miraculous miracle has gradually taken place during these seemingly wasted eons. Through the orderly sequences of unmentionable time EVOLUTION HAS REPEATED ITSELF FROM THE BEGINNING. . . . Every step once taken in the first advance of the human race, from the amoeba to the highest type of intelligence, has been duplicated, every step exactly paralleling the one that preceded in the dead ages gone by. A perfect plagiarism results. Everything is and is new. Only the imagination is undeceived. (8, 9)

The imagination is undeceived because it can see that nothing has been accomplished; there has been no return to a primal novelty. Nature is capable only of a dead imitation of that which was. This doubling brings into the open nature's sterility. Nature cannot return to an origin which is other than a repetition of something that has already happened innumerable times before. This barrenness in nature is also a limitation in the imagination, that derived force of nature. The enormous energy of the imagination is able to destroy everything, but can then create on the basis of the resulting chaos, not "the unheard of work,"[34] but only a repetition of what was there before: "Yes, the imagination, drunk with prohibitions, has destroyed and re-created everything afresh in the likeness of that which it was" (9). In the same way, the Prince's murders and burnings in Rimbaud's "Conte" leave things untouched: "The throngs, the gilded roofs, the beautiful animals still remained."[35] Williams has followed through the same line of imaginative thought as Rimbaud and has come face to face once more with the same blank wall. He repeats Rimbaud's celebrated failure to use the poetic imagination as a revolutionary force. For Williams as for Rimbaud, it seems, "There is no sovereign music for our desire."[36]

The parallel is not exact, however, and in Williams' case the impasse is not an impasse. At the moment when the repetition in nature is complete and the universe has returned to exactly the point where it was before, so that the two natures could be superimposed exactly, like two maps made to the same grid or "grate," suddenly the movement of repetition ends. The spring, so far unsuccessfully sought, miraculously appears in "By the road to the contagious hospital," following immediately after this passage in the prose:

[L]ife has now arrived for the second time at that exact moment when in the ages past the destruction of the species *Homo sapiens* occurred. / Now at last that process of miraculous verisimilitude, that grate[37] copying which evolution has followed, repeating move for move every move that it made in the past – is approaching the end. / Suddenly it is at an end. THE WORLD IS NEW. (11)

Here is revealed the sovereign power of the imagination. Left alone, nature repeats itself. Destroyed, it repeats itself again. Only when it is repeated in a certain way in words is it new: "The only means [the poet] has to give value to life is to recognize it with the imagination and name it; this is so. To repeat and repeat the thing without naming it is only to dull the sense and results in frustration" (41, 42). What is the difference between repeating and naming? It would seem that naming could only be another form of the aesthetic of imitation Williams is making every effort to reject. In elucidating the distinction between naming and repeating, Williams finds a way out of the dilemma he faces. The poems in *Spring and All* are examples of the power of imaginative naming. Or rather he finds a way to balance among the three irreconcilable and yet inextricably connected theories of art that have dominated Western thought since the Greeks. These three theories unobtrusively govern the argument of *Spring and All*. Art as *mimesis*, art as revelation, art as creation *ex nihilo* – these three regal ideas are present in the distinction Williams makes between words as repetition, words as names, and words as "unoriented sounds" (92). Though he rejects the first and last and chooses the second, he cannot free his theory or his practice from the contradictory inherence of each of these notions in the others.

In developing his version of this traditional pattern of thought, Williams makes use implicitly of two concepts of repetition. On the one hand, there is the sterile imitation of the exact copy; this form of repetition is integral to the Platonic system Williams rejects. Platonism connects the idea of repetition as the eternal return of the same with the idea of art as mimesis. Moreover, both are to be associated with the notion of a divine center that is principle and model. The cosmological image of the universe as a round in which the same eternally returns because nature is a copy of fixed ideas in the mind of the One is doubled in an aesthetic theory of art as the copy of a copy, a mirror up to nature. In both cases, legitimacy lies in the exactness of the duplication, since both nature and art are valid only insofar as they imitate a divine model.

Against this form of repetition, Williams sets the notion of a repetition based on difference. On this concept he builds his theory of imaginative naming. The poem must not be an exact repetition in words of the object it describes. On the other hand, it cannot be made of nonsense sounds –

that is, of words freed from their usual function as names of objects, words turned into sounds approaching pure music:

> According to my present theme the writer of imagination would attain closest to the conditions of music not when his words are disassociated from natural objects and specified meanings but when they are liberated from the usual quality of that meaning by transposition into another medium, the imagination. (92)

The key to Williams' theory of imagination is the idea that the imagination is a natural force making possible the re-creation of physical objects in a different form – that is, in their names. The object is a thing; it really exists. The poem is another real, existing thing. The two things echo one another at a distance. In a world where there is no divine center to control the production of meaning out of the juxtaposition of differences, they create resemblance out of difference. The destruction of nature by the imagination is both good and bad, bad because it accomplishes nothing. Nature repeats itself exactly after being destroyed. The destruction of nature is good because it is necessary to the naming that uses another form of the energies running through nature to re-create it in a new form.

Imaginative naming is creative repetition in a double sense. The verbal form duplicates what it names with a difference, and the different elements imagination gives rise to echo one another. From this echoing, meaning is created. This generation of meaning through resonance is present in *Spring and All* in two ways. In even the simplest of the poems, multiple objects from multiple sources rise into the realm of the imagination. "By the road to the contagious hospital," for example, describes the appearance all over the drab New Jersey landscape of the shrubs and weeds of spring:

> All along the road the reddish
> purplish, forked, upstanding, twiggy
> stuff of bushes and small trees . . . (12)

So much depends on the red wheelbarrow, to cite another example, not because it is supremely important in itself, but because it can momentarily be taken as the center of the world with other objects set beside it (in this case, the white chickens). In this way, meaning may arise from the juxtaposition. The other poems in *Spring and All* often work even more obviously according to a technique of the juxtaposition of the disparate: for example, the mixture of natural and urban details in the eighth poem, or the series of "unrelated" images in the eleventh, or the montage of seascape and cityscape in number thirteen, or the evocation of the crowd at a ball game in the twenty-sixth poem with its multitude of the unthinking masses which is "beautiful" "in detail" (89).

In all these poems the underlying assumption is the same. "Anywhere is everywhere" in Williams' world.[38] Williams' universe, unlike the Platonic cosmos, has no center, no reservoir of eternal models. There is only the ubiquitous life force which gives rise to differences in objects appearing side by side or in sequence from an infinity of centers. Out of the resemblances which occur by accident among these objects, meaning is created. No one place is the center or origin in this non-hierarchical world because the center is everywhere. This is why Williams pays such loving attention to random, ugly, "anti-poetical" objects. The wheelbarrow, the scrawny magnolia raising "its straggling branches of ivorywhite flowers" by the millworkers' shack (6), street signs or posters (87, 88), "the broken pieces of the city" (41), "the small / yellow cinquefoil in the / parched places" (46), "a girl with one leg / over the rail of a balcony" (48) – all are important, all equally important, because all exist, all have sprung up, from the "unfathomable ground"[39] to manifest themselves in the open. "It is only in isolate flecks that / something / is given off" (67). Any one of these flecks may be taken as the point on which everything depends and around which it turns.

This creation of meaning by the resonance of adjacent objects is echoed by the theory of language on which these poems are based. To name things with the imagination allows them to remain as they are. It liberates words from the necessity of "describing" things that have no need of being labeled. "In description," says Williams wittily, "words adhere to certain objects and have the effect on the sense of oysters, or barnacles" (90). Naming frees words from such adhesion to become independent energies with which the poet creates a new object – the poem:

> The word is not liberated, therefore able to communicate release from the fixities which destroy it until it is accurately tuned to the fact which giving it reality, by its own reality establishes its own freedom from the necessity of a word, thus freeing it and dynamizing it at the same time. (93)

Once words have been given reality and energy by their distant attunement to the things they name, an interaction among words analogous to the interaction among things in nature creates meaning in the poem. Words set side by side are forces that jostle one another. Out of this jostling of differences grows a new energy exceeding the sum of forces going into it. This dynamism gives the poem as a whole an exorbitant movement in one direction or another, all the words rising together to create that sense of enlargement or alleviation, the essential effect for Williams of a successful poem. This movement of the words together affirms simultaneously the reality of the objects named and the separate reality of the poem:

> Either to write or to comprehend poetry the words must be recognized to be moving in a direction separate from the jostling or lack of it which occurs within the piece. . . . As birds' wings beat the solid air without which none could fly so words freed by the imagination affirm reality by their flight. (86, 91)

I have tried elsewhere to show that Williams' best lyric poetry exemplifies his theory of naming.[40] These extraordinarily beautiful poems almost successfully resist analysis because in them, as Williams said there should be, there are "no ideas but in things." Their beauty depends on a delicate harmony of rhythm and sound pattern as much as on any analyzable meaning. The placing of the words on the page, especially at the ends of lines, makes these words (often articles, adverbs, pronouns, or prepositions little noticed in our speech) stand out in their verbal power as nodes of linguistic energy. Each word has the power to combine with other words in that jostling which produces meaning:

> Now the grass, tomorrow
> the stiff curl of wildcarrot leaf
>
> One by one objects are defined –
> It quickens: clarity, outline of leaf
>
> But now the stark dignity of
> entrance – Still, the profound change
>
> has come upon them: rooted they
> grip down and begin to awaken
>
>   ("By the road to the contagious hospital," 12, 13)

Or this, from "The farmer in deep thought," the third poem in *Spring and All*, in which the antagonist farmer, as the obstetrician, elsewhere, is an allegory for the poet. Both poet and farmer bring things out in the open, coax them into the light from their occultation in "the earth under our feet":[41]

> Down past the brushwood
> bristling by
> the rainsluiced wagonroad
> looms the artist figure of
> the farmer – composing
> – antagonist (17)

In their use of words, such poems as these have, more than the poems of Yeats, Stevens, Eliot, or Frost, fathered what is most vital in poetry being written today in the United States and even in England, where Williams' importance has recently been recognized and his influence spread. The prose in *Spring and All* is the discursive statement of doctrine, a doctrine, moreover, that is divided against itself, split into several incompatible strands. The poems emerge suddenly out of the lively ruminations of this prose as another sort of thing altogether, as the happening which the prose attempts to describe and justify. The poems are the abrupt opening of the luminous space of poetry – like the unforeseen appearance of the "radiant gist" in the bottom of Marie Curie's retort.[42] In the best of Williams' poems, the ideas expressed in the prose do become things, verbal substances composed or incarnated out of the syntactical energy of words. Such word-things reconcile in their visible presence the contradictions and tensions of the prose. The poems are imitations, in their movement, in their diction, and even in their shape on the page, of the things they name. They are also a manifestation of those things in their radiance, as they emerge out of the ground beneath. In addition, through the interaction of the words, they create separate and new objects.

Nevertheless, it is not clear what Williams means when he says that in poetry words "affirm reality by their flight." He has repeatedly asserted that "reality needs no personal support but exists free from human action" (91). The imagination seems no more than a mode of the life force that has the power to create "new forms as additions to nature" (78). Williams, however, grants the imagination a special, one might even say "extra-natural," function. Once more, his thought is traditional, its roots reaching back to the beginnings of Western thought. Like the tradition lying behind it, his theory of art is unable to free itself from the theories it rejects.

In Aristotle's *Poetics*, imitation is natural to man and, therefore, a part of nature. The pleasure man takes in performing or in witnessing acts of imitation is also natural and, therefore, also part of nature. This delight is man's natural pleasure in learning. In the words of Aristotle:

> As to its general origin, we may say that Poetry has sprung from two causes, each of them a thing inherent in human nature. The first is the habit of imitation; for to imitate is instinctive with mankind; and man is superior to the other animals, for one thing, in that he is the most imitative of creatures, and learns at first by imitation. Secondly, all men take a natural pleasure in the products of imitation. . . . The explanation of this delight lies in a further characteristic of our species, the appetite for learning; for among human pleasures that of learning is the keenest. . . .[43]

Aristotle, therefore, grants a sovereign role in human life to the *mimesis* enacted in a poem, in a play, or even in a simple metaphor. Metaphor he rightly sees as basic to poetry. "A command of metaphor," he says, is "the mark of genius" in a poet, for metaphor is "the application to one thing of the name that belongs to another," and "to coin good metaphors involves an insight into the resemblances between objects that are superficially unlike."[44] In *mimesis* the underlying *logos* of nature is destroyed in its sovereign oneness by being differentiated into the multiplicity of individual words. In the metaphoric interaction of words, the *logos* is brought into the open by mimetic repetition, but it is uncovered in a transferred form. In metaphor, the *logos* is destroyed and revealed at once.[45]

The same structure of thought organizes *Spring and All*, in spite of the violence of Williams' attack on the aesthetic of imitation. The key terms he uses to describe the action of imagination – "value," "life," "truth" – are again traditional. Though there may be an echo of Wordsworth in his formulation, his claim that reality is revealed and therefore brought into existence for man only in the work of art is as Aristotelian as it is romantic:

Taught by the largeness of his imagination to feel every form which he sees moving within himself, he must prove the truth of this by expression. . . . Only when this position is reached can life proper be said to begin since only then can a value be affixed to the forms and activities of which it consists. . . . It is not necessary to count every flake of the truth that falls; it is necessary to dwell in the imagination if the truth is to be numbered. . . . [I]n great works of the imagination A CREATIVE FORCE IS SHOWN AT WORK MAKING OBJECTS WHICH ALONE COMPLETE SCIENCE AND ALLOW INTELLIGENCE TO SURVIVE. . . . [L]ife becomes actual only when it is identified with ourselves. When we name it, life exists. (27–8, 36, 37, 41)

Only in the poem or painting is the truth of nature "elucidated" in the sense of "brought to light," made available to human intelligence. This elucidation, in a recurrent theme of *Spring and All*, produces the "enlargement" or lightening men feel "before great or good work, an expansion" (29). It is as if men had been released from a great burden and had come into an open space – it is the opening of revelation. Though value, life, and truth are already in nature, they are hidden, coming into existence only when the poet names natural objects. This naming brings them into that domain of the imagination where they may, in their jostling, transcend themselves in the creation of meaning. Such an art is at once *mimesis*, for "the same things exist, but in a different condition when energized by the imagination" (75), and *aletheia*, for in art alone is the hidden truth of nature uncovered, and creation, since in art a new object is brought into existence. The "truth" exists only when it is "numbered," named, "invented," and given compositional form. In its naming it becomes "actual" – that is, present. In poetic naming Williams at last takes possession of the presence of the present, "that eternal moment in which we alone live." He takes possession of it in the imagination – that is, as translated into the secondary reality of its image. This new or secondary reality performs the essential function of poetry, which for Williams, as for so many writers before him, is to be a mediator between man and primary reality. Great works of art "stand between man and nature as saints once stood between man and the sky" (38), and the authentic art work "is new, immediate – It is so because it is actual, always real. It is experience dynamized into reality" (68). Like Aristotle's *mimesis*, Williams' imagination is both part of and more than nature, both immediate and mediatorial – imitation, revelation, and creation at once. Like the long tradition he echoes, Williams remains caught in the inextricable web of connection among these concepts.

This returns us to the question of progress in the humanities. Is *Spring and All* an example of the progress of poetry? Does it transcend or improve upon its predecessors? Does it do something never done before? Has my interpretation of it, my unweaving or following through of some of its threads, accomplished anything? Have I destroyed the text, distorted it, elucidated it, preserved it, created it anew, or copied it? The answer to all these questions is both yes and no. Williams' insight into the relation between his poems and the objects they name will suggest how this is so. A poem in *Spring and All* is apposed to the natural objects it names. The same forces flow through it as flow through nature, so it is an object in its own right, and yet it is also a repetition in another form of the object it names. It is a natural object, but more than a natural object. The meaning of the poem arises from the juxtaposition of differences, not from the exact duplication of the same. For Williams difference is the basis of resemblance, not sameness the basis of difference. In a similar way the relation of *Spring and All* to its antecedents is an example of repetition with a difference, a new weaving of old threads which keeps the old meanings alive. This is both progress and stasis. My interpretation, in its turn, both destroys the text it interprets and, I hope, revivifies it. Such a "deconstruction" puts in question the received ideas of our tradition. At the same time my reading keeps the text alive by reliving it. It works back through its texture, repeats it once more in a different form, in a version of that transit through the texts of our heritage called for by Jacques Derrida:

It is necessary . . . to remain within the difficulty of the passage [through the tradition of Western ontology], to repeat it in a rigorous reading of metaphysics wherever it normalizes occidental discourse and not only in the texts of the "history of philosophy."[46]

This "rigorous reading" is not a demolition in the sense of going beyond or outside the tradition; it is not a question of a breakthrough beyond metaphysics or of a "reversal of Platonism." This reversal has been performed over and over through the centuries, from the Stoics to Neitzsche and the radical philosophers of our own day, and yet Platonism still reigns. In fact, the reversal of Platonism is perhaps performed first within the Platonic dialogues themselves.[47] It remains inscribed within the Platonic tradition as its double, inextricably part of it through two and half millennia. It is impossible to go beyond or outside this tradition because there is, for Western man, nothing outside the structure of the various languages that limits the possibilities of this thought. (I leave aside the challenging question of whether extra-European languages, Far Eastern or primitive tongues, for example, are outside these limits.) Nor can interpretation succeed in explaining a text away by identifying its origin, its "profound meaning." The interpreter of a given text can only in one way or another enter inside its play of language. "Progress" in humanistic studies does not mean discovering new facts or offering a definitive explication of one text or another. It means uncovering what has been there all along written into the words. In the same way there is no progress in human history, no unfolding or gradual perfection of the spirit. There are only endlessly varied ways to experience the human situation. Constitutive of this situation is the opening through language of temporality and a consequent distance from any origin or end. Beginning and end are exposed for the first time as shadows generated by language itself. This "first time" has always already happened, even with the first poems or with the first cave paintings. There is no progress because there is no beginning, no fixed center outside the interaction of words or signs on the basis of which progress could be measured.

The humanist must try to achieve as fully as possible a possession of the systematic connection of words and images within our tradition. If there has been "progress" in interpretation in the last century and a half, a progress sometimes associated with the names of Marx, Freud, and Nietzsche,[48] this advance has not been a movement beyond the tradition, the founding of a new historical era. It is, at most, a new way of possessing where we are and what we are, a way that more clearly understands the network of metaphors and concepts within which we live. Such a way recognizes as already present in the texts, part of their self-interpretative integument, the concepts of interpretation, history, progress, text, presence, consciousness, and temporality, which are our indispensable instruments of interpretation. Meaning is not something already there, outside the work as its center or model. It springs from within the text. As Gilles Deleuze puts it, "meaning is never a principle or origin, it is a product. It is not something to discover, to restore, nor to re-employ, it is something to produce by new mechanisms."[49] The business of the humanistic scholar is the appropriation of the texts of the past. This is an unending process of interpreting that which is itself an interpretation. In this process the same is maintained by means of the differential repetition which destroys and creates meaning at once. The meaning exists, as Williams says, only when we name it – that is, in the difference.

Notes

1. From one of the "lettres du voyant." See Arthur Rimbaud, *Illuminations and Other Prose Poems*, tr. Louise Varèse (revised ed., New York, 1957), p. xxxi.
2. *The Letters of Matthew Arnold to Arthur Hugh Clough*, H. F. Lowry, ed. (London and New York, 1932), p. 65.
3. *ibid.*, p. 124.
4. *ibid.*, p. 158.
5. *ibid.*, p. 65.
6. *ibid.*, p. 64.
7. In *Aspects of the Eighteenth Century*, Earl R. Wasserman, ed. (Baltimore, Maryland, 1965), pp. 245–64. This essay has now been supplemented by Bate's more extensive treatment of the theme in his Alexander Lectures for 1969, *The Burden of the Past and the English Poet* (Cambridge, Massachusetts, 1970). For a discussion of a similar topic, see Harold Bloom, "Keats and the Embarrassments of the Poetic Tradition," *From Sensibility to Romanticism: Essays Presented to Frederick A. Pottle*, Frederick W. Hilles and Harold Bloom eds (New York, 1965), p. 513–26.
8. Walter Jackson Bate, "The English Poet and the Burden of the Past, 1660–1820," p. 245.
9. *ibid.*, p. 246.
10. *ibid.*, p. 258.
11. *ibid.*, p. 263, 264.
12. *ibid.*, p. 262.
13. In addition to "Toward Literary History," see Geoffrey Hartman, "False Themes and Gentle Minds," *Philological Quarterly*, XLVII, 1 (January, 1968), pp. 55–68; "Romantic Poetry and the Genius Loci," in Peter Demetz, Thomas Greene, and Lowry Nelson, Jr, eds, *The Disciplines of Criticism: Essays in Literary Theory, Interpretation, and History Honoring René Wallek on the Occasion of His Sixty-fifth Birthday* (New Haven and London, 1968), pp. 289–314; "Blake and the 'Progress of Poesy,'" in Alvin S. Rosenfeld, ed., *William Blake: Essays for S. Foster Damon* (Providence, Rhode Island, 1969), pp. 57–68.
14. Hartman, "False Themes and Gentle Minds," *op. cit.*, p. 59.
15. *ibid.*: see also "Blake and the 'Progress of Poesy,'" *passim*, and "Romantic Poetry and the Genius Loci," *op. cit.*, p. 296: "From Milton through

Thomson, Gray, Collins, and the Romantics, the idea of a Progress of Poetry from Greece or the Holy Land to Britain is essential."

16. "False Themes," p. 57.
17. *ibid.*, p. 60.
18. *ibid.*
19. *ibid.*, p. 67.
20. *ibid.*, p. 60.
21. Quoted from an unpublished essay by Hartman.
22. "False Themes," p. 61.
23. See "Romantic Poetry and the Genius Loci," pp. 309ff.
24. William Carlos Williams, *Spring and All* (Dijon, 1923), p. 61. I am grateful to my colleague, Richard A. Macksey, for making available to me a copy of the rare first edition of *Spring and All*. It is now available in *Imaginations* (N.Y., 1970).
25. See Bate, "The English Poet and the Burden of the Past," *op. cit.*, pp. 248, 256.
26. *ibid.*, pp. 262, 263.
27. "False Themes," p. 60.
28. William Carlos Williams, *I Wanted to Write a Poem: The Autobiography of the Works of A Poet*, reported and edited by Edith Heal (Boston, 1967), p. 36.
29. Williams, *Spring and All*, *op. cit.*, pp. 7–8. All further citations from *Spring and All* will be identified by page numbers in parentheses after each quotation.
30. See Williams, *I Wanted to Write a Poem*, *op. cit.*, pp. 29, 30.
31. See Paul De Man, "The Rhetoric of Temporality," in Charles S. Singleton, ed., *Interpretation: Theory and Practice* (Baltimore, MD, 1969), pp. 173–209, especially pp. 190–1.
32. The phrase is borrowed from Wallace Stevens' "The Comedian as the Letter C."
33. Rimbaud, *Illuminations, ed. cit.*, pp. 17, 19: "Toutes les femmes qui l'avaient connu furent assassinées: quel saccage du jardin de la beauté! . . . Il s'amusa à égorger les bêtes de luxe. Il fit flamber les palais. Il se ruait sur les gens et les taillait en pièces."
34. Rimbaud, "L'oeuvre inouïe," *Illuminations*, p. 40, and see the "lettres du voyant," *passim, ibid.*, pp. xxvi–xxxv.
35. *ibid.*, p. 19: "La foule, les toits d'or, les belles bêtes existaient encore."
36. *ibid.*: "La musique savante manque à notre désir."
37. Thus in the text. Possibly this is a misprint for "great," but I have tried to suggest above a possible meaning that would allow it to stand. There are many misprints or downright errors in the text of *Spring and All*, some of which I have silently corrected in my citations. Slashes in my quotations correspond to paragraph breaks in the original.
38. William Carlos Williams, *Paterson* (New York, 1963), p. 273.
39. William Carlos Williams, *The Collected Later Poems* (New York, 1963), p. 23.
40. See "William Carlos Williams," *Poets of Reality: Six Twentieth-Century Writers* (Cambridge, Massachusetts, 1965), pp. 285–359 (also available in Atheneum paperback), and the introductory essay to *William Carlos Williams: A Collection of Critical Essays*, Twentieth Century Views (Englewood Cliffs, N.J., 1966), pp. 1–14, reprinted in this volume. *William Carlos Williams* also reprints for the first time some of the prose from *Spring and All*.

41. Williams, *Collected Later Poems*, *op. cit.*, p. 256.
42. Williams, *Paterson*, *op. cit.*, p. 133.
43. *Aristotle on the Art of Poetry*, tr. Lane Cooper (New York, 1947), pp. 9–10.
44. *ibid.*, pp. 68, 74.
45. For my discussion of Aristotle, I am indebted to an unpublished lecture by Jacques Derrida.
46. "La 'différance,'" *Bulletin de la Société française de Philosophie*, 62ᵉ Année, No. 3 (Juillet–Septembre, 1968), p. 96: "Il faut . . . séjourner dans la difficulté de ce passage, le répéter dans la lecture rigoureuse de la métaphysique partout où elle normalise le discours occidental et non seulement dans les textes de 'l'histoire de la philosophie.'"
47. See Jacques Derrida, "La pharmacie de Platon," *Tel Quel*, 32 and 33 (1968), pp. 3–48, 18–59, and Gilles Deleuze, "Platon et la simulacre," *Logique du sens* (Paris, 1969), pp. 292–307.
48. See Michel Foucault, "Nietzsche, Freud, Marx," *Nietzsche* (Paris, 1967), pp. 183–92.
49. Deleuze, *Logique de sens*, *op. cit.*, pp. 89, 90: "le sens n'est jamais principe ou origine, il est produit. Il n'est pas à découvrir, à restaurer ni à reemployer, il est à produire par de nouvelles machineries."

7

History as repetition in Thomas Hardy's poetry

The example of "Wessex Heights"

I

Wessex Heights (1896)

There are some heights in Wessex, shaped as if by a kindly hand
For thinking, dreaming, dying on, and at crises when I stand,
Say, on Ingpen Beacon eastward, or on Wylls-Neck westwardly,
I seem where I was before my birth, and after death may be.

In the lowlands I have no comrade, not even the lone man's friend –
Her who suffereth long and is kind; accepts what he is too weak to
    mend:
Down there they are dubious and askance; there nobody thinks as I,
But mind-chains do not clank where one's next neighbour is the sky.

In the towns I am tracked by phantoms having weird detective ways –
Shadows of beings who fellowed with myself of earlier days:
They hang about at places, and they say harsh heavy things –
Men with a wintry sneer, and women with tart disparagings.

Down there I seem to be false to myself, my simple self that was,
And is not now, and I see him watching, wondering what crass cause
Can have merged him into such a strange continuator as this,
Who yet has something in common with himself, my chrysalis.

I cannot go to the great grey Plain; there's a figure against the moon,
Nobody sees it but I, and it makes my breast beat out of tune;
I cannot go to the tall-spired town, being barred by the forms now
    passed
For everybody but me, in whose long vision they stand there fast.

There's a ghost at Yell'ham Bottom chiding loud at the fall of the
    night,
There's a ghost in Froom-side Vale, thin-lipped and vague, in a
    shroud of white,

There is one in the railway train whenever I do not want it near,
I see its profile against the pane, saying what I would not hear.

As for one rare fair woman, I am now but a thought of hers,
I enter her mind and another thought succeeds me that she prefers;
Yet my love for her in its fulness she herself even did not know;
Well, time cures hearts of tenderness, and now I can let her go.

So I am found on Ingpen Beacon, or on Wylls-Neck to the west,
Or else on homely Bulbarrow, or little Pilsdon Crest,
Where men have never cared to haunt, nor women have walked with
    me,
And ghosts then keep their distance; and I know some liberty.

The opening stanza of "Wessex Heights" identifies precisely the pervasive quality of consciousness in all Hardy's poetry. Throughout his almost nine hundred pages of lyric poetry the voice the reader hears is that of a man who muses alone, a detached spectator of human life and of human history. He is a man who lives "in quiet, screened, unknown" (*CP*, 885). The unassertive, laconic, yet garrulous voice which speaks throughout Hardy's poetry is that of a man talking not so much to other people as to himself.

As other critics have noted, the rhythm, diction and syntax of a line like the eighth in "Wessex Heights" ("But mind-chains do not clank where one's next neighbour is the sky") is that of a man so anxious to speak honestly of his experience that he must discard all attempts to achieve Tennysonian euphony. These are replaced with simple words in the plainest order, each monosyllable forced by its harsh consonants (often consonants which give the word a dead ending: "not," "clank," "next"), to be pronounced slowly and in relative isolation from the words which surround it. The sound and meaning of the words stand out starkly, as well as the "naked thew and sinew," to borrow Gerard Manley Hopkins's phrase, of its syntactical connections to other words in the phrase: "But mind-chains do not clank where one's next neighbour is the sky."

It would be a mistake, however, to think of Hardy as a simple countryman who says what he means in words of one syllable and in stark declarative sentences. Like many lines in poetry built around "not," line eight of "Wessex Heights" affirms in its sound and language what it denies. A straightforward paraphrase of the line might be: "Isolation from other people on the heights provides mental freedom." In asserting that mind-chains do not clank there, however, the sound of the lines and their abrupt rhythm puts that fettered clanking kinesthetically and audibly within the reader's experience. In poetry, as in dreams, there are no negations. To assert with appropriate strength what does not exist is to bring it into existence in the words. The mind-chains which the speaker claims to escape on the heights clank through the harsh dentals and fricatives in the line, and his bondage hums resonantly in the repetitions of the "n" sound which echoes through the line like the vibration after metal has struck metal. Only after the final roughly stopped sibilation of the "sk" in the last word does the line broaden out into the limitless freedom of the vowel in "sky." Such subtle embodiments of the qualities of mental experience are characteristic of the meditative toughness of Hardy's best poems.

This toughness is turned somewhat masochistically in on itself. By means of the words of his poems Hardy's own mind seems to become aware of itself and of its texture. The reader of these poems has the feeling not that he is being spoken to, but that he is overhearing the unceasing private ruminations of a solitary, brooding mind, a mind which speaks for itself and for the various people who throng within it and constitute its *dramatis personae*. Hardy's poems are perhaps, as he often insisted, "to be regarded, in the main, as dramatic monologues by different characters" (*CP*, 175); but whereas Browning's dramatic monologues, for example, are the result of a propulsive energy of the will by which the poet goes outside himself, enters into the lives of other people, and speaks for their private experiences, in Hardy's case the various speakers are already contained within the wide bounds of the poet's "spacious vision" (*CP*, 483). Though the poet lives in a "house of silence," within that quiet place "figures dance to a mind with sight" (*CP*, 445). Hardy's poems are as often speech of these figures as they are speech in his own proper voice. In speaking for them, however, he speaks for himself. Their experiences are aspects of his own inner experience. Their voices have the same tones as his voice when he speaks for himself, as, for example, in the *Life*. Their adventures fall into repetitive patterns, and their lives are parts of his inner world.

Hardy's habitual way of looking at life is defined exactly by the opening stanza of "Wessex Heights." The speaker of this poem is so withdrawn a watcher of life that it is as if he stood on a high place and looked at human existence spread out below him as a panoramic spectacle. Ingpen Beacon, or Inkpen Beacon, in Berkshire, the highest chalk-down in England (1011 ft), and Wylls-Neck, or Will's Neck, in Somerset, the highest of the Quantock Hills (1261 ft), form the eastward and westward boundaries of the central region of Hardy's Wessex. Though the grammar of l. 3 says that the speaker sometimes stands either on one of these high places or on the other, the naming of both of them and the suggestions of the word "say" at the beginning of the line put the speaker by implication on both heights at once. In fact the present location of the speaker is never specified. He is not in the lowlands because he speaks of them as "down there," but he is not on the heights either, since he speaks retrospectively of what it is like to be there. He is in fact in some undefined place telling what happens when during times of crisis he stands on one height or another of Wessex. This place is the locus of the poem itself, a place which exists only in the language of poetry. This language, in "Wessex Heights" at least, is spoken by an indeterminate "I" from an indeterminate place at an indeterminate time to an indeterminate auditor. In poetry generally language is often cut off from its usual contexts of person, place, and time, but this detachment is in "Wessex Heights" strikingly expressed by the strange displacement or ubiquity of the speaker. So vivid is his imaginative memory of these times of crisis in his life that he speaks of them in a kind of collective present tense as if he were standing on both heights at once, adding in the final stanza two additional heights, until it seems that the speaker of the poem is a kind of pervasive spiritual presence brooding on all the high places of Wessex, overlooking from above the towns and rivers of the central plain. As Arnold's gipsy is the *genius loci* of all the places named in "The Scholar Gipsy," present simultaneously in all of them, so the "I" of Hardy's poem is a local deity to be found on all the heights in Wessex. His placement there expresses his stubborn disengagement from life on the plain:

> So I am found on Ingpen Beacon, or on Wylls-Neck to the west,
> Or else on homely Bulbarrow, or little Pilsdon Crest . . .

The place names which echo through "Wessex Heights" have another connotation, a connotation which is reinforced by other elements in the first stanza. The names seem chosen partly because they have associations with times long gone by. Ingpen Beacon is so named because it was used as a place to burn signal fires, and one remembers Hardy's description of the long tradition of such fires in an early chapter of *The Return of the Native*. Though the "barrow" in "Bulbarrow" (a hill in Dorset) is the modern form of the Old English "beorg," for "hill" or "mountain," the word also means "burial mound" or "tumulus," and thus, like the Rainbarrow of *The Return of the Native*, is associated with the prehistoric inhabitants of Britain. Pilsdon Crest is presumably Hardy's name for Pillesdon Pen, the highest hill in Dorset (907 ft) and site of the ruins of an ancient British fort. To climb to the heights of Wessex is paradoxically to descend into the immemorial depths of the past and to reach at the summit a place where all times even before recorded antiquity are present in layered proximity:

> It was as if these men and boys [says Hardy of the bonfire builders on

Rainbarrow in *The Return of the Native*] had suddenly dived into past ages, and fetched therefrom an hour and deed which had before been familiar with this spot. The ashes of the original British pyre which blazed from that summit lay fresh and undisturbed in the barrow beneath their tread. The flames from funeral piles long ago kindled there had shone down upon the lowlands as these were shining now. Festival fires to Thor and Woden had followed on the same ground and duly had their day. Indeed, it is pretty well known that such blazes as this the heathmen were now enjoying are rather the lineal descendents from jumbled Druidical rites and Saxon ceremonies than the invention of popular feeling about Gunpowder Plot.

Like the heathmen in *The Return of the Native*, the speaker in "Wessex Heights" has reached a place where all times are contemporaneous, a place of repetition where events from the past may be fetched to the present and re-enacted there. Here, as throughout his work, Hardy's fascination with the pre-Roman past of Britain is not an antiquarian interest in its mysterious distance, but rather a recognition of its proximity and tangible presence. Even the distant past is present to a man who can describe himself as "where I was before my birth, and after death may be." If the location of the speaker of this poem is at such a spatial distance from life that it appears as a faraway panorama, this spatial distance is in turn the symbol of a more important temporal distance. From the heights in Wessex all the times of history and of pre-history seem equally close and equally far away. The speaker has reached a place out of place which is also a time out of times, a no-time before birth and after death from which all times may be seen at once, as from the perspective of eternity.

This escape from space and time, however, does not involve an ascent to some transcendent realm, as the poem makes clear. The speaker's consciousness itself involves this extravagant detachment. To be conscious, for Hardy, means to be separated from life, as if one were at an infinite distance from it, able to see it clearly, but having no part in it, like a ghost in broad daylight. The temporal and spatial distances which are such salient motifs in "Wessex Heights" are ways of expressing, not some supernatural perspective, but a withdrawal from life which, for Hardy, is native to the mind. The word "crises" in l. 2 plays an important role in defining this withdrawal. The times when the speaker climbs to the heights are especially those of crisis. The word comes from the Greek χρίσις, which is the noun formed from χρίνω, to separate, divide, choose, judge, decide, think, believe. The same source lies behind the word "critic." A crisis is, among other things, "the turning point for better or worse in an acute disease or fever," "an emotionally significant event or radical change of status in a person's life," "decisive moment: turning point," "such a point in the course of the action of a play or other work of fiction" (*Webster's International Dictionary*). One crisis in Tess Durbeyfield's life, to take an example from Hardy's fiction, is her deflowering. It marks a turning point in her life, dividing it into a "before" and an "after": "An immeasurable social chasm was to divide our heroine's personality thereafter from that previous self of hers who stepped from her mother's door to try her fortune at Trantridge poultry-farm." But Tess's deflowering is also in itself a dividing or marking, the inscription on her pure flesh of the stigma of impurity, according to the metaphor of writing or tracing which recurs in "Tess's Lament," the poem written as it were as a footnote or marginal comment for *Tess of the d'Urbervilles*. The paradox of this dividing point in Tess' life is that it is at once a unique event, a decisive moment which makes a permanent change and creates an immense chasm in the linear sequence of her destiny, and at the same time exists, as soon as it happens, not as a unique event but as repetition, as the retracing of a pattern of violent misappropriation which has already occurred many times before, echoing down through the generations:

> Why was it that upon this beautiful feminine tissue, sensitive as gossamer, and practically blank as snow as yet, there should have been traced such a coarse pattern as it was doomed to receive; why so often the coarse appropriates the finer thus, the wrong man the woman, the wrong woman the man, many thousand years of analytical philosophy have failed to explain to our sense of order. . . . Doubtless some of Tess d'Urberville's mailed ancestors rollicking home from a fray had dealt the same measure even more ruthlessly towards peasant girls of their time.

In the same way, the "crises" which lead the speaker of "Wessex Heights" to withdraw to Ingpen Beacon or to Wylls-Neck are presumably watersheds, decisive moments in his present life. Far from taking him to a direct confrontation of his immediate situation, however, they lead him to a place of repetition. There all his past history occurs and recurs within his brooding meditation and within the language of the poem. Far from being solely a center, pivot, or "turning point," each crisis is also peripheral, extreme, outside the circle of life altogether: "I seem where I was before my birth, and after death may be." These crises are both central and eccentric at once, each one a "center on the horizon," in Wallace Stevens' phrase.[1] Just as Tess' deflowering is both a unique event, a crisis, an experience which happens to her only, and at the same time exists only as the tracing of a pre-existing pattern, so the speaker of "Wessex Heights," at the moment when he is confronting a crisis in his life and is most engaged in his immediate situation, is also least engaged in his immediate situation. He sees the present from the perspective of all his past and, beyond that, he sees it, like little Father Time in *Jude the Obscure*, from the perspective of death.

The odd sequence of present participles in the second line of "Wessex Heights" therefore expresses not so much a crescendo of escapes from life as a series of implicit equivalences: "thinking, dreaming, dying." The heights of Wessex seem "as if shaped by a kindly hand." (The reader of Hardy's poems about the "unweeting" mechanisms of the "Immanent Will that stirs and urges everything" (*CP*, 289) will know what irony there is in that "as if.") The heights seem, by reason of their separation from life, especially appropriate places on which to think, to dream, and to die. For Hardy, to think is to be detached from life. But to think is to dream, that is, to enter some imaginary or insubstantial world, perhaps a world of remembered images. And to dream is to die, as did the old Britons buried in their tumuli on the heights. From thinking it is only two short steps to dying, since thinking is itself already a kind of death. By the mere act of taking thought the speaker of the poem is thrown in an instant to such a distance from life that he seems not yet born or already dead.

This extreme separation of the mind from life is the persistent quality of consciousness expressed throughout Hardy's work. It is present in the point of view of the narrators of the fiction, for example, or in the perspective of the Choruses of Spirits in *The Dynasts*, as well as in the stance of the speakers of the lyric poems. Nor can one doubt that it was a mode of existence both natural to Hardy in his own life and also deliberately chosen by him. Hardy often thinks of himself as a disembodied spectator of life, who has no real part in the present, but "travel[s] as a phantom now," and "visit[s] bodiless / Strange gloomy households often at odds" (*CP*, 429). The fullest expression of this characteristic strategy of disengagement is a passage in *The Life of Thomas Hardy* which is a perfect gloss on the first stanza of "Wessex Heights":

> For my part, [says Hardy] if there is any way of getting a melancholy satisfaction out of life it lies in dying, so to speak, before one is out of the flesh; by which I mean putting on the manners of ghosts, wandering in their haunts, and taking their views of surrounding things. To think of life as passing away is a sadness; to think of it as past is at least tolerable. Hence even when I enter a room to pay a simple morning call I have unconsciously the habit of regarding the scene as if I were a spectre not solid enough to influence my environment; only fit to behold and say, as another spectre said; 'Peace be unto you!' (*Life*, 209–10)

A curious and revealing text! As in the first stanza of "Wessex Heights," Hardy here defines his state of mind in hyperbolic terms.

Though he is still in the flesh, it is as if he were already dead, a ghost returned to life from the past who looks upon the present without concern for what happens now or in the future. This assumption of the manners and views of ghosts avoids the fundamental sadness of human existence, which is its bondage to time. Even while something is happening it is already passing away. This painful fluidity of the present means that no person and no allegiance can remain the same. The discontinuity of time is the primary source of suffering for Hardy and for his characters. To die before one is out of the flesh, to see things as if one were a ghost, is to escape from this pouring by of the present by seeing it as if it were already past.

But how can this be? To look at the present as if one were a ghost is certainly to see it with calm disengagement, as though it had nothing to do with oneself, but this hardly seems to mean seeing it as if it were past. The ghostly spectator is a revenant from the past, but what he sees in the present, so it would seem, has still the quality of passing. The apparent contradiction vanishes when one recognizes that for Hardy ghosts are out of time altogether. Like the protagonist of "Wessex Heights,." they have returned to the place where man is before birth and after death. If in one sense Hardy's ghosts return to the present from the past, as beings whose lives are already over, in another sense their perspective on the present is from the future. They see things from before and after time. From the infinite distance of death they view the present as something which has already happened and which has already been followed by its inevitable consequences. This, says Hardy, is the only way to make the present tolerable.

Such a perspective on the present is pervasive in Hardy's work, both in the poetry and in the fiction. Even in those poems, like "The Wind's Prophecy," which express directly the present experience of the speaker, an experience oriented towards a hoped-for future, a retrospective consciousness is also present, that consciousness which has foreseen the end and looks at the present from the point of view of the future, as something which has already taken place in the ineluctable sequences of the past. "The Wind's Prophecy" may describe Hardy's first trip to Cornwall, where he met Emma Lavinia Gifford, who was to become his first wife, and so was led to betray his love for his cousin, Tryphena Sparks. The speaker of this poem moves across the landscape on a journey away from his black-haired beloved, but he affirms and reaffirms his determination to remain true to her. The wind, however, speaks for its foreknowledge of the future and of the as yet unknown fair-haired beauty who awaits the lover at the end of his journey:

'I roam, but one is safely mine,'
I say, 'God grant she stay my own!'
Low laughs the wind as if it grinned:
'Thy Love is one thou'st not yet known.' (*CP*, 465)

There are further elements in the text from the *Life*, however, and further connections of that text with "Wessex Heights." When Hardy makes a morning call he thinks of himself as a spectre not solid enough to influence his environment. If he cannot touch what is around him, so also it cannot touch him. All his life Hardy hated to be touched.[2] To think of himself as a bodiless ghost is to escape into intangibility and to be no longer at the mercy of the bodies of others. *Noli me tangere* might have been his device, and the search for some form of invulnerability is the chief motivation of the retreat to high places of the speaker of "Wessex Heights."

Noli me tangere – this is one of the motifs in the Biblical passage to which Hardy so oddly refers at the end of the text in the *Life*. The play on touching in this part of the gospel is echoed in Hardy's words. "Touch me not; for I am not yet ascended to my Father," said Jesus to Mary Magdalene when he appeared to her in the garden after his resurrection, and he said, "Peace be unto you!" on his first two appearances to his disciples (John 20: 17, 19, 26). Though Jesus may have said, "Touch me not," to Mary, he could yet breathe on the disciples (John 20: 22), and he could also let Thomas Didymus thrust his hand into the wound in his side (John 20: 27). In the same way, Hardy thinks of himself as both dead and alive, both in the body and outside it. He has died, so to speak, before he is out of the flesh. Though he has been resurrected from the dead he has not ascended to any distant spiritual realm. He remains within the world as a spectral looker-on at life, unfit to affect it in any way, but able to bring peace to it by seeing it with a vision so wide and all-inclusive that it views each partial instant in the perspective of the vast whole of time and space of which it is a helpless and minuscule part.

II

"I seem where I was before my birth, and after death may be" – the innate standing-back of the mind symbolized by the high places of "Wessex Heights" or by the imagery of ghosts in the passage in the *Life* gives Hardy the power to escape triumphantly from the present. There is one dimension of time, however, from which he is unable to escape: the past. The impossibility of freeing oneself wholly from the past is the fundamental theme of "Wessex Heights," and without exaggeration it may be said to be the central theme of all his work. In Hardy's fiction there are many characters like Henchard in *The Mayor of Casterbridge* or Tess in *Tess of the d'Urbervilles* who strive earnestly to free themselves from their own pasts and from the past of humanity, yet are condemned to repeat not only patterns from their own past lives, but also the more general patterns into which the universal experience of mankind has fallen. Henchard not only repeats compulsively a sequence of love and rejection, but also repeats in these repetitions the experiences of Cain, Job, Oedipus, and Lear. Tess can free herself from her past only by re-enacting the murder which is the family curse and so condemning herself to a sacrificial death which recalls that of Christ or those in Greek tragedy or even those ritual executions supposed to have been performed in prehistoric times on the altar at Stonehenge.

The formal structure of Hardy's fiction is generated by the juxtaposition of the retrospective view of the narrator, who sees clearly from the beginning each episode in the life of the protagonist in the perspective of the pattern the whole makes, and the narrow, mystified vision of the protagonists. The latter live absorbed in the present, and in the future goals which they hope to reach by actions in that present. The narrator resurrects those lives from the past by an act of the historical imagination, presenting them to the reader as completed totalities, the perfected destinies of the main characters.

In the lyric poetry these two perspectives are joined in a single mind. Many of the poems set side by side two times in the speaker's life, a past time when he was caught up in some human relationship, usually a love affair, and was centering his whole life on attaining the goal of his desire, and a present time when he looks back on that episode in the perspective of its end in separation, betrayal, or death. This juxtaposition creates the characteristic formal structure of the lyric poems, most notably of the admirable sequence written after the death of Hardy's first wife, the "Poems of 1912–13," but also of dozens of other poems, including "Wessex Heights."

If the speaker in "Wessex Heights" can escape from the present by going up on Ingpen Beacon or on Wylls-Neck, and if even in the lowlands he has no present attachments to life ("In the lowlands I have no comrade . . . ; there nobody thinks as I"), he is unable ever to escape completely from his past. In spite of his claim that "mind-chains do not clank where one's next neighbour is the sky," the poems shows him even when he stands in imagination on the heights obsessed with the past, haunted by it, bound to it, able to think of nothing else. Hardy is a man "To whom to-day is beneaped and stale, / And its urgent clack / But a vapid tale" (*CP*, 332). On the other hand, for him the things of the past, things "that nobody else's mind calls back," "Have a savour that scenes in being lack, / And a presence more than the actual brings" (*CP*, 332).

He is the man who knows "something of ecstasy" in the "companion-ship" of "the ghost of the past." All the past still exists in his memory "just as it was" (*CP*, 290). So in one of his most beautiful poems, "In Front of the Landscape" (*CP*, 285–7), "scenes miscalled of the bygone" return with such vividness "before the intenser / Stare of the mind" that they roll like a great ocean wave between the poet and the "customed landscape" of Wessex, thinning that reality to "ghost-like gauze." The poet is inundated with such an overwhelming abundance of images from the past that he walks "plunging and labouring on in a tide of visions."

In "Wessex Heights," however, the companionship of the past brings not ecstasy but acute suffering. This suffering has three interrelated aspects. If the passage from the *Life* discussed above shows Hardy escaping from the present by imagining himself as a ghostly visitant within the actual, "Wessex Heights" shows the speaker in his turn haunted by ghosts from the past whenever he is so unwary as to descend from his heights to the lowlands. In the second stanza of the poem the speaker says he has "no comrade, not even the lone man's friend," the charitable woman, perhaps Charity herself, who is described in l. 6 in words which echo I Corinthians 13: 4: "Her who suffereth long and is kind; accepts what he is too weak to mend." In the lowlands, says the speaker, "nobody thinks as I." If anyone down there notices him at all, they are "dubious and askance." They look upon him as an odd fellow with whom there can be no possibility of mental harmony or communion. This is followed by a line which seems a *non sequitur*: "But mind-chains do not clank where one's next neighbour is the sky." So far in the poem the poet has described his isolation in the lowlands, the fact that he has no neighbor there to whom he is bound by ties of love or hate. Only if one thinks about the same things as one's neighbors can one, so it would seem, be bound to them by "mind-chains." Being surrounded by neighbors who think differently from oneself seems more a kind of freedom than a kind of servitude, and it is not immediately apparent why the speaker should flee the lowlands in order to escape "mind-chains." "Thou shalt love thy neighbour as thyself" – the speaker does not fulfil this commandment to charity in the lowlands, where he has no-one who accepts him as a neighbor, nor does he love his neighbor on the heights, where his next neighbor is the sky, the silence and solitude of infinite space. In both places he is alone, and though it might be better to have so quiet and so vacuous a neighbor as the sky than to be surrounded by people who are dubious and askance, it is still not clear why this should constitute mental servitude.

The following stanza, however, shows that the speaker is by no means alone in the lowlands. If he has ties there to no living neighbor, he is surrounded by swarms of ghosts from the past who exist only for him and who are thinking about the same things which obsess him. His mental bondage to these specters constitutes the fetter whose clank he hopes to escape on the heights. The ghosts of the lowlands, it is evident, in their weird detective ways are bent on confronting the protagonist of the poem and apprehending him for the guilt involved in his betrayal of them. Shadowily suggested behind the reticent imagery of "Wessex Heights" may be glimpsed one of those tales of love leading to betrayal, to separation, estrangement, anguish, and loss, which are so characteristic of Hardy's work both in fiction and in verse. Hardy's major theme is love. Love, for him, falls again and again into the same pattern. It begins in a fascination in which the lover fixes his whole life on the beloved. His desire for her makes her seem the radiant center of the world. This seemingly divine glow radiates outward to transfigure everything around her and make it a sign of her presence. "Love," however, "lives on propinquity, but dies of contact" (*Life*, 220). As soon as the lover reaches his goal the lady he has so loved loses all her numinous power. In one way or another he is led to betray her or to be betrayed by her and to suffer lifelong remorse for the suffering this infidelity causes. This story is repeated with variations throughout Hardy's fiction, for example, in the tangled skein of crossed fidelities in *Far from the Madding Crowd*, which leaves Bathsheba, after destroying two lovers, joined to the faithful Gabriel Oak in a marriage whose permanence will depend ironically on the psychological distance between the newlyweds, or in the waverings from Wildeve to Clym Yeobright and back to Wildeve or Eustacia Vye in *The Return of the Native*, or in the crisscross of mismatched loves in *The Woodlanders* which leaves Grace Fitzpiers at the end, as Hardy said, "doomed to an unhappy life with an inconstant husband" (*Life*, 220).[3] A similar tale of estrangement lies behind the "Poems of 1912–13." "Summer gave us sweets," Hardy wistfully asks the ghost of his dead wife in "After a Journey," "but autumn wrought division?" (*CP*, 328). It is only by going back before the autumn time of cooling love that Hardy can in these poems recover the ecstasy of his courtship of Emma by the sea. A similar story of betrayal is hinted at in the third stanza of "Wessex Heights," and must be supposed to account for the harsh heavy things the detective ghosts from the past have to say to him.[4]

III

Hardy's betrayal of others is also self-betrayal, which is perhaps more painful, as the next stanza of the poem suggests:

> Down there I seem to be false to myself, my simple self that was,
> And is not now, and I see him watching, wondering what cross cause

Can have merged him into such a continuator as this,
Who yet has something in common with himself, my chrysalis.

These admirably concentrated lines shift the focus of the poem to a second source of suffering caused by the passing of time. To betray others is bad enough, but to betray oneself is even worse. It is worse because rather than establishing a fissure between oneself and others, time now opens up a gap within the self itself. If the man who escapes from the pain of passing time by thinking of himself as a spectral visitant in the present can then become the victim of ghosts haunting him from the past, the worst form of this is to be subject to the watching, wondering disdain of his own past self. The usual relationship between present self and past self is reversed. Rather than the present conscious-ness being the spectator, looking back from the outside at one of his past selves, the reader shares with the speaker the uncomfortable experience of being subject to the watching scrutiny of an earlier self. The watcher becomes the watched. He is observed by a lucid detective vision which is closely and inescapably part of himself. This is an especially unpleasant version of the Sartrean reversal in which the man spying through a keyhole at another man, secretly stealing the other's freedom, suddenly realizes that he has himself been caught in the act of spying by another spy and so changed in his turn into an object.

This strange form of self-torture is possible because the present self of the speaker is both continuous with and discontinuous with his past self. If he were entirely different from his past self the continuity would be broken, and the past self would presumably no longer concern him at all. If he had been able to remain the same self then past and present would be perfectly in harmony, and no problem would arise. Neither of these happy possibilities has occurred. He is both the same self and a different self, false to his past self and yet forced to recognize his obligation to it. The past self "is not now" and yet still exists as an accusing spectator. That present self, in Hardy's precise definition, is a "strange continuator" of itself.

The language of this stanza is a good example of a tension between the illicit use of physical language to describe human existence and the use of language more appropriate to the actual nature of experience. This tension is fundamental to many nineteenth-century works of literature. It usually involves questions of temporality, of causality, and of freedom. The tension arises from the conflict between the writer's conscious adherence to scientific models, whether those of the physical or of the biological sciences, to describe human life and, on the other hand, his insight into the true nature of that life. Such insight means a recognition that human beings cannot be described in language appropriate for inanimate objects or for organisms. One example of this is George

Eliot's struggle in *Adam Bede* or in *Middlemarch* to reconcile her sense of human existence with a language of causality taken from nineteenth-century science. Another example is the dialectical structure of George Meredith's *The Ordeal of Richard Feverel*. That novel begins with a conflict between mechanical and organic ways of describing Richard's growing up, only to transcend both these languages in the authentically existential language of human choice and human temporality in the twenty-ninth chapter. This chapter defines Richard's decision to marry Lucy as the irreversible crossing of his Rubicon, "the River of his ordeal," after which he is no longer the same man and can never return to the other shore or to his earlier self.

Such a conflict between a false assimilation of man to physical nature and insight into the temporal structures of human experience is of great importance in Hardy's work too, for example, in the tension in *Jude the Obscure* between the various (and contradictory) attempts to locate the causes of Jude's suffering in the bad structure of society, in biological urges and their incompatibility with social law, in the incompatibility of human desire and the impersonal operations of nature, and so on, and, on the other hand, the underlying dramatic pattern of the novel. This drama focuses, like all Hardy's fiction, on the individual's ever-renewed, ever-unsuccessful attempt to escape the void in his heart by means of a happy relation to another person. The theme of interpersonal relations can become, as in Hardy's treatment of the story of Jude Fawley and Sue Bridehead, an indirect way of presenting the actual structure of human experience, in particular its temporality.

In the same way the fourth stanza of "Wessex Heights" hovers between a physical or biological picture of human time and Hardy's deeper intuition of the strange combination of presence and absence, continuity and discontinuity, which characterizes human time. On the one hand, the third line of the stanza asserts that the earlier simple self has "merged" into the present "strange continuator," as if there had been a gradual and unbroken process of change, like that of organic growth. If this is the case, it is hard to see how the present continuator of the past self could ever have become "strange." On the other hand, the final line of the stanza ("Who yet has something in common with himself, my chrysalis") proposes another model for human change through time, still an explicitly organic one, but nevertheless a model drawn from that kind of organic change which is least "natural" and most like the discontinuities of mental life and of human time. *Natura nihil facit per saltum* – this law of natural continuity is most strikingly broken by the transmogrification of chrysalis into butterfly, and it is this model of natural yet discontinuous change which Hardy finally calls on to describe the relation between present self and past self. The present self both has something in common with its past self and yet is as unlike it as butterfly is unlike its chrysalis, both connected to it and yet divided from it by an abrupt break, a temporal division which leaves the two parts of the mind staring at one another across an open space. From simplicity to complexity, from the naïve assumption of a linear temporality allowing the self to remain true to itself, to a sophisticated self-consciousness aware of its inner doubleness and aware also of the paradoxical relation between past self and present self – the two selves confront each other from opposite sides of the mind in a reflexive relation of accusation and mute confession of guilt which recalls the traditional confrontation of a man and his double, or Baudelaire's insight into the '*dédoublement*' natural to human consciousness. Like Baudelaire, Hardy glimpses *dans l'être humain l'existence d'une dualité permanente, la puissance d'être à la fois soi et un autre* (the existence of a permanent duality in the human being, the power to be at once oneself and another).[5]

Only the wondering and accusing simple self that was assumes that the change from simple self to complex self can be explained by some "crass cause" external to the self, a cause like that which accounts for the linear sequence of natural change. The phrase "crass cause" recalls a crucial line from one of Hardy's earliest poems, "Hap." That poem says it is worse to live in a universe governed by the blind impulsions of the Immanent Will than it would be to live in a world governed by a deliberately wicked god. Not intentional cruelty but meaningless physical necessity causes man's suffering: "Crass Casualty obstructs the sun and rain" (*CP*, 7). In both phrases the word "crass" suggests an energy which is unthinking, inhuman, without intention or meaning, mere brute force.[6] In "Wessex Heights," however, though the simple self still expects to find some crass cause external to itself which will account for his later self's infidelity, the present self from his position on the heights knows – as the poem as a whole makes clear – that there is no cause, no explanation, nothing outside the self to blame. However hard a man tries to remain true to himself he becomes different, so different that he is at best a strange continuator of himself. Human temporality is characterized by a paradoxical combination of presence and absence, continuity and discontinuity, similarity and difference. Time itself is the "cause," the source of self-division. The reaching out of the present towards the past inevitably opens up within the self as it exists in any given moment a hollow, a distance, a wound which can never be healed.

IV

The following two stanzas of the poem, the fifth and sixth, return with great intensity to the theme of the third stanza, the way in which the speaker when he is in the lowlands is confronted by ghosts from the past who reproach him for his infidelity to them. These stanzas are the emotional climax of the poem. In a crescendo of fear and self-disgust the speaker describes the way he encounters in the lowlands new ghosts wherever he turns, ghost upon ghost, crowds and shoals of spirits who multiply in every direction, rising like a spectral tide or fog to block his way and to stand between him and the landscape. As in "In Front of the Landscape" the poet shows himself overwhelmed by a tide of visions, so here, though as a frightening rather than pleasurable experience, the forms from the past rise up from the lowlands like ground mist and keep the speaker from living, as others do, unequivocally engaged in the present. These forms, in a splendid phrase, are said to stand fast, fixed immovably in the speaker's "long vision." The word "long" here vibrates between its spatial and its temporal connotations. The speaker's vision is long because, as the movement from place to place in the two stanzas suggests, he can simultaneously see ghosts in many different locations in the lowlands. It is long also in the sense that it persists unchanging through time and sees things from the past as vividly as if they were still real, standing fast in the atemporal fixity of the speaker's farsightedness, just as in "The Phantom Horsewoman," one of the "Poems of 1912–13," the poet says his dead wife "still rides gaily / In his rapt thought / On that shagged and shaly / Atlantic spot / And as when first eyed / Draws rein and sings to the swing of the tide" (*CP*, 333).

Here another subtle sound effect may be seen working in "Wessex Heights." If the openness and clearness of the vowel in "sky" seems to embody the limitless expanse of the air above the heights, the "i" sound is also present in the word "heights" itself, and other high vowels dominate in the place names of the heights Hardy chooses to mention: Ingpen Beacon and Wylls-Neck. By contrast the place names cited for the lowlands ("Yell'ham Bottom" and "Froom-side Vale"[7]) have low vowels, "o's" and "a's," and a thick consonant, "m," recurs, as if these low places were an appropriate spot for ghosts to congregate and multiply, or as if these spectres might have risen up like fog out of mud or out of a low-lying river. The structure of the whole poem (the heights of consciousness surveying from a distance the survivors from the past who remain the inescapable content of the mind) is echoed in this contrast in sound between "Wylls-Neck," on the one hand, and "Yell'ham Bottom" on the other.

The two stanzas end with a fine reversal. What has been a list of specters who remain unmistakably ghosts, with all the usual appurtenances of ghosts – shrouds, chattering speech, vague forms, association with night-time – suddenly becomes in the final two lines a realistic image of a reflection in the window of a railway car. The reflection in the window saying what the speaker does not like to hear is presumably the speaker's own, and the poem returns full circle at the end of the two stanzas back to a haunting of the self by itself, which is for the protagonist that form of haunting most to be feared.

V

Unfaithfulness to others, unfaithfulness to one's past self – these two forms of suffering are completed by a third form of disjunction. If love for Hardy means taking another person as the radiant center of the world, the person on whom this radiance has the most effect is the lover himself. For the Christian, God is seen as the source of selfhood for the men and women he has created; for Hardy's lovers the "well-beloved" is a substitute god and has the power over her lover to confer or to withhold being. A crucial moment in the lives of Hardy's protagonists, both in the fiction and in the poetry, is the time when they fall out of love. To fall out of love is to recognize that the seemingly divine power of the beloved has been appearance, not reality, a false energy conferred on her by the imagination of the lover rather than something she has intrinsically possessed. Then not only the lady but also the whole surrounding world is drained of its glowing lines of force, and the lover finds himself back in the real world, a world without order or meaning. "The glory which had encircled him as her lover was departed," says the narrator of Eustacia Vye in *The Return of the Native* when her marriage to Clym Yeobright has turned rapidly to indifference. And in poems like "At Waking," "He Abjures Love," or "I Was the Midmost" (*CP*, 208–9, 220–21, 630), the same change in lover, beloved and the world around her is described. The disillusioned lover in "He Abjures Love," for example, has achieved at last "clear views and certain." The scales have fallen from his eyes, and he can see things as they are, in all their barrenness:

> No more will now rate I
>   The common rare,
> The midnight drizzle dew,
>   The gray hour golden,
> The wind a yearning cry,
>   The faulty fair,
> Things dreamt, of comelier hue
>   Than things beholden! . . . (*CP*, 220–21)

In "Wessex Heights" this theme, so important to Hardy's work as a whole, takes a curious form. The speaker of the poem from the height of his temporal and spatial detachment has achieved the wisdom of a total disengagement from life. He knows now that all love is folly. Nevertheless, as I have shown, the self of the past remains still contained within the present self of the speaker, and the whole poem dramatizes the speaker's inability to escape altogether from the past even on the heights. One form of pain which the present self can suffer vicariously by means of his participation in the still-enduring attitudes of the past self is the pain caused not by the self's betrayal of others but by their betrayal of him. If the past self when in love had given himself wholly into the keeping of the beloved, so that her love of him in return had seemed almost to create him and to sustain him in being, nothing is more unpleasant than for the lady to cease that loving. If I exist in the other, my self so alienated from itself that I might say of myself, "She thinks of me, therefore I exist," then if she ceases to think of me I am, so to speak, annihilated. I go out like a snuffed candle, as in Tweedledum's interpretation of the Red King's dream of Alice. I come into existence and go out of existence as she happens to think of me or stops thinking of me. Just this cruel form of intersubjectivity is described in the penultimate stanza of "Wessex Heights." It constitutes the final form of lowland suffering which the speaker seeks to escape by going up to the heights:

> As for one rare fair woman, I am now but a thought of hers,
> I enter her mind and another thought succeeds me that she prefers;
> Yet my love for her in its fulness she herself even did not know;
> Well, time cures hearts of tenderness, and now I can let her go.

Part of the pain of this servitude is the fact that even the lady did not know the completeness of the lover's commitment to her and therefore is not aware of the power she has to bring him into existence or to annihilate him by the mere power of her thought. This ignorance makes her so irresponsible that she replaces him by another thought with carefree willfulness. The deep anguish which this insouciance causes rings through the first three lines of the stanza and gives the final line a hollow ring. It is all very well for him to say that time cures hearts of tenderness and that now he can let her go, but the preceding lines have shown that time has by no means cut him off from the tender feelings of his past self. With a part of himself he loves the woman still. And it is not so much a question of letting her go as of getting her to let him go. This, the preceding lines have shown, is impossible. Whenever she happens to think of him, he becomes enslaved once more to her power of thinking, and his knowledge of this makes it impossible for him to forget her. Here, as in the other two kinds of relation to the past, the speaker of "Wessex Heights" shows himself to be in the lowlands unable to escape from his bondage to his past self and to its entanglements with other people.

VI

The long middle section of "Wessex Heights" ends with the speaker's ironic claim that the passage of time has freed him from his enslavement to the past, so that, as he says, "now I can let her go." This is followed in the grammatical and logical armature of the poem by the pivot of the sequence, the first word of the last stanza: "So." The logical structure of the poem says: "There are some heights in Wessex where one can withdraw from life and escape from time. In the lowlands my bondage to the past causes me great suffering. *So* I go up on the heights." The poem concludes with a choice of disengagement from life which is characteristic of Hardy's protagonists near the end of their lives. When the time of complete disillusionment comes to them, as it has come to the speaker of "Wessex Heights," they can look back over the course of their lives "with telescopic sight high natures know" (*CP*, 218). When they see the complete patterns these lives make, what they see fills them with such disgust at the burden of betrayal and suffering they carry with them that they wish to escape altogether from these pasts. In order to escape wholly from themselves they must not only free themselves from all memory of the past but also obliterate that past from the memory of others. To forget and to be forgotten is their ultimate aim. So Henchard, in *The Mayor of Casterbridge*, makes in his will an ultimate request for obliteration: "& that no man remember me"; so Jude Fawley, in *Jude the Obscure*, murmurs as he dies, in echo of Job, "Let the day perish wherein I was born, and the night in which it was said, There is a man child conceived"; and so Tess, in "Tess's Lament," asks for the total effacement of her life:

> I cannot bear my fate as writ,
>   I'd have my life unbe;
> Would turn my memory to a blot,
> Make every relic of me rot,
> My doings be as they were not,
>   And gone all trace of me! (*CP*, 162)

The speaker of "Wessex Heights" seeks this kind of freedom from his past through an ascent to high places which seems the symbolic expression of a total detachment of the mind from life. The mind withdraws into its own emptiness where it can be outside time altogether, dead before it is out of the flesh. On the heights can be enjoyed that irresponsibility which only the dead, in Hardy's world, possess, as the dead folk in the churchyard in the admirable poem called "Friends Beyond" bid a gay farewell to all that they most cared about when they were alive. They live now "with very god's composure," "ignoring all that haps beneath the moon" (*CP*, 53).

This freedom from the past, however, cannot really be attained, neither in "Wessex Heights" nor in any other work by Hardy. The most the speaker of "Wessex Heights" can obtain is the modified freedom described so exactly in the final phrase of the poem as "some liberty." This theme of the impossibility of freeing oneself from the past may be approached from a number of different directions. It may be noted that the dead people in "Friends Beyond" spend most of their time talking about the things they most loved in life. Their claim that they are freed from those preoccupations contains its own denial in the vividness with which their speech brings the past back. This is another case of the difficulty of saying "not" in poetry. In the same way most of "Wessex Heights" is taken up by a description of the speaker's entanglements in that past from which he claims at least partially to have escaped. Why is it that for Hardy the past cannot be left behind?

One answer to this question is suggested in a reason the speaker gives for the relative freedom he attains on the heights. These are places, he says, "Where men have never cared to haunt, nor women have walked with me." The weird detective ghosts are present in the lowlands because that is where the speaker encountered these people in the first place. He is relatively free on the heights because they were not the scene of any of the episodes of the past from which he so wishes to escape. This theme of the embodiment of the past in the scene where it once took place recurs all through Hardy's work in prose and verse. It can be demonstrated in abundant examples and is one of his most important and persistent ideas. The "Poems of 1912–13," for example, are structured around the poet's visit to the Cornish coast which was the scene of his courtship of his first wife. Returning to the place is also a return to the past time which is embodied in it. The climax of the group of poems comes in "After a Journey" (*CP*, 328–9) when the poet recovers by means of the landscape not only his wife in all her youth and beauty but also his own past self. "I see what you are doing," says the poet to his wife's ghost, "you are leading me on / To the spots we knew when we haunted here together." The fine irony of "haunted," which speaks of the young lovers as if they had already been ghosts when they first enacted the scenes the poet is now resurrecting from the past, prepares for the final lines of the poem, in which the poet by returning to the location of those scenes becomes once more, so to speak, the living ghost of his young self:

> Trust me, I mind not, though Life lours,
>   The bringing me here; nay, bring me here again!
>   I am just the same as when
> Our days were a joy, and our paths through flowers.

The same theme lies behind that passage in *The Mayor of Casterbridge* in which the narrator describes the Roman amphitheatre at Casterbridge as at certain moments reinhabited by ghosts from the far past, "the slopes lined with a gazing legion of Hadrian's soldiery as if watching the gladiatorial combat." Other expressions of this idea are the beautiful poems "Old Furniture" and "Haunting Fingers." The idea in both poems is the same. In one the poet says that old furniture keeps present for him all the dead folk who once used them. In the other, old musical instruments in a museum are in the quiet of the night played by the long dead musicians who once owned them:

> I see the hands of the generations
>> That owned each shiny familiar thing
> In play on its knobs and indentations,
>> And with its ancient fashioning
>>> Still dallying . . . (*CP*, 456)

> And they felt past handlers clutch them,
>> Though none was in the room,
> Old players' dead fingers touch them,
>> Shrunk in the tomb. (*CP*, 559)

One reason the past is indestructible, then, is the fact that human history gets incarnated in the physical things forming the scenes in which it is enacted. As long as these things continue to exist, even in the form of archeological debris, the history they embody can be resurrected in the retrospective eye of someone with the poet's long vision. Though the speaker in "Wessex Heights" can achieve *some* liberty from his haunters by going up on the heights, nevertheless the lowlands too form, as I have tried to show, an inescapable part of his mind. As long as the Plain, the tall-spired town, and the other places continue to exist they will maintain in existence for the "intenser stare" of the speaker's mind the specters from the past.

This motif slips over into another idea. One rather unexpected notion occurs so often in Hardy's poetry that it must be accepted as an integral part of his world. This is the idea that, once an event has happened, it not only can never be undone but enters a spacious realm containing all times where it goes on happening over and over again forever. In the *Life* Hardy tells how Leslie Stephen called him unexpectedly to his house to ask Hardy to witness his resignation from holy orders. The two men sat up far into the night discussing "theologies decayed and defunct, the origin of things, the constitution of matter, the unreality of time" (*Life*, 105). Time is unreal for Hardy, in spite of his obsession with time, because once something happens it never ceases to exist but repeats itself forever. Two late poems, "The Absolute Explains" and "So, Time" (*CP*, 716–19) are the fullest and most conceptual expressions of this spatialization of time in Hardy, but it occurs in many slighter poems too. A kiss, for example, does not cease when it is over, but becomes, in a charmingly whimsical poem, "One of a long procession of sounds / Travelling aetherial rounds / Far from earth's bounds / In the infinite" (*CP*, 438). In the same way the poet affirms in the poem called "In a

Museum" that the song of an extinct fossilized bird and the voice of a woman he has heard singing the night before have now both joined that realm where all times are preserved side by side in spatial juxtaposition:

> Such a dream is Time that the coo of this ancient bird
> Has perished not, but is blent, or will be blending
> Mid visionless wilds of space with the voice that I heard,
> In the full-fugued song of the universe unending. (*CP*, 404)

If time is a dream, then what has once happened goes on happening and can never be escaped by someone with the wide vision of the speaker in "Wessex Heights." It goes on happening in a realm which is like that of astronomical space as it was seen by the science of Hardy's time. Astronomical space, however, is only a metaphor for a universal mind capacious enough to contain and keep in existence all the times of human history. Far from escaping from the past by his withdrawal to the heights where his next neighbour is the sky, the speaker of "Wessex Heights" has by an inadvertent progression from thinking to dreaming to dying entered that space where all dead things dwell forever in undying resurrection. The poet's mind comes to coincide with the universal mind. It expands to overlap with that reservoir within which all the past in a tide of visions is preserved, revivified, and given order. Within the poet's mind "there pass, in fleet arrays, / Long teams of all the years and days, / Of joys and sorrows, of earth and heaven, / That meet mankind in its ages seven, / An aion in an hour" (*CP*, 445).

The poet's mind is the world turned inside out. It is an infinitely wide expanse which contains all time and space, all history in a single imagination, an aeon in an hour. Having died in reality, each event or person rises up again within the poet's mind and within the language which embodies the visions of that mind. Each rises up to be preserved forever in the perpetual repetition which goes on within the covers of a book, as Tess' wish to have her life unbe is ironically thwarted as long as there remains a copy of *Tess of the d'Urbervilles* and someone to read it. Such a space of perpetuation the reader enters when he opens Hardy's *Complete Poems*. All Hardy's poems juxtaposed side by side constitute by synecdoche that infinite space outside of time within which all the events of time go on occurring, surrounded and embraced by the detached, ghostlike mind of the poet. If the poet's mind is the contents of all past years in their fleet arrays, it is also the distance and clarity of the container of those years. If the speaker of "Wessex Heights" cannot by his withdrawal to high places escape from the past he can at least get enough distance from it to escape blind enslavement to the entanglement of time. From his detachment he can see time with lucid insight, as it is.

In this sense "Wessex Heights" may be said to oppose, not servitude to time and escape from time, but inauthentic and authentic experiences of temporality. In place of a time which seems the intolerable burden of an inevitable sequence of sufferings and betrayals leading to a predestined present of self-loathing and desire for annihilation, there is the time of "some liberty," the liberty of a free assumption of the burden of the past. With this goes an openness towards a future which will be a never-ending repetition of the events of the past. Here the importance of the word "seem" in the fourth line of the poem appears. The speaker only *seems* on the heights to be where he was before his birth and after death may be. If he were to describe himself as out of time altogether, seeing all the past as a completed totality, he would be claiming to have obtained an escape from time which is impossible for a man while he is still alive. In fact the poem shows the speaker still very much involved in time, still open towards a future which will be constituted by the re-enactment of episodes from the past, in an always-unsuccessful attempt to free himself from them completely, so turning "some liberty" into complete freedom. This perpetual present of repetition is one version of authentic human temporality, which, as long as a man is alive, is an endless movement towards a future which will be, but never yet is, the perfected assumption of the past. The speaker in the final stanza of "Wessex Heights" has come full circle. He returns with deeper insight to the situation described in the first stanza. On the heights he is dead while still in the flesh. By surviving his own death he has freed himself from the bewildered involvement in time of his simple self that was. He remains both out of time and within it, out of the uncomprehending pain of sequential time in the lowlands, but within the lucid suffering of an unending confrontation, at a distance, of specters from the past.

VII

One question remains to be raised. What is the energy determining this unending repetition of the past in the present? Why are Hardy's personages destined to go through life in one way or another re-enacting the past? The answer one gives to this question is crucial to any interpretation of Hardy's work. Hardy's critics may be characterized according to the answers they explicitly or implicitly make. The question of the "source" of repetition is a difficult one, and the problem of repetition in literature is fundamental to the methodology of criticism. The function of figurative language, the question of sources, the role of allusion or citation, the question of representation or of mimetic "realism," the status of consciousness and of "immediate experience" (whether of the author or' of his fictive spokesmen or invented characters), the concept of uniqueness or singularity (whether as an aesthetic norm or as an aspect of personality) – all are involved. Only a preliminary suggestion of the lines to be followed in investigating the role of repetition in Hardy's work can be offered here.

Several modes of repetition in Hardy's writing may be distinguished. Each would merit extended analysis. Repetition may occur within a single text or narrative, as in the recurrent episode which structures Henchard's life in *The Mayor of Casterbridge*, or as in the way Tess' life is organized around repetitions of an event "first" enacted in the death of Prince. Recurrent motifs in a novel or poem are another form of repetition. Examples are the many occurrences of the color red which punctuate *Tess*, like so many crimson signs or marks, or the recurrences of the motif of somnolence in the same novel. The past may be repeated in the memory of a character or a narrator, as it is in "Wessex Heights." Each poem or novel is a repetition, whether one thinks of it as Hardy's transformation of events in his own life or as the recording by a fictive narrator of events which are to be taken, within the fiction, as having already happened in history. This repetition is repeated in its turn whenever the book is reprinted or read. Events within a novel or poem may repeat events outside the text, sometimes previous episodes in earlier generations of the same family (as Tess' murder of Alec re-enacts the family legend of the coach and murder), sometimes previous literary texts, Biblical, classical, or from folklore (as is again the case with Tess or Henchard), or sometimes, if the distinction is allowed, historical or mythological figures. So Tess, with pathetic prescience, does not want to read history, "because," as she says, "what's the use of learning that I am one of a long row only – finding out that there is set down in some old book somebody just like me, and to know that I shall only act her part; making me sad, that's all." All Hardy's writings, moreover, repeat one another. The same configurations recur from one end to the other of his work. Each poem or novel must be interpreted in terms of its similarity to other poems or novels. In all these kinds of repetition the meaning of a singular element in a text – character, gesture, detail, event – arises from its echoing of a previous character, gesture, detail, or event. Meaning, in Hardy's writings as in any other works of literature, arises from the relation of one feature to another. This relation may most inclusively be defined as repetition with a difference.

Various formulations have been proposed of the principle underlying these reverberations. They may be seen as a deliberate strategy employed by Hardy to obtain organic unity and richness of meaning for his texts. They may be seen as evidence of the relation of Hardy's writings to their "sources" in the Bible, in Greek tragedy, in Shakespeare, in folklore, and so on. They are, according to this explanation, traces in the texts which betray Hardy's borrowings from his reading. They may be seen as evidence of the inadvertent poverty of Hardy's imagination. Hardy's creativity, it might be said, worked in narrow channels. Whatever he wrote tended to fall into the same configurations. These are evidence of an underlying structuring unity in "the mind of Thomas Hardy." Within this mind a latent patterning form was present from the beginning. It possessed an inaugurating power as the "origin" of Hardy's works. The repetitions, on the other hand, may be seen as evidence of Hardy's conscious or unconscious insight into the coercions of the Freudian "compulsion to repeat." This is often misinterpreted as a psychological mechanism originating in childhood traumas and driving its victims to repeat unconsciously earlier episodes in their lives, as a man may contract a series of marriages which follow the same disastrous trajectory. The repetitions may be seen as evidence of Hardy's recognition of the determining pressure of historical or sociological forces, changes in agricultural practice, economic forces, and so on. The repetitions may be seen as evidence of Hardy's mythical imagination, his ability to form works according to universal patterns, so that Tess, for example, is a fertility goddess. Or it may be argued that Hardy's imagination was in resonance with the racial or collective unconscious and so repeated unintentionally archetypes from that universal pool of designs for human experience. Or, finally, the repetitions may be seen as a deliberate demonstration by Hardy that the underlying energy of the universe, the power which he called the Immanent Will, coerces each human life to trace out once more patterns which must follow one or another of a limited number of pre-existing models. Such models are written out, to use the metaphor of "Tess's Lament," as the universal fate of all mankind.

These interpretations form the spectrum of possible readings of Hardy's work. In each case the repetitions, in their diverse forms, are seen as governed in one way or another by some already existing center or patterning form. This form exists outside the chain of repetitions and directs it. There is, however, another form of repetition. This second form has been present, since the beginning of the Western tradition, alongside the first as its shadow or double, its subversive simulacrum. In the first version of repetition, within which all the major interpretations of Hardy's work have fallen, the similarities are seen as determined by their resemblance to a fixed model. Their authenticity is measured by their correspondence to this model. The validity of the repetition is always secondary in relation to the primary type which it doubles. In the second theory of repetition similarity is seen as generated out of difference, out of a chain of events, characters, or gestures which are always different from one another. The links of this chain are created or measured by no pre-existing archetype. They create in their "casual" similarities a meaning which lies only in the relations within their linear multiplicity. This meaning arises from a play of repetitions in difference controlled by no fixed or transcendent center. Each repetition has exactly the same status as all the others. All are on the same plane of immanence. So, according to this interpretation, the meaning of Tess' life is controlled by no antecedent patterning force but emerges in unforeseen ways from the "true sequence of things" she experiences, as one episode follows another and is later given "artistic form" by the narrator's retracing of one aspect of the pattern they happen to make.[8] In spite of the presence of elements inviting an interpretation according to the first mode of repetition, as in Tess' misinterpretation of her relation to her predecessors, the textual configurations of Hardy's work, as well as what he says overtly about the Immanent Will in *The Dynasts*, in the *Life*, and in the novels and lyrics themselves, confirm a reading according to the second concept of repetition. Such a reading would see the first concept of repetition as always present in human experience and in literature, but as a necessary illusion, a mystification, like Henchard's belief that "even I be in Somebody's hand!" or Eustacia Vye's feeling that the patterns of her life have been manipulated: "O, how hard it is of Heaven to devise such tortures for me." Such a reading would allow an understanding of the displacement in sentiment and evaluation which Hardy, in the Preface to the fifth edition of *Tess of the d'Urbervilles* (July, 1892), defends so discreetly and yet with such firm irony as his impurity to match Tess' impurity, his sin to match her sin, perhaps the original sin, his repetition of the sin of Shakespeare and of the historical Lear of Wessex before that.[9] This change of positions, of ownership and of assessment of "purity" is not so much the replacement of the first theory of repetition by the second as the reduction of the first to the status of a function of the second. It sees the first as an illusion developed by the play of differences in repetition.

Human history, as Hardy sees it, is a pattern of sameness emerging from difference. Differences are the initial data from which come designs of repetition. In this process the "first" datum is without originating power but is given the status of a disseminating element in a chain of repetitions when the "second" datum happens, in the random sequence of "crass casualties," to iterate it at a distance. The "first" red in *Tess* is revealed as already a repetition when the "second" red repeats it. The place of repetition which the speaker of "Wessex Heights" enters when he withdraws to the heights is the space of literature and also the space of human history. It is the place of spacing, a place not of organic unity or of satisfaction, but of gaps and fissures, of discontinuities and dis-symmetries, of perpetually unsatisfied desire. In this place of differing or deferring, any presence or continuity is permanently disrupted by the crises engraving the "traces" of human experience. These traces are both historical events – always already repetitions – and their reiteration in writing. This writing prolongs and maintains the impossibility of any event ever to coincide wholly with itself in an immediacy without repetition.

Notes

1. "A Primitive Like an Orb", *The Collected Poems of Wallace Stevens* (New York, 1954), p. 443. Citations from Hardy's poems are identified by page number in *The Collected Poems* (London, 1952).
2. See *Life*, p. 25: "He tried also to avoid being touched by his playmates. One lad, with more insight than the rest, discovered the fact: 'Hardy, how is it that you do not like us to touch you?' This peculiarity never left him, and to the end of his life he disliked even the most friendly hand being laid on his arm or his shoulder."
3. I have discussed these patterns in the fiction in *Thomas Hardy: Distance and Desire*.
4. See the discussion of "Wessex Heights" in J. O. Bailey, *The Poetry of Thomas Hardy: A Handbook and Commentary*, pp. 274–80. Bailey presents some additional information about geographical features in the poem: "Each of the heights was in ancient times a hill-fort, and each exhibits tumuli and ramparts built by the Britons before the Roman conquest" (p. 275). Bailey also argues, on the basis of a letter of December 6, 1914, from Mrs Florence Hardy to Alda, Lady Hoare, for an autobiographical interpretation of the poem. Following Mrs Hardy's hint in her letter that "the four people mentioned are actual women", Bailey suggests that there are possible references in the poem to four women who had been important to Hardy: the poet's first wife, Emma Hardy; his mother, Jemima Hardy; his cousin, Tryphena Sparks; and his friend Mrs Arthur Henniker. These identifications may be correct, but they seem more or less irrelevant to the explication of the poem as the reader encounters it in *The Collected Poems*. There it is cut off from such biographical "sources" as it may have had and presented as a text among other texts, to be read and interpreted on its own. The poem was written, according to the manuscript, in December, 1896, but Hardy withheld it from publication until the volume of 1914, *Satires of Circumstance: Lyrics and Reveries* – that is, he withheld it until its connections to his 'real life' could be less easily identified. The poem is deliberately detached from these connections. One further difficulty with Bailey's identifications is the fact that three of the four women supposedly in Hardy's mind when he wrote it were not ghosts at all in 1896, when the poem was written, though they are spoken of as such. At the least one would have to say that the poem is not about Hardy's immediate relation to these women but about his memory in 1896 of the role they had played earlier in his life.
5. Charles Baudelaire, *Oeuvres Complètes* (Paris, 1954), p. 728.
6. "Insensible", as Hardy put it in his comment on the word in the margin of F. A. Hedgcock's discussion of it in *Thomas Hardy: Penseur et artiste*. See J. O. Bailey, *op. cit.*, p. 52.
7. Yell'ham Bottom is perhaps the valley below Yellowham Hill, and Froomside Vale is the valley of the River Frome or, as Hardy spells it and as it is pronounced, Froom, in Somerset. The "Plain" in l. 17 is, it is usually

assumed, Salisbury Plain, and the "tall-spired town" in l. 19 is presumably Salisbury, with its cathedral tower, the highest of any cathedral in England. See Bailey, *op. cit.*, p. 277, for the identification of Yell'ham Bottom and for the suggestion that both Yell'ham Bottom and Froom-side Vale are places where Hardy courted his cousin Tryphena Sparks.

8. The quoted phrases come from the "Explanatory Note to the First Edition" of *Tess of the d'Urbervilles* (1891), p. xv.

9. "(T)o exclaim illogically against the gods, singular or plural, is not such an original sin of mine as he [Andrew Lang in a review of *Tess*] seems to imagine. True, it may have some local originality; though if Shakespeare were an authority on history, which perhaps he is not, I could show that the sin was introduced into Wessex as early as the Heptarchy itself. . . . However, they [the 'manipulators of *Tess*'] may have causes to advance, privileges to guard, traditions to keep going; some of which a mere tale-teller, who writes down how the things of the world strike him, without any ulterior intentions whatever, has overlooked, and may by pure inadvertence have run foul of when in the least aggressive mood. Perhaps some passing perception, the outcome of a dream hour, would, if generally acted on, cause such an assailant considerable inconvenience with respect to position, interests, family, servant, ox, ass, neighbour, or neighbour's wife. . . . So densely is the world thronged that any shifting of positions, even the best warranted advance, galls somebody's kibe. Such shiftings often begin in sentiment, and such sentiment sometimes begins in a novel" (*Tess of the d'Urbervilles* [1892 edn], pp. xix–xx).

8

Parable and performative in the Gospels and in modern literature

A large contradictory modern secondary literature now exists on the parables of Jesus in the New Testament and on their relation to the tradition of secular parable in modern writers like Kleist and Kafka.[1] Since I am not a biblical scholar, I cannot hope to add much to this discussion except possibly from the point of view of secular literature; but I can begin here with several axioms or presuppositions to guide my investigation, if only as grounds to be ungrounded by what is discovered later on.

The first presupposition is the assumption that it ought to be possible to identify specific differences, in the language, between the parables of Jesus and any secular parables whatsoever. Much is at stake here. The distinction between sacred scripture and secular literature would seem to depend on being able to identify the difference. The authority not only of the Bible as in some sense or other the word of God but more specifically of the words of Jesus as speech of God would seem to hang in the balance here. If the Middle Ages needed a distinction between "allegory of the poets" and "allegory of the theologians," we moderns would seem to need a firm distinction between "parable of the poets" and "parable of the theologians."

The second presupposition is no more than a definition of parable. Etymologically the word means "thrown beside," as a parabolic curve is thrown beside the imaginary line going down from the apex of the imaginary cone on the other side of whose surface the parabola traces its graceful loop from infinity and out to infinity again. Comets on a parabolic trajectory come once, sweep round the sun, and disappear forever, unlike those on a large elliptical orbit which return periodically, Halley's Comet for instance. When this is taken as a parable of the working of parable in literature or in scripture, it suggests that parable is a mode of figurative language which is the indirect indication, at a distance, of something that cannot be described directly, in literal language, like that imaginary invisible cone or like the sun, single

135

controlling focus of the comet's parabola, which cannot be looked in the eye, although it is the condition of all seeing, or like that inaccessible place from which the comet comes and to which it returns. A parabolic narrative is, my parable of the comet would suggest, in some way governed, at its origin and at its end, by the infinitely distant and invisible, by something that transcends altogether direct presentation. The correspondence between what is given in parable – the "realistic" story represented in a literal language – and its meaning is more indirect than is the case, for example, in "symbolic" expression, in the usual meaning of the latter, where, as the name suggests, one expects more of interpretation, of participation, and of similarity. One German name for parable is *Gleichnis*, "likeness." This is what Luther calls a parable of Jesus. The paradox of parable is that it is a likeness that rests on a manifest unlikeness between what is given and what cannot by any means be given directly. A parabolic "likeness" is so "unlike" that without interpretation or commentary the meaning may slip by the reader or listener altogether.

Hegel's discussion of what he called "conscious symbolism" provides a definition of parable that corresponds to the one I have been making. The sublime (*das Erhabene*) is, strangely enough, included by Hegel with fable, parable, apologue, proverb, and metamorphosis as a mode of "conscious symbolism."

> What has emerged from sublimity as distinct from strictly unconscious symbolizing consists on the one hand in the *separation* [*in dem Trennen*] between the meaning, explicitly known in its inwardness, and the concrete appearance divided therefrom; on the other hand in the directly or indirectly emphasized non-correspondence of the two [*Sichnichtentsprechen beider*] wherein the meaning, as the universal, towers above individual reality and its particularity.[2]

If "separation" and "non-correspondence" characterize all such forms of symbolism, including parable, then the meaning of the parable can hardly be expected to be perspicuous to eyes that cannot see the tenor of which such symbols are the vehicle. For example, says Hegel when he comes to discuss parable in particular:

> The parable of the sower [in all the Synoptics] is a story in itself trivial in content [*für sich von geringfügigem Gehalt*] and it is important only because of the comparison with the doctrine of the Kingdom of Heaven. In these parables the meaning throughout is a religious doctrine to which the human occurrences in which it is represented [*vorgestellt*] are related in much the same way as man and animal are related in Aesop's Fables, where the former constitutes the meaning of the latter.[3]

In parable, human is to religious doctrine as animal is to human. The latter constitutes the meaning of the former across the gap of their separation and non-correspondence.

On the basis of this definition, a distinction, in principle at least, between sacred parable and secular parable may be made. The parables of Jesus are spoken by the Word, the Logos, in person. Even if this terminology is fully present only in the Gospel of John, it is already implicit in the characterization in the first three Gospels of Jesus as the Messiah. The fact that the Messiah speaks the parables guarantees the correspondence between the homely stories he tells of farming, fishing, and domestic economy on the one hand, and the spiritual or transcendent meaning on the other, the meaning that tells of things beyond the threshold of the domestic and visible, the meaning that nevertheless can be spoken only in parable, that is, indirectly. Christ as the Logos is not only the basis of the analogies, echoes, and resemblances among things of the world created in his name and between things created in his name and things hidden since the creation of the world. Christ as Logos is also the basis of the correspondence within the realm of language, for example the correspondence between visible vehicle and invisible and unnamed tenor in a parable. When Jesus speaks the parables, Christ the Word stands visibly before his auditors, for those who have eyes to see and ears to hear, as support of the correspondence between his realistic narrative of sowing, fishing, or household care and those unseeable things of which the parable "really" speaks. This guarantee is, I take it, one of the fundamental meanings of the Incarnation. Believing in the validity of the parables of the New Testament and believing that Jesus is the Son of God are the same thing.

The speakers or writers of secular parables stand in a different place, even though their parables too may deal with religious or metaphysical matters. They are down here with us, and their words about things visible can only be thrown beside things invisible in the hope that their narratives of what can be spoken about, the fencing bear in Kleist's "Über das Marionettentheater," for example, will magically make appear the other invisible, perhaps imaginary, line to which their realistic stories, they hope, correspond. The editor of the Greek New Testament I have consulted, Henry Alford, a nineteenth-century Anglican biblical scholar, put this clearly in his preliminary note on Matthew 13. A parable, he says,

> is *a serious narration within the limits of probability, of a course of action pointing to some moral or spiritual Truth* ("Collatio per narratiunculam fictam, sed veri similem, serio illustrans rem sublimiorem." Unger, de Parabolis Jesu [Meyer]) ["some moral or spiritual truth," it might be noted, is a loose

translation of "rem sublimiorem"]; and derives its force from real analogies impressed by the Creator of all things on His creatures. The great Teacher by parables therefore is He who needed not that any should testify of man; for He knew what was in man, John ii.25: moreover, He *made* man, and orders the course and character of human events. And this is the reason why no one can, or dare, teach by parables, except Christ. We do not, as He did, see the inner springs out of which flow those laws of spiritual truth and justice, which the Parable is framed to elucidate. *Our* parables would be in danger of perverting, instead of guiding aright.[4]

The fact that Alford a page later commits the crime he warns against is an amusing example of the *odium theologicum* but also an example of a problem with Christ's parables. Any interpretation of these parables is itself parabolic. In one way or another it must do what Henry Alford warns against, that is, claim to understand "the inner springs out of which flow those laws of spiritual truth and justice, which the Parable is framed to elucidate." Which of us, reading Matthew 13, would admit to being one of those who seeing see not, and hearing hear not, neither understand? So Alford, speaking of that terrifying law of parable Jesus enunciates whereby "For to him who has will more be given, and he will have abundance; but from him who has not, even what he has will be taken away" (Matthew 13:12), applies it to the biblical commentators of his own day, doing in the process what he has said a page before no mere human being should dare do, namely, teach by parable: "No practical comment," says Alford, "on the latter part of this saying can be more striking, than that which is furnished to our day by the study of German rationalistic (and, I may add, some of our English harmonistic) Commentators; while at the same time we may rejoice to see the approximate fulfilment of the former in such commentaries as those of Olshausen, Neander, Stier, and Trench."[5] No doubt Olshausen, Neander, Stier, and Trench were worthy scholars, but there is also no doubt a grotesque incongruity or bathos in using the parable of the sower as a means of dividing the sheep from the goats in the parochial warfare of biblical scholarship. In any case, there is great temerity in doing so, just that merely human preaching by parables against which Alford has warned on the page before. Yet it is obvious that whoever speaks of the parables at all runs the risk, perhaps must endure the necessity, of doing this. The language of parables contaminates, or perhaps it might be better to say inseminates, impregnates, its commentators. Such language forces them to speak parabolically, since it is by definition impossible to speak of what the parables name except parabolically. Commentary on the parables is, or ought to be, an example of the dissemination of the Word, its multiplication thirty- , sixty- , or a hundredfold.

This need to distinguish secular from sacred parable and yet difficulty in doing so leads to my third presupposition. This is that the two kinds of parable may be distinguished by recognizing that both are performative rather than constative utterances but that two radically different kinds of performative would appear to be involved. A parable does not so much passively name something as make something happen. A parable is a way to do things with words. It is a speech act. In the case of the parables of Jesus, however, the performative word makes something happen in the minds and hearts of the hearers, but this happening is a knowledge of a state of affairs already existing, the kingdom of heaven and the way to get there. In that sense, a biblical parable is constative, not performative at all. A true performative brings something into existence that has no basis except in the words, as when I sign a check and turn an almost worthless piece of paper into whatever value I have inscribed on the check, assuming the various contexts for this act are in correct order – even though as the phenomenon of counterfeit money or the passing of bad checks indicates, the performative may make something happen even when some aspect of the contexts is amiss. Secular parable is a genuine performative. It creates something, a "meaning", that has no basis except in the words or something about which it is impossible to describe whether or not there is an extralinguistic basis. A secular parable is like a piece of money about which it is impossible in principle to know whether or not it is true or counterfeit. Secular parable is language thrown out that creates a meaning hovering there in thin air, a meaning based only on the language itself and on our confidence in it. The categories of truth and falsehood, knowledge and ignorance, do not properly apply to it.

My final presupposition is that both kinds of parable tend to be parables about parable. They are about their own efficacy. Jesus' parable of the sower in Matthew 13:1–23, with its parallels in Mark and Luke, is a well-known example of this.[6] Its topic is the efficacy of the word. The distinction is between those who have eyes and ears for the Word and those who do not, or rather the parable distinguishes four possibilities, that the seed will fall by the wayside, in stony places, among thorns, and in good ground, with an appropriate psychological interpretation for each of the different predispositions to receive the Word, as the thorns stand for "the care of this world, and the deceitfulness of riches," which "choke the word" (Matthew 13:22). What in fact is the "word"? It is the good news, the gospel of salvation, the "secrets of the kingdom of heaven" (Matthew 13:11), "what has been hidden since the foundation of the world" (Matthew 13:35). A whole series of paradoxes operates at once in this parable about parable.

First paradox: The presupposition is that the mysteries of the kingdom of heaven cannot be spoken of directly. The things that have been kept secret from the foundation of the world can only be spoken of in parable. Christ as the Logos is in the awkward position of not being able to speak the Logos directly but of being forced to translate it into a form suitable for profane ears. The Word cannot speak the Word as such.

Second paradox: Unless you understand the Word already as such, unless you are already fertile ground for the Word, which means somehow already grounded in it, sown by it, you will not understand it when it is expressed in parable. When the disciples ask, "Why do you speak to them in parables?" Christ's answer is: "To you it has been given to know the secrets of the kingdom of heaven, but to them it has not been given. For to him who has will more be given, and he will have abundance; but from him who has not, even what he has will be taken away. This is why I speak to them in parables, because seeing they do not see, and hearing they do not hear, nor do they understand" (Matthew 13:10–13). The parables are posited on their own inefficacy. If you have knowledge of the kingdom of heaven already, you do not need them. The parables are superfluous, a superabundance, a surplus, a gift beyond gift. If you do not have that knowledge, you will not understand the parables anyhow. They will be a way of covering your eyes and ears further, not a breaking of the seals or a form of unveiling, of revelation. The things that have been kept secret from the foundation of the world will remain secret for most people even after they are spoken in parable. Such things are perhaps made secret by that foundation, veiled by the creation itself rather than revealed by it, and so kept secret by parables that name those secret things with names drawn from familiar created things. The parables translate the Word, so to speak, into the language of familiar things, sowing, fishing, household work. Even so, those for whom the parables are intended are like those to whom one speaks in a foreign language or like someone who does not know Greek presented with the Gospel of Matthew in Greek. The parable, as they say, is all Greek to that person. Such persons lack the gift of tongues or the gift of translating the parable back into the original word. "Hearing they do not hear, nor do they understand." Such people are like Belshazzar confronted by the handwriting on the wall, or they are like those auditors who are not going to understand the prophecy of Isaiah, a failure in understanding that Jesus says the failure of his parables will fulfill. Here is the great text in Isaiah on which Jesus' parable of the sower is a commentary:

> Then flew one of the seraphims to me, having in his hand a burning coal which he had taken with tongs from the altar. And he touched my mouth, and said: "Behold, this has touched your lips; your guilt is taken away, and your sin forgiven." And I heard the voice of the Lord saying, "Whom

shall I send, and who will go for us?" Then I said, "Here am I! Send me."
And he said, "Go, and say to this people: 'Hear and hear, but do not
understand; see and see, but do not perceive.' Make the heart of this people
fat, and their ears heavy, and shut their eyes; lest they see with their eyes,
and hear with their ears, and understand with their hearts, and turn and be
healed." (Isaiah 6: 6–10)

The parables, however, are intended for just such people, and so they are
posited on their own inevitable misreading or nonreading. The problem,
once more, is how to cross over from one kind of language to the other,
from the word of God, "Whom shall I send?" to the word of the human:
"Here am I! Send me." If you can understand the parables, you do not
need them. If you need them, you cannot hope to understand them. The
parables are not a way of giving the Word but a way of taking away, a
way of adding further deprivation to a deprivation that is already total:
"From him who has not, even what he has will be taken away."

Third paradox: The disciples are said by Jesus to be those to whom it is
given to know the mysteries of the kingdom of heaven. It would seem
that this means they already have the Word and therefore have open eyes
and ears, are able to understand the parables spontaneously, translate
their displaced language back to the original tongue, and at the same time
do not need the parables. The parables give them more when they
already have and so do not need. For them the parables are superfluous.
"For to him who has will more be given, and he will have abundance."
The paradox is that, having said that, Jesus proceeds to explain to the
disciples the parable of the sower, spelling it out, translating it back into
the language of the kingdom of heaven, as if they could not understand it
without his interpretation. He has said they understand, but he goes on
to speak as if they could not possibly understand: "Truly, I say to you,
many prophets and righteous men have longed to see what you see, and
did not see it, and to hear what you hear, and did not hear it. Hear then
the parable of the sower. When any one hears the word of the kingdom
and does not understand it, the evil one comes and snatches away what is
sown in his heart; this is what was sown along the path . . ." and so on
through the explicit application of each of the clauses of the parable to
each of the four kinds of people in relation to the proffered insemination
or dissemination of the Word, down to: "As for what was sown on good
soil, this is he who hears the word and understands it; he indeed bears
fruit, and yields, in one case a hundredfold, in another sixty, and in
another thirty" (Matthew 13:17–23).

Fourth paradox: The economy of equivalence, of giving and receiving,
of equable translation and measure, of the circulation of signs governed
by the Logos as source of proportion and guarantee of substitution or
analogy, is upset by the parables. Although the parables of Jesus are

spoken by the Word, they are not logical. They are not governed, as, say, medieval allegory is said to be, whatever Henry Alford affirms, by the "real analogies impressed by the Creator of all things on his creatures." Or, if they are so governed, they function by a choice of alogical moments in systems of circulation and exchange in the familiar domestic world to indicate the failure of analogy between anything human, including human languages – Aramaic, Greek, Latin, English, or whatever – and the divine Logos, the Word of the kingdom of heaven. If allegory and symbolism in one way or another work by analogy or by correspondence, resonance, or participation between one thing and another thing on a different level, or between one word and another word, as in the proportionalities of metaphor, the parables of Jesus are ana-analogical, or rather, since "ana" is already a double antithetical prefix, which may mean either "according to" or "against," it may simply be said that the parables are "analogical" in the sense of "against logic," "counter to logic." "Paradox": the word means etymologically, "against teaching," or against the received opinion of those in authority. The words or parables of Jesus are a stumbling block to the Greeks because they go against the habits of logical thinking. The Logos in the sense of Jesus as the Word contradicts *logos* in the sense of Greek reason, or reasoned thinking, which is reason as such in the West.

The "literal" language of the parables of Jesus and of his actions themselves as described by the gospel makers is drawn from various realms of domestic economy, production, consumption, and exchange in the family or in the immediate social group such as a household with servants or a farm with hired workers. These various realms include eating, sowing and reaping, fishing, sexual reproduction, the donation and receiving of gifts, the exchange of words, translation from one language to another, counting, and the exchange of money, its use and its usury. In all cases the example chosen breaks down the pattern of a closed circuit of exchange of the same for the same or its equivalent. The fisherman draws fish abundantly from the salt and inhospitable sea. A single seed cast in fertile ground reproduces a hundred- , sixty- , or thirtyfold, and a tiny mustard seed produces an enormous tree. He who saves his life will lose it. To save it, it must be thrown away, and the same thing may be said of virginity, which is of value or use only if it is given up, just as money has the power of reproducing itself magically but not if it is hoarded, only if it is invested, put out at risk, used. The distinction between male potency and female passive receptivity is broken down in sexual reproduction, since the female must be fertile ground for the seed and thus in a sense already contain its potentiality, as only fertile ground will multiply the seed cast on it and as only those who already have the Word can receive it and multiply it. Although the image

Jesus uses in his exegesis of the parable of the sower is that of sexual reproduction, the sexes are strangely reversed, as they are in the image of the soul as the bride of Christ. Jesus speaks of the different persons who receive the seed of the Word as "he": "But he that received the seed into stony places . . ." and so on, but that fertile ground must in some sense be a feminine matrix, an egg ready to receive the seed. A genuine gift, like the other elements upsetting any domestic economy of equivalence and exchange, is, as Marcel Mauss and Jacques Derrida have in different ways argued, always something incommensurate with any recompense, something suspending the circuit of obligation, of payment and repayment.[7] A true gift can never be returned. It creates an infinite obligation and is not restitution for any claim I have on another. The gift leads to such absurdities as the Northwest American Indian potlatch, in which one man vies with another in destroying great heaps of valuable property.

The power of the gift to break down logical equivalences in social exchange is shown in reverse in what might be called the living parable of the story of the loaves and fishes in Matthew 14. Jesus blesses the bread, breaks it, and gives the five loaves and the two fishes to the disciples. The disciples give them to the multitude. In that double process of giving, the loaves and fishes become multiplied beyond any rational calculation so that there is always enough and some over – twelve baskets of fragments – though about five thousand have been fed. In this case, as in the parables generally, for example the parable of the sower, several different realms, of the ones I have listed, come together: gift giving and receiving, agriculture and fishing in the bread and fishes, and the illogic of an arithmetical sum in which five loaves and two fishes become a countless number with twelve basketsfull left over. In the case of the parable of the sower, sowing and reaping, on the one hand, and sexual reproduction on the other, are used each as a figure for the paradoxes of the other. There is a contamination of the "literal" language of each of the realms, in any vernacular, with figures drawn from others of the realms, as when we speak of "seed money," or of the "dissemination" of the seed in sowing, as well as of the dissemination of doctrine, or of sexual reproduction in terms of "getting" and "spending," and so on, in a perpetual round in which no one set of these terms is the purely literal language that provides figures for the others. Another way to put this is to say that ordinary language, the language Jesus must use to speak to the multitude or to the disciples, is already irremediably parabolic.

The final realm in which rational equivalence and exchange breaks down is then that of language itself, that dissemination of the Word for which all these other realms are not so much figures as living and material hieroglyphs, that is, places where the paradoxes of sign-making and sign-using enter into the actual process of the living together of men and women in family and community, to be incorporated inextricably into that process. In the realm of language, too, the giving of the Word introduces a form of sign into the rational exchanges of word for word in ordinary communication which breaks open that circuit with the alogic of parable. The Word is like a tiny mustard seed which produces a huge tree, and although it is demonstrably untranslatable, "the propagation of the gospel in foreign lands" depends on its translatability and on the gift of tongues to the apostles and their dissemination, carrying the Word into the four corners of the world. The limitations of a given translation are not contingent but absolute. The failure of translation is not a result of the incompatability of one idiom and another or between a proper original and some improper transfer or *Übersetzung*, as they say in German for translation, "setting over." The failure of translation is the result of the absence of any adequate original in any humanly comprehensible language. When I read the King James Bible today, or some other English Bible, it has behind it the Vulgate, the Greek, the hypothetical Aramaic versions of what Jesus said, language behind language behind language. However, the inadequacy of any translation and the way the propagation of the Gospel is a triumph over its own manifest impossibility lie not in the incorrectness of this or that detail in, say, the King James Bible in relation to the Greek or Aramaic "original", but in the fact that even the words of the parable of the sower, for example, as Jesus originally spoke them, were not an original but already the translation of an untranslatable original Word, which is what Jesus in the parable of the sower "says": "That is why I speak to them in parables, because seeing they do not see, and hearing they do not hear, nor do they understand. With them indeed is fulfilled the prophecy of Isaiah which says: 'You shall indeed hear but never understand, and you shall indeed see but never perceive'" (Matthew 13:13–14).

In all these realms the pattern of alogic is "the same." It is analogical, an analogy among ana-analogies or an analogy in one sense among analogies in the antithetical sense. In each case the pattern expresses a strange arithmetic in which one will get you not two but a hundredfold in return, or rather in which something so tiny that it is in effect zero will multiply infinitely, as in that equation Paul Claudel makes among things globular and null or almost null: "*oeuf, semence, bouche ouverte, zéro,*" "egg, seed, open mouth, zero," where the open mouth that proffers the word, "Here am I, send me," is equated not only with the egg and seed of sowing and sexual reproduction but also with the zero that divides an infinite number of times even into a single unit, as a single word may be broken, divided, and scattered in all languages to the four winds.[8]

I turn now to modern secular parable, which should in principle, I have suggested, function differently, since a secular parable is not spoken by the Word itself translating itself to human ears and human understanding but is spoken by some all-too-human person casting out figurative language toward something across the border from any direct seeing, hearing, or understanding.

In *Von den Gleichnissen* ("On Parables") Franz Kafka develops a characteristically mind-twisting paradox that turns on the distinction between whether something happens in reality or in parable. It is a triple distinction: a distinction between everyday reality and "some fabulous yonder"; a distinction between the everyday person and that person transfigured; a distinction between literal language and parabolic language:

> When the sage says: "go over," he does not mean that we should cross to some actual place, which we could do anyhow if the labor were worth it; he means some fabulous yonder (*irgendem sagenhaftes Drüben*), something unknown to us (*das wir nicht kennen*), something that he cannot designate more precisely (*von ihm nicht näher zu bezeichnen ist*), and therefore cannot help us there in the very least.[9]

The word "over" (*hinüber*) in parabolic speech refers not to some real place "over there" but to a place out of this world. It is a place, moreover, that cannot be designated more precisely than in topographical terms drawn from the real world and applied figuratively to the place out of the real world. There are no literal terms for the places in parable. They cannot be designated more precisely than by the transferred terms of metaphor or rather of catachresis, which is the proper term for a figure that does not replace any existing proper word. The question posed by Kafka's little text is a double one: What kind of action is performed by the sage when he wrests words from their normal usage and says, "Go over"? What kind of actions should we perform if we wish to obey the sage's injunction?

The answer seems obvious enough. We have only to follow the parables in order to become parables. We would then enter into the realm of parable, and escape cares of real life in the actual place where we are: "Concerning this a man once said: Why such reluctance? If you only followed the parables you yourselves would become parables and with that rid of all your daily cares."[10]

The question about this commentary is also obvious enough. Is the remark by "a man" in itself literal, or is it parabolic? This in turn is a displacement of a more general question. Is Kafka's "On Parables" as a whole literal or is it parabolic? Is it possible to speak of parables literally, or is the language of the commentators on parables always contaminated

by what they talk about, subdued to what they work in, so that their
language becomes in its turn inevitably parabolic? Would that necessarily
be a bad thing? These are the questions raised by the little alternating
dialogue that ends Kafka's "On Parables." In this dialogue two more
voices are heard, and the voice of "Kafka" himself, which spoke at first,
as well as the voice of the "man" who said we only need to "follow" the
parables, vanishes entirely. The little dialogue has to do with the
linguistic status of the exhortation to follow the parables and has to do
with winning and losing not in the parables themselves but in the
interpreter's stance in relation to them and in his language about them:

> Another said: I bet that is also a parable.
> The first said: You have won.
> The second said: But unfortunately only in parable.
> The first said: No, in reality: in parable you have lost.[11]

The reader (I hope) will be able to follow this somewhat bewildering
alternation to the point of blinding clarity it reaches. To say something is
a parable can only be done from the point of view of reality and of literal
language, since the realm of parable and the language of parable are
defined by their difference from the real and the literal. They are a
transfer from it, a "going over." To say that by following the parables
one becomes a parable is a parable all right, but it is a saying that remains
immovably still in the realm of everyday life, which, after all, as "On
Parables" says at the beginning, "is the only life we have." One wins the
bet ("I bet that is also a parable") but only in reality, which means that
one loses in parable. The parables ask to be taken literally. The only way
they can become efficacious is for them to become literally true, so that
one does literally "go over." As long as they are seen as figures of speech,
as merely parabolic, one loses in parable, one has failed to enter into the
realm of parable. But they cannot be seen otherwise. They produce
neither action nor knowledge. To know that fabulous realm over there is
to cross over into it, but the parables merely throw out incomprehensible
figures in the direction of the incomprehensible. They are like parables
proffered by one of the multitude who hear Jesus speak or at best like a
parable given out by one of the disciples. "All these parables really set
out to say merely that the incomprehensible is incomprehensible
(*unfassbar*), and we know that already."[12]

"On Parables" is a characteristic example of the specifically Kafkan
double bind. Either way you have had it. You lose by winning and lose
by losing too. If you take the parable literally, then you must understand
it as naming some literal crossing over from one place to another in
reality, in which case you remain in reality, "the only life we have"; so
following the parables does not make anything happen. If you take

parable parabolically, then it is seen as merely figurative. In that case neither the parable itself nor following the parable makes anything happen, and so you have lost in parable, since winning in parable could only occur if the crossing over promised in the parable were occur in reality. Either way you lose, since winning in reality is losing in parable, and the one thing needful is to win in parable, to find a joy whose grounds are true.

This may perhaps be made clearer by a return to my comparison with performative language. It would seem at first that two kinds of language, the creative *Fiat lux* of God and statements made by human beings like "I pronounce you husband and wife" are the same. Both are ways of doing things with words. There is, however, an essential difference. The "Let there be light" of God produces the basic condition of visibility and therefore of knowledge. It allows things to stand in the sunlight and be seen. To use the distinction employed also by Nietzsche, as well as by Kafka in the phrase *das wir nicht kennen*, God's *Fiat lux* leads to an act of knowledge, an *Erkennen*. Human performatives, on the other hand, can never be the object of an epistemological act whereby subject confronts something that has been brought to life and knows it. Human performatives are always from beginning to end baseless positings, acts of *Ersetzen* rather than of *Erkennen*.[13] A secular parable is an *Ersetzen* that must, impossibly, become an *Erkennen*. It must actually create a new realm into which we might cross over. It remains a merely human positing, the making of a realm created by language, existing and sustained only in language. In this it is no different from the complex social world made by promising, contracting, naming, and so on, the "daily life" with all its "cares" "which is the only life we have," and which we would do anything to cross over out of. No speech act, no poetic or parabolic performative can help us one bit to do that. "Over out of": The multiplication of adverbs is meant to mime the repeated unsuccessful attempts to go somewhere with language.

I shall now attempt to draw such conclusions as I can from my brief side-by-side discussion of sacred parable and secular parable. My primary motivation, it will be remembered, has been to identify distinguishing marks that would allow a firm division between one and the other. I claim to have done this in identifying a different nature and standing place in each case for the speaker or writer of the parable and in identifying a different relation in each case to the distinction between performative and constative language. The latter difference may be phrased by saying that both kinds of parables are catachreses, the throwing out of language toward an "unknown X" which cannot be named in proper or literal language. In the case of secular parable it cannot be known for certain, even by the one who invents the parable, whether or not there is something out there, across the frontier, which pre-exists the language for it. Such language may be a true performative, bringing something into being that exists only in the words or by means of the words. Sacred parable is in principle spoken by someone who has that knowledge to start with, by someone who *is* that knowledge, by someone who is the Logos itself in all the sense of that word: mind, reason, knowledge, speech, measure, ratio, ground of all things.

The distinction seems clear, but the distinction itself involves a double paradox, one on each side of the line separating secular from sacred parable. On the one hand, Christ the Word must in the parables translate the Word into humanly comprehensible language. He is in himself both sides of the dialogue between Jehovah and Isaiah that he says his parables are meant to fulfill. Christ is both the Word of God, "the voice of the Lord" called in vocation or in invocation to Isaiah, "Whom shall I send?" and Isaiah's answering voice in acceptance of vocation, "Here am I! Send me." Christ's words are therefore subject necessarily to the limitations of human language in whatever language they are spoken or into which they might be translated, in spite of the suprahuman standing place from which he speaks. Christ's dissemination of the Word is therefore performed over its logical impossibility, as he says in the parable of the sower. This impossibility may be expressed by saying that the parables of Jesus are not properly performative. They do not in themselves make anything happen, since their auditors must already know the Word to be fertile ground for the Word the parables speak. The parables of Jesus are constative, but they provide knowledge that for many is spoken in a foreign tongue, a tongue that is not going to be understood. The paradox of the parables of the Gospels as at once Word of God and at the same time humanly comprehensible words is "the same as," analogical to in one or the other meaning of the word analogy, the mystery of the Incarnation, in which God and humanity become one across the barrier of the impossibility of their union.

Of another "analogous" problem with the parables in the Gospels I have not even spoken here, and can only indicate a line to be followed. Do the citations of the parables by the authors of the Gospels have the same efficacy as the parables had when they were originally spoken by Jesus to his auditors, or are they only the report of a form of language that has its efficacy elsewhere? Are they still the Word of the kingdom of heaven, the good news itself, or are they only the translation of that Word so it may be disseminated in another tongue? To employ the terminology of the speech-act theorists, are they "use" or only "mention" of Christ's language? These questions, it will be seen, are analogous to, although not quite the same as, the problem of translation on the one hand and the problem of distinguishing sacred from secular parable on the other.[14]

On the other side of the line separating secular and sacred parable, the paradox is that no purely human parable-maker, even though that person may be someone who, like Kafka, fully accepts the limitations of humanity, can avoid the temerity of at least tentatively, implicitly, or hypothetically putting himself in Christ's place and claiming to serve as an intermediary between this everyday world and the kingdom of heaven on the other side of the frontier of which all parables bring word. Secular parable may be, strictly speaking, a true performative, the creation of something that exists, for humanity at least, only in the words, but this purely performative function is always contaminated by an implicit claim to be based on knowledge and to bring knowledge, even if that knowledge is the negative knowing of the apparent impossibility of "going over." Kafka was fully aware of this danger. It is in fact the fundamental burden of *Von den Gleichnissen.*

Any commentator on parables, secular or sacred, is in the situation of Kafka, or indeed of such a commentator as Henry Alford. One should be anxious to avoid the danger of being parabolic oneself and yet one is unable certainly to do so. The question of the relation between secular and sacred parable is a tiny seed that generates a long line of thought, multiplying itself thirty- , sixty- , or a hundredfold, of which this paper is only a preliminary segment. Such a line of thought is like a parabolic trajectory, sweeping in from an infinite distance and back out again. That my discourse on parable is itself parabolic there can be no doubt, although whether I have been able to keep safely on this side of the line separating secular from sacred parable is not so certain. The uncertainty derives from the difficulty – perhaps the impossibility – in spite of all efforts and in spite of the high stakes involved, of keeping the two kinds of parable absolutely distinct.

Notes

1. See, for example, William Beardslee, *Literary Criticism of the New Testament* (Philadelphia, 1970); Charles Carlston, *The Parables of the Triple Tradition* (Philadelphia, 1975); Dominic Crossan, *In Parables* (New York, 1973); *idem, Raid on the Articulate* (New York, 1976); C. H. Dodd, *The Parables of the Kingdom* (New York, 1961); Robert W. Funk, *Language, Hermeneutic, and the Word of God* (New York, 1966); J. Jeremias, *The Parables of Jesus* (New York, 1972); Norman Perrin, *Jesus and the Language of the Kingdom* (Philadelphia, 1976); Norman Petersen, *Literary Criticism for New Testament Critics* (Philadelphia, 1978); Jean Starobinski, "Le Combat avec Légion," *Trois fureurs* (Paris, 1974) pp. 73–126; Mary Ann Tolbert, *Perspectives on the Parables: An Approach to Multiple Interpretations* (Philadelphia, 1979); Dan O. Via, *The Parables* (Philadelphia, 1967); Andrzej Warminski, "'Patmos': The

Senses of Interpretation," *MLN*, 91 (1976) pp. 478–500; Amos Wilder, "The Parable," *Early Christian Rhetoric: The Language of the Gospel* (Cambridge, 1971) pp. 71–88. A collection may also be mentioned, *Analyse structurale et exégèse biblique* (François Bovon, ed.; Neuchâtel, 1971), which also contains the essay by Jean Starobinski listed above. In addition, two journals, *Semeia* and *Linguistica Biblica*, have contained many essays on the parables of Jesus. I owe most of this brief bibliography of recent work on the parables to Amos Wilder, who has kindly assisted in educating me in this area, as he has educated me in other ways over the years. I am glad to be able to thank him here for manifold kindnesses.

2. G. W. F. von Hegel, *Aesthetics: Lectures on Fine Art* (tr. T. M. Knox; 2 vols; New York, 1975) l. 378; *Vorlesungen über die Ästhetik, Werkausgabe* (Frankfurt am Main, 1970) l. 486.

3. *ibid.*, English, p. 391; German, pp. 502–3.

4. *The Greek Testament* H. Alford, ed. (4 vols; Boston; New York, 1874) l. 136–7.

5. *ibid.*, p. 138.

6. As Jean Starobinski observes, "Le Combat," 111ff.

7. See Marcel Mauss, *The Gift* (tr. Ian Cunnison; New York, 1967); the seminars by Jacques Derrida at Yale University in the fall of 1980 focused on Mauss' book.

8. Paul Claudel and André Gide, *Correspondance 1899–1926* (Paris, 1949) p. 91.

9. Franz Kafka, *Parables and Paradoxes*, in German and English (New York, 1971) pp. 10–11.

10. *ibid.*

11. *ibid.*

12. *ibid.*, p. 258.

13. See Paul de Man's discussion of Nietzsche's use of this distinction in "Rhetoric of Persuasion (Nietzsche)," *Allegories of Reading* (New Haven and London, 1979) pp. 119–31.

14. Werner H. Kelber has completed a study of the parables of the Synoptic Gospels which makes the distinction between citation and original oral utterance suggested in this paragraph.

9

Mr Carmichael and Lily Briscoe

The rhythm of creativity in *To the Lighthouse*

There is such a thing as being too profound. Truth is not always in a well. In fact, as regards the more important knowledge, I do believe she is invariably superficial.

Dupin, in "The Murders in the Rue Morgue"

Creativity for Virginia Woolf is a matter of an extending or buoyant élan. It is not so much, as I have argued elsewhere,[1] a matter of interpolation, the filling in of gaps between here and there, this and that, as it is a matter of extrapolation, the projection out into the unknown of a life force, a constructive force, whether moral, collective, or artistic. For Virginia Woolf this force, in all its dimensions, is liable to falter, fail, and drop, plunging the one who is dependent on it into an abyss of despondency, even of inexplicable terror, despair, or fear of death, desire for death. "We perished, each alone." Near the beginning of *To the Lighthouse* Mrs Ramsay thinks:

> . . . so that the monotonous fall of the waves on the beach, which for the most part beat a measured and soothing tattoo to her thoughts and seemed consolingly to repeat over and over again as she sat with the children the words of some old cradle song, murmured by nature, "I am guarding you – I am your support," but at other times suddenly and unexpectedly, especially when her mind raised itself slightly from the task actually in hand, had no such kindly meaning, but like a ghostly roll of drums remorselessly beat the measure of life, made one think of the destruction of the island and its engulfment in the sea, and warned her whose day had slipped past in one quick doing after another that it was all ephemeral as a rainbow – this sound which had been obscured and concealed under the other sounds suddenly thundered hollow in her ears and made her look up with an impulse of terror.[2]

I have interrupted a long sentence in the middle with the "so that" which follows "this sound . . . had ceased": "This sound . . . had ceased;

so that . . ." Virginia Woolf's style is characterized by this prolonged, sustained rhythmical movement, drawing breath again just when it seems about to stop, and continuing beyond a semicolon or even beyond a full stop or the numbering or naming of a new section. It is as though Woolf or "the narrator," whoever it is who speaks the words of the novel, were afraid that if she (he? it?) were to stop, the sound of the waves breaking would intervene as the terror of an imminent fall. Woolf's work throughout is dominated by the question of whether there is beneath the manifold human activities of doing, thinking, talking, writing, creating, a rhythmical groundswell which is comforting and sustaining; or whether such rhythm as there is outside human constructing beats out no more than the measure of approaching death. To go on talking, thinking, doing, writing, creating, is either a way of warding off the fall, of sustaining onself over the abyss, or if there is somewhere support, comfort, a "wedge-shaped core of darkness," the groundswell before, beneath, or ahead, to rest in that movement and share in it, to incarnate the secret rhythm of creation, out there, in what creates, in here.

To the Lighthouse contains many examples of this effort of rhythmic extrapolation reaching out from what is now and here toward what is there and not yet. The form of novel is made up of these parallel analogous strands of creativity interacting, wound together, each pursuing its separate course toward its goal. The interpretation of *To the Lighthouse* is the interpretation of the meanings of each of these various examples of creative energy, both separately and in its relation to the others. Mrs Ramsay gives her dinner party with its triumphant *Boeuf en daube*. She has brought eight children into the world, nurtured and sustained them. She has given her self-pitying and insecure husband "this delicious fecundity, this fountain and spray of life," into which "the fatal sterility of the male plunge[s] itself, like a beak of brass barren and bare" (58). The goal Mrs Ramsay reaches in the novel, however, is death. The novel turns on the vanishing of her consciousness from the world and from the lives of the other characters. Her vanishing coincides with the vanishing in the catastrophe of the Great War of all that Victorian and Edwardian world of assured social order. The emblematic expression of this vanishing in the novel is that extraordinary representation, in the "Time Passes" section of the novel, of the world without any witnessing consciousness other than the ubiquitous mind of the narrator. There is in this section, to put it more precisely, no witnessing mind watching the gradual decay of the Ramsay's summer house, none but that anonymous mind of the narrator, that and the intermittently present cleaning woman, Mrs McNab, who comes creaking and groaning now and then to make a momentary stay against entropy.

Mr Ramsay's sense of failure results from his unsuccessful attempt to reach all the way to Z in his philosophical thinking. He too tries to extrapolate out into the void, but he gets stuck at Q: "A shutter, like the leathern eyelid of a lizard, flickered over the intensity of his gaze and obscured the letter R. In that flash of darkness he heard people saying – he was a failure – that R was beyond him. He would never reach R. On to R, once more. R – " (54). If Mr Ramsay does not ever reach even R, much less Z, chanter of poetry though he is, he does get finally, with James and Cam, to the lighthouse.

Mr Ramsay's setting foot on the little island, as any reader of the novel knows, coincides with Lily Briscoe's putting the finishing stroke on her painting, the line that stands for the dead Mrs Ramsay and substitutes for her, that replaces the missing shadow on the step cast by Mrs Ramsay, the wedge-shaped core of darkness which had been present there when Lily began her painting and Mrs Ramway sat knitting the reddish-brown stocking and reading to James: "With a sudden intensity, as if she saw it clear for a second, she drew a line there, in the centre. It was done; it was finished. Yes, she thought, laying down her brush in extreme fatigue, I have had my vision" (310). Lily's vision, before she has even had it, is proleptically compared to Mrs Ramsay's establishment of order and stability in chaos by placing herself as the wedge-shaped core of darkness in the midst of the flow. This comparison is proof of that principle of analogy among the various acts of creativity which holds the diverse strands of *To the Lighthouse* together: "Mrs. Ramsay bringing them together; Mrs. Ramsay saying, 'Life stand still here'; Mrs. Ramsay making of the moment something permanent (as in another sphere Lily herself tried to make of the moment something permanent) – this was of the nature of a revelation. In the midst of chaos there was shape; this eternal passing and flowing (she looked at the clouds going and the leaves shaking) was struck into stability. Life stand still here, Mrs. Ramsay said" (240–1).

Lily's act of painting is presented explicitly as a rhythmical movement which carries her forward through time and seems perhaps to be sustained by an impersonal transcendent rhythm which is beyond her yet in which she nevertheless participates:

The brush descended. It flickered brown over the white canvas; it left a running mark. A second time she did it – a third time. And so pausing and so flickering, she attained a dancing rhythmical movement, as if the pauses were one part of the rhythm and the strokes another, and all were related; and so, lightly and swiftly pausing, striking, she scored her canvas with brown running nervous lines which had no sooner settled there than they enclosed (she felt it looming about her) a space . . .

Then, as if some juice necessary for the lubrication of her faculties were spontaneously squirted, she began precariously dipping among the blues and umbers, moving her brush hither and thither, but it was now heavier and went slower, as if it had fallen in with some rhythm which was dictated to her (she kept looking at the hedge, at the canvas) by what she saw, so that while her hand quivered with life, this rhythm was strong enough to bear her along with it on its current. (235–6, 237–8).

The word *rhythm*, one can see, is the key term and concept in this remarkable passage. If "stability" names the fixed stay against chaos, as of a stake planted firmly in the swift current of life, "rhythm" for Woolf is the name for the shaping forward movement through time, scoring it in both senses, of the creative impetus in all its forms. An example is the choreographed and choreographing dance of Lily's hand. The fundamental question is whether, for Woolf, this movement is based on a ground, a fundament or principle outside itself, or whether its power is merely intrinsic, the imposition of a pulsating formal pattern on a formless background, as one scores a piece of music or scores a sign on featureless rock.

There is, however, yet a fourth example of creativity in *To the Lighthouse*, one more covert, muted, obscure: the poetry writing of Augustus Carmichael. If Mr Ramsay sustains himself by rhythmically chanting poetry, Tennyson's "The Charge of the Light Brigade" or Cowper's "The Castaway," as he paces up and down the terrace, or as they go to the lighthouse, if Mrs Ramsay brings people together and gives her egotistical husband sympathy, and if Lily Briscoe paints, Mr Carmichael is presented in the first section of the book, "The Window," as a silent, ineffectual, and not altogether pleasant old man. He shuffles about in yellow slippers, dislikes Mrs Ramsay, takes opium, and has cat's eyes and a cat's manners. In the last section, "The Lighthouse," the reader learns somewhat to his surprise (to my surprise at least) that Mr Carmichael has become a successful, even a famous, poet. When Mr Carmichael sits there catching words out of the air like a cat catching birds, he is gradually assembling words which are perhaps the most successful example of creativity in the novel: "And there he would lie all day long on the lawn brooding presumably over his poetry, till he reminded one of a cat watching birds, and then he clapped his paws together when he had found the word" (145).

I have said that the presentation of Mr Carmichael's creativity in the novel is obscure. The sign of this obscurity is the curious fact that Mr Carmichael, almost alone of all the characters in *To the Lighthouse*, is never or scarcely ever presented from the inside by way of that indirect discourse, the consciousness of the narrator married to the consciousness of the character and speaking for it, which is the usual mode of presentation of people in this novel. I note only one time when the reader enters Mr Carmichael's mind in this way: "And it all looked, Mr. Carmichael thought, shutting his book, much as it used to look" (214). Why this relatively complete effacement of Mr Carmichael should occur, what significance it may have, can only be speculated about at a later point in this essay.

If these diverse acts of creativity are presented in the novel as they are embodied in the characters, what about the act of representation represented by the novel itself? Is not the novel an act of rhythmic extrapolation out into the future, making form? Should the reader not think of all the forms of creativity within the novel – Mrs Ramsay's, Mr Ramsay's, Lily Briscoe's, Augustus Carmichael's – as oblique representations of the act of creativity represented by the novel itself? A distinction must be made here, as always, between Virginia Woolf sitting at her desk with a blank sheet of paper before her, composing *To the Lighthouse*, extending the line of words further and further out into the void of not-yet-written-on paper, and, on the other hand, the imagined and imaginary narrator of the novel. The latter is a different person, is located in a different place, and possesses quite different powers. Whatever may be said of Lily, Mr Ramsay, Mrs Ramsay, or Augustus Carmichael, both Virginia Woolf and her imagined narrative voice, in their quite different ways, succeed admirably in fulfilling the creative impetus which carries them out into the future or from one moment in the past up to another moment in the past. The novel creates an imagined world. It gets written, printed, published, reviewed. It makes Woolf famous, more famous than her father. The narrator retraces with patient completeness a stretch of time past, thought of now as having really happened. The narrator retraces this stretch of time all the way from the moment when Mrs Ramsay sits with James, knitting the brown stocking, up to the moment when Mr Ramsay, James, and Cam reach the lighthouse at last, and Lily puts the finishing stroke on her painting. All these diverse materials are gathered together, organized formally or rhythmically, and moved forward toward an end, the reaching of the lighthouse, the finishing of Lily's picture. All are recorded and preserved in words for the reader to resurrect once more in his turn.

Exactly who, or what, is the narrator of *To the Lighthouse*? Where is she, he, or it located? What powers does the narrator have? Whatever may be said of Woolf herself, the narrator of *To the Lighthouse* has extraordinary powers. The narrator enters at will into the minds of all the characters, or perhaps it might be better to say that the narrator is located already within all those minds and is able to speak for them in that strange third-person, past-tense form of narration: indirect discourse, *erlebte rede,* or *style indirect libre* (each of these nomenclatures has a different nuance of implications). Indirect discourse, along with dialogue, is the main resource of the tradition in the English novel that Woolf inherited and exploited so admirably. *To the Lighthouse* is a masterwork of exploration of the consciousness of others with the tool of indirect discourse, or to put this another way, it is a masterwork of the creation of the imaginary consciousness of others by means of this technique.

The past tense of the indirect discourse and indeed of all the narration of *To the Lighthouse* places the narrator of the novel at some indeterminate point after the action is over, looking back retrospectively at the events narrated. Exactly how long after or exactly where in space the "now" of the narrator is placed there is absolutely no way to tell. She, he, or it is nowhere and everywhere, located at no identifiable time except at an indeterminate "after." The narrator of *To the Lighthouse* has none of the characteristics of a person except voice and tone. The reader learns nothing of the narrator's history, dress, opinions, or family relations. She, he, it is anonymous, impersonal, ubiquitous, subtle, penetrative, insidious, sympathetic, and indifferent at once, able to plunge into the depths of any character's thoughts and feelings but liable to move without warning out of one mind and into another in the middle of a sentence, as in the shift from James' to Mr Ramsay's mind in the fourth paragraph of the novel. Or the narrator may move without warning from one time to another time within the mind of a single character or group of characters, as in that sequence in the first pages of the novel in which Mrs Ramsay reproves her daughter Nancy for saying that the atheist Tansley has chased them all the way to the Hebrides (13). This must have occurred at an earlier time than the "now" in which Mrs Ramsay sits watching James cut out pictures from the catalogue of the Army and Navy Stores.

The voice of the narrator is subtly subversive of the thoughts and feelings of the characters. The sign of this undercutting is the greater or lesser degree of irony and distance involved not only in repeating these thoughts and feelings in the past tense but also in repeating them in the third person. The signal of this somewhat insolent distance is the locution: "he thought" or "she thought" or "X thought": "[Mr Ramsay] standing, as now, lean as a knife, narrow as the blade of one, grinning sarcastically, not only with the pleasure of disillusioning his son and casting ridicule upon his wife, who was ten thousand times better in every way than he was (James thought), but also with some secret conceit at his own accuracy of judgment" (10). The narrator, it seems, is a ubiquitous mind, present everywhere at all times of the past, but condemned to know and feel only what the characters know and feel, and condemned also to hollow out these thoughts and feelings in the act of reliving them and repeating them in words.

The narrator, it appears, is a collective consciousness, dependent on the consciousnesses of the various characters for its existence. The narrator is without life, personality, opinions, feelings of its own, and yet is doomed to see all the lives, personalities, opinions, and feelings which it relives from the perspective of that prospective death toward which they all move, and where the narrating mind already is. Woolf's work can in this be defined as a magnificent exploitation and bringing out into the open of the implications of the Victorian convention of the "omniscient narrator," the narrator of *Middlemarch,* or of *The Last Chronicle of Barset,* or of *Our Mutual Friend.* The most disquieting of these conventions, it may be, is the way, if one thinks of it for a moment from the point of view of the characters, it can be seen that each of them is, without knowing it, overlooked, overfelt, if that may be said, penetrated through and through by an invisible, inaudible, wholly undetectable mind. That mind is gifted with terrifying clairvoyant insight, a kind of one-way television, telepathy, telethinking. The location of that "afar," the *tele* in all these words, is the future place of death which sees things as already part of the lost and irrevocable past. There is an indescribable pathos in this instantaneous transformation, by the impersonal conventions of storytelling, of flesh and blood immediacy into long-lost, impalpable ghosts.

Take, as one example, of this, the following joining of the narrator's mind to Lily Biscoe's mind. The passage is a segment of extraordinarily supple and expert free indirect discourse from early in the novel. Once again my citation is broken out of a much longer continuous following of Lily's thoughts and feelings as she walks with Mr Bankes and compares him to Mr Ramsay:

> How then did it work out, all this? How did one judge people, think of them? How did one add up this and that and conclude that it was liking one felt, or disliking? And to those words, what meaning attached, after all? Standing now, apparently transfixed, by the pear tree, impressions poured in upon her of those two men, and to follow her thought was like following a voice which speaks too quickly to be taken down by one's pencil, and the voice was her own voice saying without prompting undeniable, everlasting, contradictory things, so that even the fissures and humps on the bark of the pear tree were irrevocably fixed there for eternity. You [Mr Bankes] have greatness, she continued, but Mr Ramsay has none of it. His is petty, selfish, vain, egotistical; he is spoilt; he is a tyrant; he wears Mrs Ramsay to death; but he has what you (she addressed Mr Bankes) have not; a fiery unworldliness; he knows nothing about trifles; he loves dogs and his children. He has eight. Mr Bankes has none. Did he not come down in two coats the other night and let Mrs Ramsay trim his hair into a pudding basin? All of this danced up and down, like a company of gnats, each separate, but all marvellously

controlled in an invisible elastic net – danced up and down in Lily's mind, in and about the branches of the pear tree, where still hung in effigy the scrubbed kitchen table, symbol of her profound respect for Mr Ramsay's mind, until her thought which had spun quicker and quicker exploded of its own intensity; she felt released; a shot went off close at hand, and there came, flying from its fragments, frightened, effusive, tumultuous, a flock of starlings. (40–41)

In this admirable passage, one among so many similarly admirable passages in *To the Lighthouse*, the narrator has entirely penetrated within the mind and feelings of the character, occupied them from within, down to every crevice, like the tide rising along the shore. The narrator repeats the character's thoughts and emotions for the reader in language composed in the past tense and in the third person, or at least without ever using "I." This repetition alienates the thoughts and feelings from Lily in the act which does her homage by so sympathetically identifying with her. That is, the narrator alienates the contents of Lily's consciousness by displacing them into that vast, capacious, impersonal mental–verbal reservoir of the narrator's collective consciousness. Within that manifold mind every thought and feeling that has ever occurred goes on happening over and over in an eternal repetition of itself in the mode of having always already happened when the reader encounters it. Within that all-embracing collective mind everything is permanently preserved, as even the fissures and humps on the bark of the pear tree seem to Lily "fixed there for eternity," and as her inner voice seems to her to be saying "everlasting" things, but they are preserved as fixed and dead. Within the narration every "I," "is," or "now" becomes "he" or "she," "was," or "then." For Lily the fissures and humps on the bark of the pear tree *are* fixed there for eternity; for the narrator and the reader they *were* so fixed.

I say "for the reader" too. What is performed by the narrator within the novel, the simultaneous alienation and preservation of the characters' affective thoughts, is performed by the novel for the reader in the most concrete and material way. Any copy of *To the Lighthouse* I hold in my hand encloses within itself, like a fly in amber, along with all its other contents, this particular sequence of moments in Lily Briscoe's mental life, eternally preserved in the words on the page, at least as long as this or at least one copy of the novel exists somewhere. The sequence is stored up, ready to be resurrected again in the mind of any reader whenever the paragraph is reread. The two forms of preservation are symmetrical, but they exist on opposite sides of the looking glass of fiction, one performed within the imaginary world of the novel, the other performed by the novel as a strange kind of physical object in the real world, paper marked all over with small black designs and bound in sheafs or stacks with cardboard covers.

The passage I have quoted is especially useful because it contains explicit notations of the mode of existence of the character's mind and a hint of the relation of that mind to that ubiquitous, all-knowing mind of which she is totally unaware. If the major narrative lines of *To the Lighthouse* are large-scale examples of creativity, abortive or unsuccessful, the small-scale existence of each character's mind from moment to moment is no less an example of a specific kind of creative élan, one repeating in miniature the formal structure of the book as a whole. Like the book, Lily's mind in these moments is made up of a large number of separate and contradictory thoughts and feelings all going on at once, a bundle or bunch of fragmentary details. At the same time the human mind, for Woolf, has a constantly acting power of rhythmically unifying these fragments, sweeping them into a measured, ongoing, alternating oneness, and holding them together within it, as all the words of a poem are held within that poem's organizing metrical scheme. This conception of the mind is precisely expressed in the double figure of the dancing gnats and the elastic net: "All this danced up and down, like a company of gnats, each separate, but all marvellously controlled in an invisible elastic net – danced up and down in Lily's mind."

The other crucial formulation here is the one in which the narrator says: "To follow her thought was like following a voice which speaks too quickly to be taken down by one's pencil, and the voice was her own voice saying without prompting undeniable, everlasting, contradictory things." There is no way to tell whether the infinitive phrase "to follow her thought" is to be thought of as Lily's own mental activity following that stream of thoughts which is like a rapid, unprompted, continuous, unstanchable murmur within her, or whether it is to be thought of as the narrator's activity of following and recording that murmuring voice within Lily, not by pencil but by means of that vast, all-inclusive, all-preserving sensorium or ubiquitous bugging apparatus which tapes everything but by some miracle of word-processing turns every present tense to past, every "I" to "he" or "she." The voice within Lily is both those voices at once, her own voice and what her own voice, like the inner voices of all the other characters, participates in without knowing it – the inaudible, all-absorbing voice of the narrator, that voice the reader is uniquely privileged to hear.

I have said that all the characters participate without knowing it in the voice and mind of the narrator, according to the assumption Woolf notes in her diary that a "tunnelling process" deep into the minds of all her characters would reach a point where they all connect, all have the same or similar thoughts, all move to the same profound rhythm, which is

the rhythm of that impersonal narrator's way of thinking.³ Might it not
be that this impersonal, all-inclusive all-keeping, all-annihilating perspective is covertly embodied in the person of Augustus Carmichael?
The paradox then would be that although in one sense the mind of Mr
Carmichael is the one mind that the narrator hardly ever recounts from
within for the reader in that indirect discourse which is her (or his or its)
main resource, in another sense there is evidence that Mr Carmichael's
mind coincides (perhaps with the help of opium) more closely than that
of any other character with the mind of the narrator. To read the novel,
to dwell within the narrator's mind and share the narrator's perspective,
is to be within something closely approximating Mr Carmichael's mind
and perspective. Early in the novel the reader is shown Mr Carmichael
"basking with his yellow cat's eyes ajar, so that like a cat's they seemed
to reflect the branches moving or the clouds passing, but to give no
inkling of any inner thoughts or emotion whatsoever." Mr Carmichael is
unable to respond to Mrs Ramsay's blandishments, "sunk as he was in a
grey-green somnolence which embraced them all, without need of
words, in a vast and benevolent lethargy of well-wishing; all the house;
all the world; all the people in it" (19). Does this not covertly describe the
narrator's perspective, or one aspect of it at least? Much later in the
novel, after the reader has been told that Mr Carmichael has become a
famous and successful poet, Lily Briscoe muses about him and his
poetry:

> She had never read a line of his poetry. She thought that she knew how it
> went though, slowly and sonorously. It was seasoned and mellow. It was
> about the desert and the camel. It was about the palm tree and the sunset.
> It was extremely impersonal; it said something about death; it said very
> little about love. There was an impersonality about him. (289–90)

The rhythm of successful creativity in Mr Carmichael, it may be,
coincides as closely or even more closely than that of Lily Briscoe to the
rhythm of creativity in the novel through which the narrator's
impersonal voice transforms everything into pastness and sees everything from the perspective of death.   '

In what I have said so far I have suggested that the mind of the narrator
is dependent on the minds of the characters for its existence. The
narrator's mind can appear, can think or feel, can articulate itself, only in
terms of what one or another of the characters thinks, feels, or articulates
to himself or herself. There is of course a celebrated section of *To the
Lighthouse*, "Time Passes," which seems openly and aggressively
intended to contradict that generalization. Here the narrator witnesses
and narrates the rhythm of gradual dissolution of the Ramsay's summer
house when it is left empty, after Mrs Ramsay's death, bereft of any

human presence. The narrator too, it seems, is bereft, empty of any human presence, and yet still remains as a neutral witness:

> The house was left; the house was deserted. It was left like a shell on a sandhill to fill with dry salt grains now that life had left it. The long night seemed to have set in; the trifling airs, nibbling, the clammy breaths, fumbling, seemed to have triumphed. The saucepan had rusted and the mat decayed. Toads had nosed their way in. Idly, aimlessly, the swaying shawl swung to and fro. A thistle thrust itself between the tiles in the larder. The swallows nested in the drawing-room; the floor was strewn with straw; the plaster fell in shovelfuls; rafters were laid bare; rats carried off this and that to gnaw behind the wainscots. Tortoise-shell butterflies burst from the chrysalis and pattered their life out on the window-pane. Poppies sowed themselves among the dahlias; the lawn waved with long grass; giant artichokes towered among roses; a fringed carnation flowered among the cabbages; while the gentle tapping of a weed at the window had become, on winters' nights, a drumming from sturdy trees and thorned briers which made the whole room green in summer. (206–7)

In this extraordinary tour de force of language Virginia Woolf attempts a hyperbolic fulfillment of the project of Mr Ramsay's books (and no doubt also of Leslie Stephen's books as his daughter thought of them). Mr Ramsay's work, as Andrew tells Lily Briscoe, is about "subject and object and the nature of reality," and when Lily says she does not understand that, Andrew says, "Think of a kitchen table then . . . when you're not there" (38). How can this be done? It is a genuine double bind. If I think of the table, then I must somehow be "there" to think it, but if I efface myself, then it seems I must efface the table. The "reality" of the table, for me at least, depends on my being there to think it, and yet the table manifestly would go on being there even if I were not there, even if I were dead. And so I try again, like Mr Ramsay trying to get beyond Q to R, to think of the kitchen table when I am not there. The context of this difficult mental feat is of course those eighteenth-century philosophers, Locke, Berkeley, and Hume, in whom Leslie Stephen specialized, for example in *History of English Thought in the Eighteenth Century* (1876). If a tree crashed in the forest far out of earshot of any living being, would there be any noise? asked Bishop Berkeley. He answered that God's ubiquitous ear guaranteed that there would be everywhere a divine someone to hear every noise. In *To the Lighthouse* Woolf, like her father before her, attempts to do without this way out and to imagine not just the kitchen table but the whole milieu of that version of the table in the Ramsays' house at Skye, and to imagine it without any human consciousness as stay against entropy other than the intermittent and ineffectual presence of the cleaning woman, Mrs McNab.

Even on a night when the house is full of human inhabitants, darkness and sleep depersonifies these inhabitants and deprives them of the ability to say "I" or of the right to be properly described as "he" or "she": "Nothing, it seemed, could survive the flood, the profusion of darkness which, creeping in at keyholes and crevices, stole round window blinds, came into bedrooms, swallowed up here a jug and basin, there a bowl of red and yellow dahlias, there the sharp edges and firm bulk of a chest of drawers. Not only was furniture confounded; there was scarcely anything left of body or mind by which one could say, 'This is he' or 'This is she'" (189–90). What persists, in the absence of individual human minds, as witness of the gradual decay of the house is the mind of the narrator or the language of the narrator. Not only does this indicate that, in *To the Lighthouse* at least, the mind of the narrator is *not* dependent on the minds of the characters for its continued existence; it is also evidence that although what the narrator sees when all individual human consciousnesses are withdrawn is a universal and remorseless process of disintegration, a slowing down of the rhythm of creativity and a vanishing of distinctions like that in Swinburne's "A Forsaken Garden," nevertheless for Woolf the traditional "omniscient narrator" is truly omniscient, a fictional replacement of God. This narrative mind exceeds and surrounds all individual minds. It was there before those individual minds, and it is still there when they are all gone. It is anonymous, ubiquitous, impersonal – watching everything, aware of everything, turning everything into all-annihilating, all-preserving past-tense language:

> The place was gone to rack and ruin. Only the Lighthouse beam entered the rooms for a moment, sent its sudden stare over bed and wall in the darkness of winter, looked with equanimity at the thistle and the swallow, the rat and the straw. Nothing now withstood them; nothing said no to them. Let the wind blow; let the poppy seed itself and the carnation mate with the cabbage. (208)

If only living human beings, working, creating, individually or collectively, can keep nonhuman nature from an irresistible tendency to that dispersal and obliteration of boundaries for which the symbol here is unnatural love, the poppy seeding itself, the carnation grotesquely mating with the cabbage, on the other hand, even if no human being is left to say no to this unnatural propensity in nature, there will still be an inhuman witness of the universal dissolution. There will remain precisely that view and that voice which go on seeing and speaking with such impersonal clairvoyance in "Time Passes."

Is that voice in fact so impersonal, so depersonifying? One form of figuration persists through all the citations from "Time Passes" I have made – in fact it permeates the whole chapter: personification, that trope of prosopopoeia whereby we speak of the absent, the dead, or the inanimate as if they were alive, as if they were possessed of human consciousness and intent. The trifling airs nibble and fumble. They have clammy breaths. The darkness creeps, steals, swallows. The lighthouse beam stares and looks. The carnation mates with the cabbage, as though they were human beings making love. Though this prosopopoeia is present everywhere in "Time Passes," one of the most beautiful of such sequences occurs early in the second part of the section, just after the passage already quoted about the vanishing in darkness and sleep of each "he" or "she." It is as if personality vanishes from the sleeping inhabitants of the house (for in this early section of "Time Passes" the house has not yet been left derelict), only to be displaced to the inhuman entities which remain, in this case the gentle breaths of sea air which circulate through the house. The passage has importance in unostentatiously calling attention to the fictive nature of the prosopopoeia. The night breaths are not really alive, but "almost one might imagine them" to be human. It is "as if" they were able to think and act:

> Only through the rusty hinges and swollen sea-moistened woodwork certain airs, detached from the body of the wind (the house was ramshackle after all) crept round corners and ventured indoors. Almost one might imagine them, as they entered the drawing-room questioning and wondering, toying with the flap of hanging wall-paper, asking, would it hang much longer, when would it fall? Then smoothly brushing the walls, they passed on musingly as if asking the red and yellow roses on the wall-paper whether they would fade, and questioning (gently, for there was time at their disposal) the torn letters in the waste-paper basket, the flowers, the books, all of which were now open to them and asking, Were they allies? Were they enemies? How long would they endure? (190–91)

What should one say of the personification here? What is its source or justification? What significance does it have? Can "one" not almost say that the dispersed presence of these prosopopoeias, present everywhere in the language of the narration when the narrator tries to think of the kitchen table and all its surroundings when no one is there, is evidence that language itself forbids the carrying out of this project; that the narrator of *To the Lighthouse* is not a ubiquitous mind but language itself; that language therefore takes precedence over consciousness here; or, to put this another way, that the personifications present in ordinary language (so that without necessarily thinking about it one describes the wind as creeping round corners, venturing indoors, questioning, wondering, sighing) are the source of one's ideas of the personalities of "real people" (Lily Briscoe, Mr Ramsay, Mrs Ramsay, and all the rest)? The evidence for the last point is the way personality will inevitably be ascribed to inanimate objects, animating the wind for example (*anima*: wind, breath, soul in Latin) when all "real people" are asleep, absent, or dead. Wherever there is language there will be personality somewhere. The novel as a genre, "almost one might imagine," is no more than the systematic and highly conventionalized exploitation of the potentiality within ordinary language to generate and project manifold illusions of selfhood, in the wind or in the light if not in some "he" or "she" named "Mr Ramsay" or "Lily Briscoe."

It is impossible to think of the kitchen table when you are not there not so much because it is impossible to efface consciousness or to imagine the absence of some witnessing mind as because there is no thinking without language. Language always reimports some "you," some "I," "he," or "she" into whatever is turned into language, for example in speaking of the "legs" of that table or in describing the gradual deterioration under the influence of wind and weather of the Ramsays' summer house as time passes.[4] It is not entirely accurate, therefore, to speak of the mind of the narrator of *To the Lighthouse* as dependent on the minds of the characters for its existence. "Time Passes" shows that this is not the case. Language, *To the Lighthouse* implies, preexists everything human as its presupposition, for example in the universal human belief in the existence of minds or selves. Something human might remain if every separate human being were effaced. Language might remain, and with it the conditions of belief in human minds or selves. In the case of *To the Lighthouse* both the personality of the narrator and those of the characters are dependent on that ineffaceable tendency present in ordinary language to project faces and bodies (and minds or feelings behind those faces and bodies). Any speaker or writer inherits language and its pervasive prosopopoeias among all the other things already there in the world into which he or she is born. "Time Passes" is a striking confirmation of this and a demonstration of some of its effects on story-telling or novel writing.

"He or she"? "One"? A final question remains, one that will return to the fundamental question posed earlier of whether there is a fundament or ground for the rhythm of creativity in Woolf. What is the sex of the one who says of the night airs, "almost one might imagine them questioning, creeping, wondering, sighing"?[5] Is the language of narration in *To the Lighthouse* gender-specific? Is the style of *To the Lighthouse* feminine? masculine? androgynous? Does Virginia Woolf "write like a woman"? What would it mean to say, "Virginia Woolf writes like a woman"? How would one tell certainly about this or persuade another of the truth of one's judgment?

Woolf herself, of course, raised these questions, especially in *A Room of One's Own*. There on the one hand (once more with some embarrassment of pronouns: "room of *one's* own") she asserts that "it is fatal for any *one* who writes to think of *their* sex . . . It is fatal for a woman . . . in any way to speak consciously as a woman" (emphasis mine).[6] On the other hand, Woolf, apparently without irony, praises Mary Carmichael, her imaginary young woman writer, for writing unselfconsciously as a woman: "She wrote as a woman, but as a woman who has forgotten that she is a woman, so that her pages were full of that curious sexual quality which comes only when sex is unconscious of itself" (*ROO*, 96). What does this mean? How can one identify this curious sexual quality? Is there any significance in the fact that Woolf gives her aspiring woman novelist in *A Room of One's Own* the same patronymic as she gives the elusive male poet in *To the Lighthouse*? Is Mary Carmichael the daughter of Augustus Carmichael?

At the end of the printed record of the discussion following Jacques Derrida's initial presentation at Cerisy of his essay on Nietzsche and the place of woman, *Éperons: Les styles de Nietzsche*, there is an odd moment. Derrida here affirms in answer to a question that he would like to write like (a) woman and tries to do so: "J'aimerais bien écrire, aussi, comme (une) femme. J'essaie."[7] What does this mean? Can a man write like a woman, or a woman write like a man, as, for example, Mary Anne Evans called herself George Eliot and at least ostensibly "wrote like a man"? Could any writing be beyond sexual difference, truly bisexual or asexual? Would that be desirable?

The issues here are extremely complex, even if one limits oneself to the question of sexual differentiation in its relation to style. One must move carefully and tentatively, hypothetically, in these areas. Only the indication of a direction to move toward can be given here. To write like a woman might mean a number of different things, or manifest itself in a number of different ways, for example in straightforward thematic assertion. The latter is certainly present in Woolf's work – in the admirable feminist polemic of *A Room of One's Own*, or in the recurrent treatment of men in her novels as sterile egotists, overdependent on women, such as Mr Ramsay in *To the Lighthouse* or Peter Walsh in *Mrs Dalloway*. Writing like a woman might have, and in Woolf's case does have, a number of different possible contexts for discussion: biological, psychological, familial, social, historical, and so on. I suggest that perhaps Woolf's most important contribution to the question of what it might mean to write like a woman or like a man, or like some androgynous combination of the two, is her recognition that at the deepest level it is not a matter of thematic assertion but a matter of rhythm.

The problem for a woman writer, in Woolf's view, is that the rhythm of male style does not fit her natural stylistic stride and pace: "For we think back through our mothers if we are women. It is useless to go to the great men writers for help, however much one may go to them for pleasure. Lamb, Browne, Thackeray, Newman, Sterne, Dickens, De Quincey – whoever it may be – never helped a woman yet, though she may have learnt a few tricks of them and adapted them to her use. The weight, the pace, the stride of a man's mind are too unlike her own for her to lift anything substantial from him successfully. The ape is too distant to be sedulous" (*ROO*, 79). As Émile Benveniste has shown,[8] the word and the concept of rhythm arose among the Greeks as an extrapolation from the measured movements of the body in dancing, that is, from just that area from which Woolf draws her figure to explain why the standard masculine style does not work for a woman. Mary Carmichael must therefore in her writing destroy or disrupt the normal male rhythm and replace it with an abrupt, interrupted female style more suited to the biological and social conditions of a woman's life:

> The book has somehow to be adapted to the body, and at a venture one would say that women's books should be shorter, more concentrated, than those of men, and framed so that they do not need long hours of steady and uninterrupted work. For interruptions there will always be. (*ROO*, 81)[9]

Mary Carmichael in *Life's Adventure* writes like a woman not because of anything she says but because she performs successfully the double act of disrupting the inherited male rhythm and of replacing it with a new feminine rhythm appropriate for her time (as Jane Austen's Mozartean melodies would not have been):

> So I tried a sentence or two on my tongue. Soon it was obvious that something was not quite in order. The smooth gliding of sentence after sentence was interrupted. Something tore, something scratched; a single word here and there flashed its torch in my eyes. She was "unhanding" herself as they say in the old plays. She is like a person striking a match that will not light, I thought. But why, I asked her as if she were present, are Jane Austen's sentences not of the right shape for you? Must they all be scrapped because Emma and Mr Woodhouse are dead? Alas, I sighed, that it should be so. For while Jane Austen breaks from melody to melody as Mozart from song to song, to read this writing was like being out at sea in an open boat. Up one went, down one sank . . .
>
> I am almost sure, I said to myself, that Mary Carmichael is playing a trick on us. For I feel as one feels on a switchback railway when the car, instead of sinking, as one has been led to expect, swerves up again. Mary is tampering with the expected sequence. First she broke the sentence; now she has broken the sequence. Very well, she has every right to do both these things if she does them not for the sake of breaking, but for the sake of creating. (*ROO*, 84–5)

"Not for the sake of breaking, but for the sake of creating" – in what sense, exactly, can this broken, interrupted female rhythm be creative? I suggest that there are two possible concepts of rhythm. One is implicitly associated by Woolf with "writing like a man," the other with "writing like a woman." The rhythm of a piece of writing may be a way of participating, or of thinking one participates, in the pulsation of creation already there in the world outside the mind of the writer. An example would be the sprung rhythm of Gerard Manley Hopkins. This rhythm, as Hopkins affirms in "The Wreck of the Deutschland," corresponds to the intrinsic rhythm of God's immanent presence in His creation: "world's strand, sway of the sea," "ground of being, and granite of it." Such a conception of rhythm is constative. It claims to reaffirm, to echo, a pattern already present outside the writing. Woolf tends to associate such a concept of rhythm with the male writer's comforting illusion that he dwells in the truth, that he possesses the truth and sways with its deepest measures. "Indeed, it was delightful to read a man's writing again," says Woolf of Mr A's novel, her example of male writing in *A Room of One's Own*. "It was so direct, so straightforward after the writing of women. It indicated such freedom of mind, such liberty of person, such confidence in himself. One had a sense of physical well-being in the presence of this well-nourished, well-educated, free mind, which had never been thwarted or opposed, but had had full liberty from birth to stretch itself in whatever way it liked" (*ROO*, 103). The problem with Mr A's novel is that this bland assumption that he is securely in resonance with the deep rhythms of the truth is false. Mr A's novel is in fact the unjustified assertion of the sterile letter "I" shadowing everything. It expresses the ungrounded imposition of the rhythms of sexual domination over women:

> It took place on the beach under sun. It was done very openly. It was done very vigorously. Nothing could have been more indecent . . . There seemed to be some obstacle, some impediment of Mr. A's mind which blocked the fountain of creative energy and shored it within narrow limits . . . When Alan approaches what can he do? Being honest as the day and logical as the sun, there is only one thing he can do. And that he does, to do him justice, over and over (I said, turning the pages) and over again . . . He does it in protest. He is protesting against the equality of the other sex by asserting his own superiority. He is therefore impeded and inhibited and self-conscious. (*ROO*, 104–5)

Against this false rhythm of unjustified solar male superiority may be opposed the more lunar rhythm of writing like a woman. This latter is the free projection of a broken, jagged, hesitant, evanescent measure against the aimless flux and tendency toward entropy of the outside world. This projection is made by the one who writes like a woman in full knowledge of the evanescence of the rhythmic beat of the words thus constructed, and in full knowledge that this rhythm is not grounded on any corresponding rhythm outside. Such a rhythm is extrapolative, performative. It projects a measured form through time out toward an unknown end. It is a way of doing things with words that is not to be measured by its truth of correspondence to any pre-existing pattern. Such writing brings something, a repeating and repeatable pattern, into existence through the words, through the autonomous say-so of the writer. To do this, to write performatively rather than constatively, is, it may be, to write like a woman. It is to write beyond or outside the ego-tistic illusions of "phallogocentrism," that erect male letter "I" shadowing and killing everything, like a giant beech tree, and bamboozled by its confidence that it is in tune with "the truth," the *logos*.

It will be seen, however, that writing like a woman and writing like a man tend to change places or values in the moment of being defined and enacted. The male thinks he writes constatively, but in fact his affirmations are groundless performatives. The woman writer knows there is no truth, no rhythm but the drumbeat of death, but this means that her broken, hesitant rhythms are in resonance with the truth that there is no truth. Writing like a woman is superior to male writing by being truly constative rather than unwittingly performative. Back and forth from one extreme to the other Woolf's thought alternates; each side is no sooner identified with one pole of the dichotomy than it reverses into its opposite. Nor is this absence or weakness of mind on Woolf's part. Woolf is no more able than any male writer to do without some form, however surreptitious, of the constative notion of authenticity in writing.

It may be that Woolf's well-known intermittent commitment to the idea of androgynous writing, writing like a man and like a woman simultaneously, is no more than a name for this fundamental undecid-ability in her notion of what would constitute valid rhythms of style, writing with a pen and not with a pickaxe, as she puts it apropos of Mary Carmichael. The good writer writes both performatively and constatively at once, that is, both like a woman and like a man, though the definitions and the values of both kinds of writing change places constantly:

> And I went on amateurishly to sketch a plan for the soul so that in each of us two powers preside, one male, one female; and in the man's brain, the man predominates over the woman, and in the woman's brain, the woman predominates over the man. The normal and comfortable state of being is that when the two live in harmony together, spiritually cooperating. If one is a man, still the woman part of the brain must have effect; and a woman also must have intercourse with the man in her. Coleridge perhaps meant this when he said that a great mind is

androgynous. It is when this fusion takes place that the mind is fully fertilised and uses all its faculties. Perhaps a mind that is purely masculine cannot create, any more than a mind that is purely feminine, I thought . . . Coleridge certainly did not mean, when he said that a great mind is androgynous, that it is a mind that has any special sympathy with women; a mind that takes up their cause or devotes itself to their interpretation. Perhaps the androgynous mind is less apt to make these distinctions than the single-sexed mind. He meant, perhaps, that the androgynous mind is resonant and porous; that it transmits emotion without impediment; that it is naturally creative, incandescent and undivided. (*ROO*, 102)

Does not *To the Lighthouse* already fulfill Woolf's desire to write like a woman whose mind is fertilized by the presence of the man in it? In somewhat covertly granting Augustus Carmichael creative power too, along with Lily Briscoe, does Woolf not already express that desire for an equivocal androgynous rhythm of style, beyond or combining the contradictory penchants of sexual difference? And does not the identification of sexual difference in style turn out to be no more than a way of naming these two forms of rhythm in their crisscrossing relation to the presence or absence of rhythm outside language? This constantly reversing rhythm, affirming itself and at the same time interrupting itself, is the dominant measure of *To the Lighthouse* and of Woolf's work generally. An example is the quotation I made at the beginning of this essay describing Mrs Ramsay's sense of the double meaning of the beat of the waves, sustaining and devastating at once.

Notes

1. In "*Between the Acts*: Repetition as Extrapolation," *Fiction and Repetition* (Cambridge, Mass., 1982), pp. 203–31.
2. Virginia Woolf, *To the Lighthouse* (New York, 1927) pp. 27–8. Further references to *To the Lighthouse* will be identified in the text by page numbers from this edition. Reprinted by permission of Harcourt Brace Jovanovich, Inc., The Hogarth Press, and the Author's Literary Estate.
3. "I dig out beautiful caves behind my characters: I think that gives exactly what I want; humanity, humour, depth. The idea is that the caves shall connect." *A Writer's Diary* (New York, 1954), p. 59.
4. Strictly speaking, "legs" is a catachresis as well as a prosopopoeia. The region of catachresis and the region of prosopopoeia overlap but do not coincide. Their relation is a complex form of chiasmus. "Legs of a table," like "face of a mountain," goes toward effacement in one direction (prosopopoeia) and toward making present in the other (catachresis). I have written in more detail on this topic in "Catachresis and Character: The Example of Clara Middleton in *The Egoist*," forthcoming in the transactions of a symposium on catachresis and syllepsis held at the University of Toronto in June 1982. And see also, on this topic, Paul de Man, "Hypogram and Inscription: Michael Riffaterre's Poetics of Reading," *Diacritics*, 11 (Winter 1981), pp. 30–5.

5. A preliminary version of this essay was presented at the Woolf Centenary Conference at Brown University, February 26–27, 1982. The conference was supposed to ask, among other things, "whether theories of sexual difference and definition can lead to better understanding of Woolf and her milieu."
6. Virginia Woolf, *A Room of One's Own* (New York and Burlingame, n.d.; first published in 1929), p. 108; hereafter cited as *ROO*. Reprinted by permission of Harcourt Brace Jovanovich, Inc., The Hogarth Press, and the Author's Literary Estate.
7. *Nietzsche aujourd'hui?* (Paris, 1973), I, 299. The discussion at Cerisy of Derrida's lecture is not included in the English translation of the essay. Derrida has more recently returned to his essay on Nietzsche and to the issues it raises about the feminine and feminine style in "Choreographies," an interview with Christie V. McDonald, *Diacritics*, 12 (Summer 1982), pp. 66–76. This issue of *Diacritics* is devoted to the topic of feminism and literature and is an excellent representation of the state of work in this area.
8. See Émile Benveniste, "La notion de 'rhythme' dans son expression linguistique," *Problèmes de linguistique générale* (Paris, 1966), pp. 327–35.
9. Peggy Kamuf presented an excellent paper at the Brown Conference entitled "Penelope at Work: Interruption in *A Room of One's Own*."

10

Thomas Hardy, Jacques Derrida, and the "Dislocation of Souls"

My focus is a poem by Thomas Hardy, "The Torn Letter." As a way into this admirable poem, a passage from Kafka's *Letters to Milena* and a recent essay by Jacques Derrida will provide a line of communication. First Kafka:

> The easy possibility of letter-writing must – seen merely theoretically – have brought into the world a terrible dislocation [*Zerrüttung*] of souls. It is, in fact, an intercourse with ghosts, and not only with the ghost of the recipient but also with one's own ghost which develops between the lines of the letter one is writing and even more so in a series of letters where one letter corroborates the other and can refer to it as a witness. How on earth did anyone get the idea that people can communicate with one another by letter! Of a distant person one can think, and of a person who is near one can catch hold – all else goes beyond human strength. Writing letters, however, means to denude oneself before the ghosts, something for which they greedily wait. Written kisses don't reach their destination, rather they are drunk on the way by the ghosts. It is on this ample nourishment that they multiply so enormously. . . . The ghosts won't starve, but we will perish.[1]

Thinking and holding are here opposed to writing. The former belongs to "the real world" of persons, bodies, and minds, of distance and proximity. If a person is near, one can touch him, hold him, kiss him (or her). If a person is distant one can think of that person. Such thinking relates one real "soul" to another. It is as genuine a "means of communication" as touch. The souls or selves pre-exist the thinking that joins them, as much as two bodies pre-exist their kiss. Writing is another matter. Nothing is easier than writing – a letter, for example. The writing of a poem, a story, a novel, is no more than an extension of the terrible power of dislocation involved in the simplest "gesture" of writing a note to a friend. The dislocation is precisely a "dislocation of souls." Writing is a dislocation in the sense that it moves the soul itself of

171

the writer, as well as of the recipient, beyond or outside of itself, over there, somewhere else. Far from being a form of communication, the writing of a letter dispossesses both the writer and the receiver of themselves. Writing creates a new phantom written self and a phantom receiver of that writing. There is correspondence all right, but it is between two entirely phantasmagorial or fantastic persons, ghosts raised by the hand that writes. Writing calls phantoms into being, just as the ghosts of the dead appear to Odysseus, to Aeneas, or to Hardy in his poem "In Front of the Landscape." In this case, however, the ghosts are also of the witnesses of those ghosts. The writer raises his own phantom and that of his correspondent. Kafka's ghosts, in his "commerce with phantoms," drink not blood but written kisses. They flourish and multiply on such food, while the one who writes the kisses and the correspondent they do not reach die of hunger, eaten up by the very act through which they attempt to nourish one another at a distance.

Now Derrida: Some remarkable paragraphs in "Télépathie"[2] seem almost to have been written with "second sight," that is, with prophetic foreknowledge that I would need to cite them here to support my reading of Hardy. In this essay Derrida speculates on the performative power a letter (in the epistolary sense) may have in order to bring into existence an appropriate recipient. If a letter happens to fall into my hands I may become the person that letter needs as its receiver, even though that new self is discontinuous with the self I have been up till now. Derrida's argument is peripherally attached as an appendage to his polemic, in "Le facteur de la vérité",[3] against Jacques Lacan's idea that a letter always reaches its destination. For Derrida, in "Télépathie," a letter reaches its destination all right, but not because the proper recipient, the self to which the letter corresponds, is waiting there for it, already in full-formed existence as a self. No, the letter creates the self appropriate to itself. It creates it by performing (in the strict Austinian sense of performative,[4] though with a twist) the utmost violence on the already existing self of the hapless person who accidentally reads the letter. The "twist" lies in the fact that the performative power of the letter is not foreseen or intended. This is contrary to the strict concept of a performative utterance as defined by Austin, but it may be that Austin, here as in other aspects of his theory, was unsuccessfully attempting to limit the terrible and always to some degree unpredictable power of a performative utterance:

Why, [asks Derrida] do the theoreticians of the performative or of the pragmatic interest themselves so little, to my knowledge, in the effects of written things, notably in letters? What do they fear? If there is something performative in the letter, how is it that a letter can produce all sorts of these ends, foreseeable and unforeseeable, and in fact even produce its recipient? All of this, to be sure, according to a properly performative causality, if there is such a thing, and which is purely performative, not at all according to another sequence extrinsic to the act of writing. I admit that I do not fully know what I want to say by that; the unforeseen should not be able to be part of the performative structure in the strict sense, and yet. . . . ("Télépathie," 9; my translation)

As an example of this strange coercive and yet unpredictable power of the written word, Derrida has suggested on the previous page that someone might determine his whole life according to the "program" of a letter or of a postcard that he accidentally intercepts, a missive not even intended for him. The recipient becomes the self the letter invites him to be (but there is no "him" before he receives the letter), just as poor Boldwood, in Thomas Hardy's novel *Far from the Madding Crowd*, becomes the bold lover Bathsheba's valentine seems to tell him he is:

> I do not [says Derrida] make the hypothesis of a letter which would be the external occasion, in some way, of an encounter between two identifiable subjects – and which would be already determined. No, rather of a letter which after the fact seems to have been projected toward some unknown recipient at the moment it was written, predestined receiver unknown to himself or to herself, if that can be said, and who determines himself or herself, as you know so well how to do, on receipt of the letter; this is therefore an entirely different thing from the transfer of a message. Its content and its end no longer precede it. Here it is then: you identify yourself and you engage your life according to the program of the letter, or perhaps better still of a postcard, a letter open, divisible, at once transparent and encrypted. . . . Then you say: it is I, uniquely I who can receive this letter, not that it is meant especially for me, on the contrary, but I receive as a present the happenstance to which this card exposes itself. It chooses me. And I choose that it should choose me by chance, I wish to cross its trajectory, I wish to encounter myself there, I am able to do it and I wish to do it – its transit or its transfer. In short, by a gentle and yet terrifying choice you say: "It was I." . . . Others would conclude: a letter thus *finds* its recipient, he or she. No, one cannot say of the recipient that he exists before the letter. ("Télépathie," 7–8; my translation)

It almost seems, as I have said, that these sentences were written with a kind of retrospective prevision of their appropriateness as a commentary on Hardy's "The Torn Letter," or as if "The Torn Letter" had been written with foresight of Jacques Derrida's meditations on July 9, 1979, though so far as I know Derrida had not then and has not yet read Hardy's poem. Even so, Hardy's poem, which is a "letter" in the first person written to an unnamed "you," has found its proper recipient at last in the unwitting Derrida. Derrida has become its reader without even knowing it. He has been programmed by the poem to write an interpretation of it before, beside, or after the letter, so to speak, in displacement from any conscious encounter with it. He has become the person the poem-letter invites him to be, in a confirmation of his theories of which he is unaware.

Here is Hardy's poem:

> The Torn Letter
>
> I
>
> I tore your letter into strips
>   No bigger than the airy feathers
>   That ducks preen out in changing weathers
> Upon the shifting ripple-tips.
>
> II
>
> In darkness on my bed alone
>   I seemed to see you in a vision,
>   And hear you say: "Why this derision
> Of one drawn to you, though unknown?"
>
> III
>
> Yes, eve's quick need had run its course,
>   The night had cooled my hasty madness;
>   I suffered a regretful sadness
> Which deepened into real remorse.
>
> IV
>
> I thought what pensive patient days
>   A soul must know of grain so tender,
>   How much of good must grace the sender
> Of such sweet words in such bright phrase.
>
> V
>
> Uprising then, as things unpriced
>   I sought each fragment, patched and mended;
>   The midnight whitened ere I had ended
> And gathered words I had sacrificed.
>
> VI
>
> But some, alas, of those I threw
>   Were past my search, destroyed for ever:
>   They were your name and place; and never
> Did I regain those clues to you.

VII

I learnt I had missed, by rash unheed,
My track; that, so the Will decided,
In life, death, we should be divided,
And at the sense I ached indeed.

VIII

That ache for you, born long ago,
Throbs on: I never could outgrow it.
What a revenge, did you but know it!
But that, thank God, you do not know.[5]

"The Torn Letter" contains several characteristic Hardyan ironic turns away from the straightforward notion that a letter may have a performative power to determine the self of its recipient. Derrida has the general idea of the letter-poem from Thomas Hardy right, but the message seems to have got garbled or overlaid with static and interference on the way. Some parts are twisted a bit or missing entirely, perhaps because somewhere along the line they have been switched or translated from Hardy's pungent and acerb English into Derrida's idiomatic French. In the latter, for example, the recipient of a letter is called its *destinataire*, with suggestions that the receiver is predestined, a latent fatality or doomed end point of the message. These overtones are missing in the equivalent English words, such as those I have used in my translation of "Derrida's" ideas back into English.

"The Torn Letter" is spoken or written by someone who has received a letter from an unknown admirer, apparently a woman. Before concluding that the speaker-writer is "Hardy" it must be remembered that Hardy claims most of his poems are "personative," spoken or written by imaginary personages. The poem is addressed to the sender of the letter, but, paradoxically, the poem is posited on the assumption that she will never receive his message and therefore cannot learn how much her letter had made him suffer: "But that, thank God, you do not know." If the poem is thought of as spoken or perhaps as silently thought, then the woman will indeed never know. In fact it is written down (or how else could we be reading it?). The poem itself, in its physical existence, contradicts its own affirmation. It is always possible, perhaps even inevitable, that the poem will fall into the woman's hands and tell her what he says he thanks God she cannot know. If her "revenge" on him for destroying the letter is the permanent ache of a remorse for not having kept it and answered it, his revenge on her is to let her know this in the act of saying she does not and cannot know. The poem is a version of that sort of mind-twisting locution, discussed elsewhere by Derrida,[6] which imposes disobedience to its own command: "Do not read this," or "Burn this without reading it."

Ashamed or embarrassed at receiving such a letter from a stranger (though the reader is never told just what she said), the speaker-writer of the poem has turned her letter into strips, tiny unreadable fragments "No bigger than the airy feathers / That ducks preen out in changing weathers / Upon the shifting ripple-tips." The "I" has divided and subdivided the letter until its bits are mere useless objects like molted feathers. The scraps are no longer able to carry legible words or to communicate any message. The letter has been reduced to detached letters or fragments of words. The fragments are no longer able to form part of a whole and to "fly," so to speak, in the sense of rising above the matter on which the message is written into the airy freedom of meaning. Unlike Farmer Boldwood, the "I" here has such a violent resistance to receiving the letter, responding to it, becoming subject to its performative power, turning into the person it would by perlocution make him be, that he tries to destroy the letter and all its latent power. He wants to turn it back into senseless matter. This is a striking example of part at least of what Derrida may mean by the "divisibility" of the letter. Derrida has in mind a letter's detachment from any single conscious emitting mind or self. He means also a letter's readiness to divide itself indiscriminately at the receiving end and to branch out to exert its power over any number of recipients, *destinataires*. For Derrida, and for Hardy too, a letter or a poem is divisible, and divided, at its origin, in itself, and at its end. In "The Torn Letter" the initial emphasis is on its physical divisibility. The letter by no means has the "organic unity" that used to be attributed to the single text. It can be turned into a thousand tiny pieces.

It will surprise no reader of Hardy to discover that neither this theoretical divisibility, nor the fact that the "I" turns theory into practice and fragments the letter, inhibits one bit its implacable performative power. To the contrary. The message is somehow distributed throughout the whole "signifying chain," like the proper name repeated beneath the text in one of Saussure's "hypograms."[7] The message can operate through any fragment of it, as a single cell contains the DNA message for reconstructing the whole organism of which it is a minute part, or as, in one of the more grotesque experiments of modern biology, one worm may learn behavior from another worm that has been pulverized and fed to the first worm. The genetic code or imprint passes by ingestion.

The "I" regrets his rash act. His "regretful sadness" at his "derision" "of one drawn to him though unknown" deepens "into real remorse" as the night wears on. He seems to see the writer of the letter "in a vision," reproaching him. The letter has invoked this vision. It has raised the ghost or hallucination of the lady. It has operated as a prosopopoeia, a speech to the absent or dead. Or perhaps it would be better to say that the act of tearing the letter to pieces, reducing the letter to dead letters, so to speak, has made it act as a magic invocation, as a man might be haunted by the ghost of the woman he had killed, or as "Hardy," in another poem, "In Front of the Landscape," is haunted by the phantoms of those he has betrayed. The poet rises up, collects the fragments of the letter, and pieces them together again.

The "Hardyan twist" is that the speaker cannot find all the pieces of the torn letter. Those lost are the ones with the lady's name and address. The speaker's act, with a reversal of the sexes, is like that of Isis gathering up the fragments of the body of the Osiris she has murdered. In both cases something is missing, the phallus of Osiris in one case, the lady's identification in the other, head source of meaning in both cases. Once again, as in that strange myth, the story Hardy tells is of the dispersal, fragmentation, defacing, depersonification, or even unmanning of the self, since in the end the reader of the poem, as I shall argue, becomes not the speaker, receiver of the letter, but the unattainable woman to whom the poem is spoken. The speaker cannot, after all, write back to the lady. He cannot initiate a correspondence and a relationship in which he would, in spite of his initial resistance to doing so, become the self the letter invited him to be:

> I learnt I had missed, by rash unheed,
> My track; that, so the Will decided,
> In life, death, we should be divided,
> And at the sense I ached indeed.

The Will here is of course the Immanent Will, that unconscious energy within what is which, in Hardy's phrase, "stirs and urges everything."[8] The Will is Hardy's name for the fact that things happen as they do happen. This volition is will as force, not will as conscious intent. Its "decisions" are the decisions of fortuity, the fact, for example, that the poet could not find the scraps with the woman's name and address. This means that the track he should have followed, the destiny that waited for him, remains untrodden. The divisibility of the letter means that he must remain divided from the correspondent, by a "decision" that is another form of division, separating this possibility from that one, this track from that.

"I had missed, by rash unheed, / My track" – the phrasing is odd. On the one hand, the track was truly his. It was fated for him by the Will. The track pre-exists his taking it, and with the track the self appropriate to it also exists. This track is his destiny. How can a man avoid his destiny, even by the "rash unheed" of not responding to the woman's call? On the other hand, "the Will decided" that he should not, as punishment for his rash unheed, take the track that was nevertheless destined for him. It is as if he were two separate persons, or two superposed persons, the one who took the track and the one who did not take it, as in Borges' "The Garden of the Forking Paths."

Though the divisibility of the letter did not mean that its power could be destroyed, that power was partially inhibited, and so another form of division takes place, the poet's permanent division from the lady. On the other hand, the paradox of the poem, another wry ironic turn, is that by missing his track he only follows it more surely and securely. He becomes more deeply and more permanently marked by the letter just because he has lost the name and address of its sender and so cannot answer it back, follow out the track it lays out. The letter is detached from the real name and self of its sender and liberated to have an anonymous or universal power to make new selves and join them. Again, as in Saussure's hypograms, what is "proper" to the letter is not a proper name and place attached to it on the outside but a power distributed throughout its minutest parts, its letters, a power to bring into existence the phantom selves of both sender and destined receiver. The fact that the letter lacks the proper name and address is just what gives it its power of the dislocation of souls. This might be defined by saying that although the torn and then reconstructed letter operates as an apostrophe or prosopopoeia, the ghost that is invoked is that dislocated new self of the reader of the letter, the self the letter personified into existence, if such a transitive use of the word may be made. It is as though the letter were being written on my mind, inscribed there, thus giving that blank page a personality it did not have.

Had the speaker answered the letter the episode would have run its course, as always happens in Hardy. Warmth, intimacy, love perhaps, would have been followed by coolness, betrayal, the wrenching apart of a final division. For Hardy it is always the case that "Love lives on propinquity, but dies of contact."[9] If he had followed the track he would ultimately have gone off the track and ceased forever to be the self the letter commands him to be. As it is the ache remains: "That ache for you, born long ago, / Throbs on: I never could outgrow it." For Hardy, the only relation to another person that can last is one that is in some way inhibited, prevented from moving on from propinquity to contact. In this case, the ache remains, like an unhealed and unhealable wound. One part of the "I" does become and remain the self the letter "performs" into existence. I say "one part" because, as Derrida affirms, "all is not recipient [*destinataire*] in a recipient, a part only which accommodates itself to the rest" ("Télépathie," 9–10; my translation). For Hardy, as for Derrida, or as for Nietzsche in paragraph 490 of *The Will to Power*,[10] the divisibility of the self is not only along the diachronic track, but synchronically, in the moment. At any given time the "self" is a commonwealth of many citizens. The self is the locus of many different selves dwelling uneasily with one another. Each struggles to dominate the others and to become the sole ruler, the single self within the domain of the self. For the speaker-writer in "The Torn Letter," one of those selves will remain the self who would have answered the unknown woman's letter.

One more thing must be said of the significance of the missing name and address in "The Torn Letter." The fact that he cannot attach the letter to a proper name and to a specific place puts the "I" of the poem in the same situation as the reader of this or of many other poems by Hardy. The reader is told precious little of the stories at which Hardy's poems hint. He is given a fragment only, usually lacking names, dates, and places. The poem is cut off from what came before and from what came after. It is the bare sketch of an episode. Vital facts are missing that would allow the reader to attach the poem with certainty to Hardy's biography or to actual places on a map of Dorset. Far from reducing the poems' power to haunt their readers, to stick in the mind and lodge there permanently, as an ache or throb the reader can never outgrow, the absence of these specifications multiplies the poems' powers over the reader a hundredfold. The poems produce something like that tantalizing sense that there is a proper name one cannot quite remember. This incompletion gives the poems their power to dwell within the reader, like a ghost, or like an unrealized self, or like a parasite within its host. Each of Hardy's poems is an unsolved and unsolvable mystery. It is a track the reader cannot take or reach the end of, and so he remains fascinated by it. One part of the reader, too, becomes, by the law of multiple simultaneous selves, permanently the self the poem performatively creates.

As Derrida observes, it is not necessary for a letter that brings a new self into existence in me to contain detailed instructions about what that self should be. Far from it. The performative power of the letter works best if it remains a sketch, like Hardy's poems. If, as Derrida says, "you identify yourself and engage your life according to the program of the letter," it is also the case that

> the program says nothing, it announces or enunciates nothing at all, not the least content, it does not even present itself as a program. One cannot even say that it 'works' as a program, in the sense of appearing like one, but without looking like one, it *works*, it programs. ("Télépathie," 8; my translation)

"The Torn Letter" is a striking confirmation of this. Just because the poem is so bereft of details, like the torn letter itself, it is able to perform its magic on any reader who happens to read it. It is as if he had accidentally come upon a letter intended for someone else. Reading the poem, I, you, or anyone becomes its addressee, since it has no name or specified destination. Hardy is forced to communicate with his lost correspondent by sending out a general letter to the world and publishing it in a book of poems, just as radio telescopists send out messages beamed into outer space in hopes they may be intercepted by some intelligent beings, somewhere: "Is anybody there?"

The reader of "The Torn Letter" becomes not so much, through a familiar kind of negative capability, the self of the speaker-writer of the poem, the "I" who has received the letter and is haunted by it, as, by a far stranger form of metamorphosis, the "you" to whom the poem is spoken or written. The reader becomes the woman who has caused the "I" so much ache. The poem becomes a letter in its turn, a letter missing the name and address of its destined receiver, and so anyone who happens to read it is put in the place of that unnamed receiver and programmed ever after to be, a part of him or her at least, the self that letter-poem calls into being. If letters or postcards perform that fearful dislocation of souls of which Kafka speaks, putting a man beside himself, as it were, drinking his life in the creation of a phantom self and a phantom correspondent for that self, a phantom who intercepts the most passionate of written kisses so that they never reach their destination, works of literature can enact a similar dispossession. A poem, too, may dislocate its reader. It may make her someone else somewhere else, perhaps without power ever to go back to herself.

Notes

1. F. Kafka, *Letters to Milena*, W. Hass, ed., tr. T. and J. Stern (New York, 1954), p. 229. Translation slightly altered: for the German, see Kafka, *Briefe an Milena*, E. Hass, ed. (New York, 1952), pp. 259–60.
2. J. Derrida, "Télépathie," *Furor*, February 1981, pp. 5–41.
3. J. Derrida, *La carte postale* (Paris, 1980); see, for example, "Envois."
4. J. L. Austin, *How To Do Things With Words* (Cambridge, Mass., 1967).
5. T. Hardy, *The Complete Poems*, J. Gibson, ed. (London, 1976), pp. 313–14.
6. For example, in "Envois," *La carte postale*.
7. J. Starobinski, *Les mots sous les mots: Les anagrammes de Ferdinand de Saussure* (Paris, 1971).
8. "The Convergence of the Twain," *Complete Poems*, p. 307.
9. F. E. Hardy, *The Life of Thomas Hardy: 1840–1928* (London, 1965) p. 220.
10. F. W. Nietzsche, *The Will to Power*, tr. W. Kaufmann and R. J. Hollingdale (New York, 1968), pp. 279–81; for the German see *Werke*, vol. 3, K. Schlecta, ed. (Munich, 1966), pp. 473–4.

11

Heart of Darkness revisited

I begin with three questions: Is it a senseless accident, result of the crude misinterpretation or gross transformation of the mass media, that the cinematic version of *Heart of Darkness* is called *Apocalypse Now*, or is there already something apocalyptic about Conrad's novel in itself? What are the distinctive features of an apocalyptic text? How would we know when we had one in hand?

I shall approach an answer to these questions by the somewhat roundabout way of an assertion that if *Heart of Darkness* is perhaps only problematically apocalyptic, there can be no doubt that it is parabolic. The distinctive feature of a parable, whether sacred or secular, is the use of a realistic story, a story in one way or another based firmly on what Marx calls man's "real conditions of life, and his relations with his kind,"[1] to express another reality or truth not otherwise expressible. When the disciples ask Jesus why he speaks to the multitudes in parables, he answers, "Therefore speak I to them in parables: because they seeing see not; and hearing they hear not, neither do they understand" (Matthew 13:13). A little later Matthew tells the reader that "without a parable spake he not unto them: That it might be fulfilled which was spoken by the prophet, saying, I will open my mouth in parables; I will utter things which have been kept secret from the foundation of the world" (Matthew 13:34–5). Those things which have been kept secret from the foundation of the world will not be revealed until they have been spoken in parable, that is, in terms which the multitude who lack spiritual seeing and hearing nevertheless see and hear, namely, the everyday details of their lives of fishing, farming, and domestic economy. Though the distinction cannot be held too rigorously, if allegory tends to be oriented toward the past, toward first things, and toward the repetition of first things across the gap of a temporal division, parable tends to be oriented toward the future, toward last things, toward the mysteries of the kingdom of heaven and how to get there. Parable tends to express what Paul at the end of Romans, in echo of Matthew, calls "the revelation of the mystery, which was kept secret since the world began, but now is made manifest" (Romans 16:25–6). Parable, one can see, has at least this in common with apocalypse: it too is an act of unveiling.

What might it mean to speak of *Heart of Darkness* as parabolic in form? Here it is necessary to turn again to that definition by the primary narrator of *Heart of Darkness* of the difference between Marlow's tales and the tales of ordinary seamen. This passage has often been commented on, quite recently, for example, by Ian Watt in his magisterial *Conrad in the Nineteenth Century*. Watt's discussion of *Heart of Darkness* seems also the definitive placing of that novel in the historical context of the parabolic story it tells. That context is nineteenth-century world-dominating European imperialism, specifically the conquest and exploitation of western Africa and the accompanying murder of large numbers of Africans. Watt's book, along with work by Frederick Karl, Norman Sherry, and other biographers, tells us all that is likely to be learned of Conrad's actual experience in the Congo, as well as of the historical originals of Kurtz, the particolored Harlequin-garbed Russian, and other characters in the novel. If parables are characteristically grounded in representations of realistic or historical truth, *Heart of Darkness* admirably fulfills this requirement of parable.

My contention is that *Heart of Darkness* fits, in its own way, the definition of both parable and apocalypse, and that much illumination is shed on it by interpreting it in the light of these generic classifications. As Marlow says of his experience in the heart of darkness: "It was sombre enough, too – . . . not very clear either. No, not very clear. And yet it seemed to throw a kind of light."[2] A narrative that sheds light, that penetrates darkness, that clarifies and illuminates – this is one definition of that mode of discourse called apocalyptic, but it might also serve to define the work of criticism or interpretation. All criticism claims to be enlightenment, *Aufklärung*.

Conrad's narrator distinguishes between two different ways in which a narrative may be related to its meaning:

> The yarns of seamen have a direct simplicity, the whole meaning of which lies within the shell of a cracked nut. But Marlow was not typical (if his propensity to spin yarns be excepted), and to him the meaning of an episode was not inside like a kernel but outside [*MS*: outside in the unseen], enveloping the tale which brought it out only as a glow brings out a haze, in the likeness of one of those misty halos that sometimes are made visible by the spectral illumination of moonshine. (5)

The narrator's distinction is made in terms of two figures, two versions of the relation of inside to outside, outside to inside. The hermeneutics of parable is presented here parabolically, according to a deep and unavoidable necessity. The meanings of the stories of most seamen, says the narrator, are inside the narration like the kernel of a cracked nut. I take it the narrator means the meanings of such stories are easily expressed, detachable from the stories and open to paraphrase in other terms, as when one draws an obvious moral: "Crime doesn't pay," or "Honesty is the best policy," or "The truth will out," or "Love conquers all." The figure of the cracked nut suggests that the story itself, its characters and narrative details, are the inedible shell which must be removed and discarded so the meaning of the story may be assimilated. This relation of the story to its meaning is a particular version of the relation of container to the thing contained. The substitution of contained for container, in this case meaning for story, is one version of that figure called in classical rhetoric synedoche, but this is a metonymic rather than a metaphorical synecdoche. The meaning is adjacent to the story, contained within it as nut within shell, but the meaning has no intrinsic similarity or kinship to the story. The same meaning could be expressed as well in other terms. Its relation to the story that contains it is purely extrinsic or contingent. The one happens to touch the other, as shell surrounds nut, or as shrine case its iconic image.

It is far otherwise with Marlow's stories. Their meaning is outside, not in. It envelops the tale rather than being enveloped by it. The relation of container and thing contained is reversed. The meaning now contains the tale. Moreover, perhaps because of that enveloping containment, or perhaps for more obscure reasons, the relation of the tale to its meaning is no longer that of dissimilarity and contingency. The tale is the necessary agency of the bringing into the open or revelation of that particular meaning. It is not so much that the meaning is like the tale. It is not. But the tale is in preordained correspondence to or in resonance with the meaning. The tale magically brings the "unseen" meaning out and makes it visible.

Conrad has the narrator express this subtle concept of parabolic narration according to the parabolic "likeness" of a certain atmospheric phenomenon. "Likeness": the word is a homonym of the German *Gleichnis*. Both are terms for figure or parable. The meaning of a parable does not appear as such. It appears in the "spectral" "likeness" of the story that reveals it, or rather, it appears in the likeness of an exterior light surrounding the story, just as the narrator's theory of parable appears not as such but in the "likeness" of the figure he proposes. The figure is supposed to illuminate the reader, give him insight into that of which the figure is the phantasmal likeness. The figure does double duty, both as a figure for the way Marlow's stories express their meaning and as a figure for itself, so to speak, that is, as a figure for its own mode of working. This is according to a mind-twisting torsion of the figure back on itself that is a regular feature of such figures of figuration, parables of parable, or stories about story-telling. The figure both illuminates its own workings and at the same time obscures or undermines it, since a figure of a figure is an absurdity, or, as Wallace Stevens puts it, there is no such thing as a metaphor of a metaphor. What was the figurative vehicle of the first metaphor automatically becomes the literal tenor of the second metaphor.

Let us look more closely at the exact terms of the metaphor Conrad's narrator proposes. To Marlow, the narrator says, "the meaning of an episode was not inside like a kernel but outside, enveloping the tale which brought it out only as a glow brings out a haze, in the likeness of one of those spectral illuminations of moonshine." The first simile here ("as a glow") is doubled by a second, similitude of a similitude ("in the likeness of . . ."). The "haze" is there all around on a dark night, but, like the meaning of one of Marlow's tales, it is invisible, inaudible, intangible in itself, like the darkness, or like that "something great and invincible" Marlow is aware of in the African wilderness, something "like evil or truth, waiting patiently for the passing away of this fantastic invasion" (23), or like the climactic name for that truth, the enveloping meaning of the tale, "the horror," those last words of Kurtz that seem all around in the gathering darkness when Marlow makes his visit to Kurtz's Intended and tells his lie: "The dusk was repeating them in a persistent whisper all around us, in a whisper that seemed to swell menacingly like the first whisper of a rising wind. 'The horror! The horror!'" (79).

The working of Conrad's figure is much more complex than perhaps it at first appears, both in itself and in the context of the fine grain of the texture of language in *Heart of Darkness* as a whole, as well as in the context of the traditional complex of figures, narrative motifs, and concepts to which it somewhat obscurely alludes. The atmospheric phenomenon that Conrad uses as the vehicle of his parabolic metaphor is a perfectly real one, universally experienced. It is as referential and as widely known as the facts of farming Jesus uses in the parable of the sower. If you sow your seed on stony ground it will not be likely to sprout. An otherwise invisible mist or haze at night will show up as a halo around the moon. As in the case of Jesus' parable of the sower, Conrad uses his realistic and almost universally known facts as the means of expressing indirectly another truth less visible and less widely known, just as the narrative of *Heart of Darkness* as a whole is based on the facts of history and on the facts of Conrad's life but uses these to express something transhistorical and transpersonal, the evasive and elusive "truth" underlying both historical and personal experience.

Both Jesus' parable of the sower and Conrad's parable of the moonshine in the mist, curiously enough, have to do with their own efficacy, that is, with the efficacy of parable. Both are posited on their own necessary failure. Jesus' parable of the sower will give more only to those

who already have and will take away from those who have not even
what they have. If you can understand the parable you do not need it. If
you need it you cannot possibly understand it. You are stony ground on
which the seed of the word falls unavailing. Your eyes and ears are
closed, even though the function of parables is to open the eyes and ears
of the multitude to the mysteries of the kingdom of heaven. In the same
way, Conrad, in a famous passage in the preface to *The Nigger of the
"Narcissus,"* tells his readers, "My task which I am trying to achieve is,
by the power of the written word, to make you hear, to make you feel –
it is, before all, to make you *see.*" No reader of Conrad can doubt that he
means to make the reader see not only the vivid facts of the story he tells
but the evasive truth behind them, of which they are the obscure revelation, what Conrad calls, a bit beyond the famous phrase from the preface
just quoted, "that glimpse of truth for which you have forgotten to ask."
To see the facts, out there in the sunlight, is also to see the dark truth that
lies behind them. All Conrad's work turns on this double paradox, first
the paradox of the two senses of seeing, seeing as physical vision and
seeing as seeing through, as penetrating to or unveiling the hidden
invisible truth, and second the paradox of seeing the darkness in terms of
the light. Nor can the careful reader of Conrad doubt that in Conrad's
case too, as in the case of the Jesus of the parable of the sower, the goal of
tearing the veil of familiarity from the world and making us *see* cannot be
accomplished. If we see the darkness already we do not need *Heart of
Darkness.* If we do not see it, reading *Heart of Darkness* or even hearing
Marlow tell it will not help us. We shall remain among those who
"seeing see not; and hearing they hear not, neither do they understand."
Marlow makes this clear in an extraordinary passage in *Heart of Darkness*,
one of those places in which the reader is returned to the primary scene of
narration on board the *Nellie*. Marlow is explaining the first lie he told
for Kurtz, his prevarication misleading the bricklayer at the Central
Station into believing he (Marlow) has great power back home:

"I became in an instant as much of a pretence as the rest of the bewitched
pilgrims. This simply because I had a notion it somehow would be of help
to that Kurtz whom at the time I did not see – you understand. He was just
a word for me. I did not see the man in the name any more than you do.
Do you see him? Do you see the story? Do you see anything? It seems to
me I am trying to tell you a dream – making a vain attempt, because no
relation of a dream can convey the dream-sensation, that commingling of
absurdity, surprise, and bewilderment in a tremor of struggling revolt,
that notion of being captured by the incredible which is of the very essence
of dreams . . ."
    He was silent for a while.
    ". . . No, it is impossible; it is impossible to convey the life-sensation of

any given epoch of one's existence – that which makes its truth, its meaning – its subtle and penetrating essence. It is impossible. We live, as we dream – alone . . ."

He paused again as if reflecting, then added:

"Of course in this you fellows see more than I could then. You see me, whom you know . . ."

It had become so pitch dark that we listeners could hardly see one another. For a long time already he, sitting apart, had been no more to us than a voice. There was not a word from anybody. The others might have been asleep, but I was awake. I listened, I listened on the watch for the sentence, for the word, that would give me the clue to the faint uneasiness inspired by this narrative that seemed to shape itself without human lips in the heavy night-air of the river. (27–8)

The denial of the possibility of making the reader see by means of literature is made here through a series of moves, each one ironically going beyond and undermining the one before. When this passage is set against the one about the moonshine, the two together bring out into the open, like a halo in the mist, the way *Heart of Darkness* is posited on the impossibility of achieving its goal of revelation, or, to put this another way, the way it is a revelation of the impossibility of revelation.

In Conrad's parable of the moonshine, the moon shines already with reflected and secondary light. Its light is reflected from the primary light of that sun which is almost never mentioned as such in *Heart of Darkness*. The sun is only present in the glitter of its reflection from this or that object, for example, the surface of that river which, like the white place of the unexplored Congo on the map, fascinates Marlow like a snake. In one passage it is moonlight, already reflected light, which is reflected again from the river: "The moon had spread over everything a thin layer of silver – over the rank grass, over the mud, upon the wall of matted vegetation standing higher than the wall of a temple, over the great river I could see through a sombre gap glittering, glittering, as it flowed broadly by without a murmur" (27). In the case of the parable of the moonshine too that halo brought out in the mist is twice-reflected light. The story, according to Conrad's analogy, the facts that may be named and seen, is the moonlight, while the halo brought out around the moon by the reflection of the moonlight from the diffused, otherwise invisible droplets of the mist, is the meaning of the tale, or rather, the meaning of the tale is the darkness which is made visible by that halo of twice-reflected light. But of course the halo does nothing of the sort. It only makes visible more light. What can be seen is only what can be seen. In the end this is always only more light, direct or reflected. The darkness is in principle invisible and remains invisible. All that can be said is that the halo gives the spectator indirect knowledge that the darkness is there.

The glow brings out the haze, the story brings out its meaning, by magically generating knowledge that something is there, the haze in one case, the meaning of the story, inarticulate and impossible to be articulated, in any direct way at least, in the other. The expression of the meaning of the story is never the plain statement of that meaning but is always no more than a parabolic "likeness" of the meaning, as the haze is brought out "in the likeness of one of those misty halos that sometimes are made visible by the spectral illumination of moonshine."

In the passage in which Marlow makes explicit his sense of the impossibility of his enterprise he says to his auditors on the *Nellie* first that he did not see Kurtz in his name any more than they do. The auditors of any story are forced to see everything of the story "in its name," since a story is made of nothing but names and their adjacent words. There is nothing to see literally in any story except the words on the page, the movement of the lips of the teller. Unlike Marlow, his listeners never have a chance to see or experience directly the man behind the name. The reader, if he happens at this moment to think of it (and the passage is clearly an invitation to such thinking, an invocation of it), is in exactly the same situation as that of Marlow's auditors, only worse. When Marlow appeals to his auditors Conrad is by a kind of ventriloquism appealing to his readers: "Do you see him? Do you see the story? Do you see anything? It seems to me I am trying to tell you a dream – making a vain attempt." Conrad speaks through Marlow to us. The reader too can reach the truth behind the story only through names, never through any direct perception or experience. In the reader's case it is not even names proffered by a living man before him, only names coldly and impersonally printed on the pages of the book he holds in his hand. Even if the reader goes behind the fiction to the historical reality on which it is based, as Ian Watt and others have done, he or she will only confront more words on more pages, Conrad's letters or the historical records of the conquest and exploitation of the Congo. The situation of the auditors even of a living speaker, Marlow says, is scarcely better, since what a story must convey through names and other words is not the fact but the "life-sensation" behind the fact "which makes its truth, its meaning – its subtle and penetrating essence." This is once more the halo around the moon, the meaning enveloping the tale. This meaning is as impossible to convey by way of the life-facts that may be named as the "dream-sensation" is able to be conveyed through a relation of the bare facts of the dream. Anyone knows this who has ever tried to tell another person his dream and has found how lame and flat, or how laughable, it sounds, since "no relation of a dream can convey the dream-sensation." According to Marlow's metaphor or proportional analogy: as the facts of a dream are to the "dream-sensation," so the facts of a life are to the "life-sensation." Conrad makes an absolute distinction between experience and the interpretation of written or spoken signs. The sensation may only be experienced directly and may by no means, oral or written, be communicated to another: "We live, as we dream, alone."

Nevertheless, Marlow tells his auditors, they have one direct or experimental access to the truth enveloping the story: "You fellows see more than I could then. You see me, whom you know." There is a double or even triple irony in this. To see the man who has had the experience is to have an avenue to the experience for which the man speaks, to which he bears witness. Marlow's auditors see more than he could then, that is, before his actual encounter with Kurtz. Ironically, the witness cannot bear witness for himself. He cannot see himself or cannot see through himself or by means of himself, in spite of, or in contradiction of, Conrad's (or Marlow's) assertion a few paragraphs later that work is "the chance to find yourself. Your own reality – for yourself, not for others – what no other man can ever know. They can only see the mere show, and never can tell what it really means" (29). Though each man can only experience his own reality, his own truth, the paradox involved here seems to run, he can only experience it through another or by means of another as witness to a truth deeper in, behind the other. Marlow's auditors can only learn indirectly, through Marlow, whom they see. They therefore know more than he did. Marlow could only learn through Kurtz, when he finally encountered him face to face. The reader of *Heart of Darkness* learns through the relation of the primary narrator, who learned through Marlow, who learned through Kurtz. This proliferating relay of witnesses, one behind another, each revealing another truth further in which turns out to be only another witness corresponds to the narrative form of *Heart of Darkness*. The novel is a sequence of episodes, each structured according to the model of appearances, signs, which are also obstacles or veils. Each veil must be lifted to reveal a truth behind which always turns out to be another episode, another witness, another veil to be lifted in its turn. Each such episode is a "fact dazzling, to be seen, like the foam on the depths of the sea, like a ripple on an unfathomable enigma" (43), the fact for example that though the cannibal Africans on Marlow's steamer were starving, they did not eat the white men. But behind each enigmatic fact is only another fact. The relay of witness behind witness behind witness, voice behind voice behind voice, each speaking in ventriloquism through the one next farther out, is a characteristic of the genre of the apocalypse. The book of Revelation, in the Bible, is the paradigmatic example in our tradition, though of course it is by no means the only example. In Revelation God speaks through Jesus, who speaks through a messenger angel, who speaks through John of Patmos, who speaks to us.

There is another reason beyond the necessities of revelation for this structure. The truth behind the last witness, behind Kurtz for example in *Heart of Darkness*, is, no one can doubt it, death, "the horror"; or, to put this another way, "death" is another name for what Kurtz names "the horror." No man can confront that truth face to face and survive. Death or the horror can only be experienced indirectly, by way of the face and voice of another. The relay of witnesses both reveals death and, luckily, hides it. As Marlow says, "the inner truth is hidden – luckily, luckily" (34). This is another regular feature of the genre of the apocalypse. The word apocalypse means "unveiling," "revelation," but what the apocalypse unveils is not the truth of the end of the world which it announces, but the act of unveiling. The unveiling unveils unveiling. It leaves its readers, auditors, witnesses, as far as ever from the always not quite yet of the imminent revelation – luckily. Marlow says it was not his own near-death on the way home down the river, "not my own extremity I remember best," but Kurtz's "extremity that I seem to have lived through." Then he adds,

> True, he had made that last stride, he had stepped over the edge, while I had been permitted to draw back my hesitating foot. And perhaps this is the whole difference; perhaps all the wisdom, and all truth, and all sincerity, are just compressed into that inappreciable moment of time in which we step over the threshold of the invisible. Perhaps! (72)

Marlow, like Orpheus returning without Eurydice from the land of the dead, comes back to civilization with nothing, nothing to witness to, nothing to reveal but the process of unveiling that makes up the whole of the narration of *Heart of Darkness*. Marlow did not go far enough into the darkness, but if he had, like Kurtz he could not have come back. All the reader gets is Marlow's report of Kurtz's last words, that and a description of the look on Kurtz's face: "It was as though a veil had been rent. I saw on that ivory face the expression of sombre pride, of ruthless power, of craven terror – of an intense and hopeless despair" (70–71).

I have said there is a triple irony in what Marlow says when he breaks his narration to address his auditors directly. If the first irony is the fact that the auditors see more than Marlow did because they see Marlow, whom they know, or as Conrad elsewhere puts this, "the onlookers see most of the game," the second irony is that we readers of the novel, if we happen to think at this moment of our own situation, realize that we must therefore see nothing. We see and can see no living witness, not the primary narrator, not Marlow, not Kurtz, not even Conrad himself, who is now only a voice from the dead for us. We see only the lifeless words on the page, the names Marlow, Kurtz, and so on, Conrad's name on the title page. By Marlow's own account that is not enough. Seeing only happens by direct experience, and no act of reading is direct experience. The book's claim to give the reader access to the dark truth behind appearance is withdrawn by the terms in which it is proffered. The third irony in this relay of ironies behind ironies is that Marlow's auditors of course do not see Marlow either. It is too dark. They hear only his disembodied voice. "It had become so pitch dark," says the narrator, "that we listeners could hardly see one another. For a long time already he, sitting apart, had been no more to us than a voice." Marlow's narrative does not seem to be spoken by a living incarnate witness, there before his auditors in the flesh. It is a "narrative that seemed to shape itself without human lips in the heavy night-air of the river." This voice can be linked to no individual speaker or writer as the ultimate source of its message, not to Marlow, nor to Kurtz, nor to the first narrator, nor even to Conrad himself. The voice is spoken by no one to no one. It always comes from another, from the other of any identifiable speaker or writer. It traverses all these voices as what speaks through them. It gives them authority and at the time dispossesses them, deprives them of authority, since they only speak with the delegated authority of another. As Marlow says of the voice of Kurtz and of all the other voices, they are what remain as a dying unanimous and anonymous drone or clang that exceeds any single identifiable voice and in the end is spoken by no one:

A voice. He was very little more than a voice. And I heard him – it – this voice – other voices – all of them were so little more than voices – and the memory of that time itself lingers around me, impalpable, like a dying vibration of one immense jabber, silly, atrocious, sordid, savage, or simply mean, without any kind of sense. Voices, voices – . . . . (49)

For the reader too *Heart of Darkness* lingers in the mind or memory chiefly as a cacophony of dissonant voices. It is as though the story were spoken or written not by an identifiable narrator but directly by the darkness itself, just as Kurtz's last words seem whispered by the circumambient dusky air when Marlow makes his visit to Kurtz's Intended, and just as Kurtz himself presents himself to Marlow as a voice, a voice which exceeds Kurtz and seems to speak from beyond him: "Kurtz discoursed. A voice! a voice! It rang deep to the very last. It survived his strength to hide in the magnificent folds of eloquence the barren darkness of his heart" (69). Kurtz has "the gift of expression, the bewildering, the illuminating, the most exalted and the most contempt-ible, the pulsating stream of light, or the deceitful flow from the heart of an impenetrable darkness" (48). Kurtz has intended to use his eloquence as a means of "wringing the heart of the wilderness," but "the wilderness had found him out early, and had taken on him a terrible vengeance for the fantastic invasion" (59). The direction of the flow of languages reverses. It flows from the darkness instead of toward it. Kurtz is "hollow at the core" (59), and so the wilderness can speak through him, use him so to speak as a ventriloquist's dummy through which its terrible messages may be broadcast to the world: "Exterminate all the brutes!" "the horror!" (51, 71). The speaker to is spoken through. Kurtz's disembodied voice, or the voice behind voice behind voice of the narrators, or that "roaring chorus of articulated, rapid, breathless utterance" (68) shouted by the natives on the bank, when Kurtz is taken on board the steamer – these are in the end no more direct a testimony of the truth than the words on the page as Conrad wrote them. The absence of a visible speaker of Marlow's words and the emphasis on the way Kurtz is a disembodied voice function as indirect expressions of the fact that *Heart of Darkness* itself is words without person, words which cannot be traced back to any single personality. This is once more confirmation of my claim that *Heart of Darkness* belongs to the genre of the apocalypse. This novel is an apocalyptic parable or a parabolic apocalypse. The apocalypse is after all a written not an oral genre, and it turns on the "Come" spoken or written always by someone other than the one who seems to utter or write it.[3]

A full exploration of the way *Heart of Darkness* is an apocalypse would need to be put under the multiple aegis of the converging figures of irony, antithesis, catachresis, synecdoche, aletheia, and prosopopoeia. Irony is a name for the pervasive tone of Marlow's narration, which undercuts as it affirms. Antithesis identifies the division of what is presented in the story in terms of seemingly firm oppositions which always ultimately break down. Catachresis is the proper name for a parabolic revelation of the darkness by means of visible figures that do not substitute for any possible literal expression of that darkness. Synecdoche is the name for the questionable relation of similarity between the visible sign, the skin of the surface, the foam on the sea, and what lies behind it, the pulsating heart of darkness, the black depths of the sea. Unveiling or *aletheia* labels that endless process of apocalyptic revelation which never quite comes off. The revelation is always future. We must always go on watching and waiting for it, as the primary narrator remains wakeful, on the watch for the decisive clue in Marlow's narration. Personification, finally, is a name for the consistent presentation of the darkness in terms of the trope prosopopoeia. The reader encounters the darkness always as some kind of living creature with a heart, ultimately as a woman who unmans all those male questors who try to dominate her. This pervasive personification is most dramatically embodied in the native woman, Kurtz's mistress: "the immense wilderness, the colossal body of the fecund and mysterious life seemed to look at her, pensive, as though it had been looking at the image of its own tenebrous and passionate soul" (62).

Heart of Darkness is perhaps most explicitly apocalyptic in announcing the end, the end of Western civilization, or of Western imperialism, the reversal of idealism into savagery. As is always the case with apocalypses, the end is announced as something always imminent, never quite yet. Apocalypse is never now. The novel sets women, who are out of it, against men, who can live with the facts and have a belief to protect them against the darkness. Men can breathe dead hippo and not be contaminated. Male practicality and idealism reverse, however. They turn into their opposites because they are hollow at the core. They are vulnerable to the horror. They *are* the horror. The idealistic suppression of savage customs becomes, "Exterminate all the brutes!" Male idealism is the same thing as the extermination of the brutes. The suppression of savage customs is the extermination of the brutes. This is not just wordplay but actual fact, as the history of the white man's conquest of the world has abundantly demonstrated. This conquest means the end of the brutes, but it means also, in Conrad's view of history, the end of Western civilization, with its ideals of progress, enlightenment, and reason, its goal of carrying the torch of civilization into the wilderness and wringing the heart of the darkness. Or it is the imminence of that end which has never quite come as long as there is someone to speak or write of it.

I claim to have demonstrated that *Heart of Darkness* is not only parabolic but also apocalyptic. It fits that strange genre of the apocalyptic text, the sort of text that promises an ultimate revelation without giving it, and says always "Come" and "Wait." But there is an extra twist given to the paradigmatic form of the apocalypse in *Heart of Darkness*. The *Aufklärung* or enlightenment in this case is of the fact that the darkness can never be enlightened. The darkness enters into every gesture of enlightenment to enfeeble it, to hollow it out, to corrupt it and thereby to turn its reason into unreason, its pretense of shedding light into more darkness. Marlow as narrator is in complicity with this reversal in the act of identifying it in others. He too claims, like the characteristic writer of an apocalypse, to know something no one else knows and to be qualified on that basis to judge and enlighten them. "I found myself back in the sepulchral city," says Marlow of his return from the Congo,

> resenting the sight of people hurrying through the streets to filch a little money from each other, to devour their infamous cookery, to gulp their unwholesome beer, to dream their insignificant and silly dreams. They trespassed upon my thoughts. They were intruders whose knowledge of life was to me an irritating pretence because I felt so sure they could not possibly know the things I knew. (72)

The consistent tone of Marlow's narration is ironical. Irony is truth telling or a means of truth telling, of unveiling. At the same time it is a defense against the truth. This doubleness makes it, though it seems so coolly reasonable, another mode of unreason, the unreason of a fundamental undecidability. If irony is a defense, it is also inadvertently a means of participation. Though Marlow says, "I have a voice too, and for good or evil mine is the speech that cannot be silenced" (37), as though his speaking were a cloak against the darkness, he too, in speaking ironically, becomes, like Kurtz, one of those speaking tubes or relay stations through whom the darkness speaks. As theorists of irony from Friedrich Schlegel and Søren Kierkegaard to Paul de Man have argued, irony is the one trope that cannot be mastered or used as an instrument of mastery. Any ironic statement is essentially indeterminate or undecidable in meaning. The man who attempts to say one thing while clearly meaning another ends up by saying the first thing too, in spite of himself. One irony leads to another. The ironies proliferate into a great crowd of little conflicting ironies. It is impossible to know in just what tone of voice one should read one of Marlow's sardonic ironies. Each is uttered simultaneously in innumerable conflicting tones going all the way from the lightest and most comical to the darkest, most somber and tragic. It is impossible to decide exactly which quality of voice should be allowed to predominate over the others. Try reading a given passage aloud and you will see this. Marlow's description of the clamor of native voices on the shore or of the murmur of all those voices he remembers from that time in his life also functions as an appropriate displaced description of the indeterminations of tone and meaning in his own discourse. Marlow's irony makes his speech in its own way another version of that multiple cacophonous and deceitful voice flowing from the heart of darkness, "a complaining clamour, modulated in savage discords," or a "tumultuous and mournful uproar," another version of that "one immense jabber, silly, atrocious, sordid, savage, or simply mean, without any kind of sense," not a voice, but "voices" (40, 49). In this inextricable tangle of voices and voices speaking within voices, Marlow's narration fulfills, no doubt without deliberate intent on Conrad's part, one of the primary laws of the genre of the apocalypse.

The final fold in this folding in of complicities in these ambiguous acts of unveiling is my own complicity as demystifying commentator. Behind or before Marlow is Conrad, and before or behind him stands the reader or critic. My commentary unveils a lack of decisive unveiling in *Heart of Darkness*. I have attempted to perform an act of generic classification, with all the covert violence and unreason of that act, since no work is wholly commensurate with the boundaries of any genre. By unveiling the lack of unveiling in *Heart of Darkness*, I have become another witness in my turn, as much guilty as any other in the line of witnesses of covering over while claiming to illuminate. My *Aufklärung* too has been of the continuing impenetrability of Conrad's *Heart of Darkness*.

Notes

1. Karl Marx, "Manifesto of the Communist Party," in *The Marx-Engels Reader*, 2d ed., Robert C. Tucker, ed. (New York, 1978), p. 476.
2. Joseph Conrad, *Heart of Darkness*, Robert Kimbrough, ed. (New York, 1963), p. 7. Further references will be indicated by page numbers from this edition, which includes variants from the manuscript.
3. See Jacques Derrida, "D'un ton apocalyptique adopté naguère en philosophie," in *Les Fins de l'homme*, Philippe Lacoue-Labarthe and Jean-Luc Nancy, eds (Paris, 1981), pp. 445–79, especially pp. 468ff. The essay has recently been translated by John P. Leavey, Jr., and published in the 1982 number of *Semeia* (pp. 62–97).

12

Topography and tropography in Thomas Hardy's "In Front of the Landscape"

"In Front of the Landscape"

Plunging and labouring on in a tide of visions,
    Dolorous and dear,
Forward I pushed my way as amid waste waters
    Stretching around,
Through whose eddies there glimmered the customed landscape
    Yonder and near

Blotted to feeble mist. And the coomb and the upland
    Coppice-crowned,
Ancient chalk-pit, milestone, rills in the grass-flat
    Stroked by the light,
Seemed but a ghost-like gauze, and no substantial
    Meadow or mound.

What were the infinite spectacles featuring foremost
    Under my sight,
Hindering me to discern my paced advancement
    Lengthening to miles;
What were the re-creations killing the daytime
    As by the night?

O they were speechful faces, gazing insistent,
    Some as with smiles,
Some as with slow-born tears that brinily trundled
    Over the wrecked
Cheeks that were fair in their flush-time, ash now with anguish,
    Harrowed by wiles.

Yes, I could see them, feel them, hear them, address them –
    Halo-bedecked –
And, alas, onwards, shaken by fierce unreason,
    Rigid in hate,
Smitten by years-long wryness born of misprision,
    Dreaded, suspect.

Then there would breast me shining sights, sweet seasons
    Further in date;
Instruments of strings with the tenderest passion
    Vibrant, beside
Lamps long extinguished, robes, cheeks, eyes with the earth's crust
    Now corporate.

Also there rose a headland of hoary aspect
    Gnawed by the tide,
Frilled by the nimb of the morning as two friends stood there
    Guilelessly glad –
Wherefore they knew not – touched by the fringe of an ecstasy
    Scantly descried.

Later images too did the day unfurl me,
    Shadowed and sad,
Clay cadavers of those who had shared in the dramas,
    Laid now at ease,
Passions all spent, chiefest the one of the broad brow
    Sepulture-clad.

So did beset me scenes, miscalled of the bygone,
    Over the leaze,
Past the clump, and down to where lay the beheld ones;
    – Yea, as the rhyme
Sung by the sea-swell, so in their pleading dumbness
    Captured me these.

For, their lost revisiting manifestations
    In their live time
Much had I slighted, caring not for their purport,
    Seeing behind
Things more coveted, reckoned the better worth calling
    Sweet, sad, sublime.

Thus do they now show hourly before the intenser
    Stare of the mind
As they were ghosts avenging their slights by my bypast
    Body-borne eyes,
Show, too, with fuller translation than rested upon them
    As living kind.

Hence wag the tongues of the passing people, saying
    In their surmise,
'Ah – whose is this dull form that perambulates, seeing nought
    Round him that looms
Whithersoever his footsteps turn in his farings,
    Save a few tombs?'[1]

Take, as an example, Thomas Hardy's poem "In Front of the Landscape." This is put as the opening text in *Satires of Circumstance* (1914). What is its identity as a text? If this identity arises from relations to previous and later texts and readers, among the most important of these relations are those to other poems by Hardy, for example to the other poems in Hardy's volume of 1914, or, more broadly, to all the poems taken together in *The Complete Poems of Thomas Hardy*. To call "In Front of the Landscape" an example of Hardy's poetry illustrates the falsification involved in assuming that Thomas Hardy is a single person or that his poems taken together form a coherent whole. The differences of "In Front of the Landscape" from any other poem by Hardy are more important, it may be, than any similarities. The poem tells the reader things about "Hardy" she or he can learn only from this poem. If "Wessex Heights" dramatizes the relation the speaker has to the swarm of ghosts from the past when he sees them from the relative detachment of the hilltop, "In Front of the Landscape" describes what it is like, for Hardy, down there in the lowlands.

What is "in front of the landscape" for the speaker of this poem is a great "tide of visions," memories of this or that person from his past. This so overwhelms and drowns him with its immediacy that it almost hides the scene behind. What should be there in the present is rendered ghostlike and insubstantial, as though the landscape were the mist and the mist the substantial reality. Scenes, objects, and persons from the past, "miscalled of the bygone," have more presence and solidity than anything present in the present. It is the presence and force of a great flood ramping over the land and sinking it:

> Plunging and labouring on in a tide of visions,
>   Dolorous and dear,
> Forward I pushed my way as amid waste waters
>   Stretching around,
> Through whose eddies there glimmered the customed landscape
>   Yonder and near.
>
> Blotted to feeble mist. And the coomb and the upland
>   Coppice-crowned,
> Ancient chalk-pit, milestone, rills in the grass-flat
>   Stroked by the light,
> Seemed but a ghost-like gauze, and no substantial
>   Meadow or mound.

"In Front of the Landscape" is one of Hardy's most grandly rhythmical poems. It is unusually open in its expression of emotion. For once the meter does not seem an arbitrary framework into which certain material is pushed, trimmed to shape. The dactylic meter fits the thematic mood and the organizing figure, affirming that memories are like the inundating waters of great sea-swells, wave after wave. The reader will feel the swing and rise of the lines. This rhythm is punctuated by the rhyming of the last line of each stanza with the second line. Each stanza is like a wave finally breaking and crashing. The alternate long and short lines within each stanza give the rhythm of waters moving across a shallow tideland, building up in a slow mounting like a long indrawing breath: "Plunging and labouring on in a tide of visions," and then more rapidly dropping as it is exhaled: "Dolorous and dear." Within the complex wave movement of each stanza a new wave is preparing in the end-word of each fourth line: "Stretching around," "Stroked by the light." These have no rhymes within their own stanzas but hang there in the air, so to speak. They are responded to finally by the first and last short lines in the next stanza. The poem proceeds by way of a braided effect, in a complex rhythm of one wave that completes itself but always contains within itself the doubling or crossing rhythm of the next preparing wave. This interweaving is reinforced by frequent grammatical enjambment from one stanza to the next, as in the two stanzas quoted above. In the last stanza of all, the last two short lines rhyme: "Round him that looms"; "Save a few tombs?"

I have said that the poem is unusual among Hardy's in its rhythmical majesty. It is like some grand organ fugue. The poem is unusual also in its match of rhythm and theme, its frank yielding to the fallacy of imitative form. The rhythm is not only obviously meant to mime the movement of tidal waves but is also meant to mime what the figure mimes: the inundation of the poet by waves of visionary memories. There is no actual water named anywhere in the poem, only the figure of water introduced in the initial phrase "tide of visions." This is then made explicitly figurative in a simile later in the poem: – "Yea, *as* the rhyme / Sung by the sea-swell, so in their pleading dumbness / Captured me these" (my italics). To put this another way, the words of the poem are themselves the incarnation of the tide of visions. The poem is a repetition once more, after the fact (since the poem is in the past tense), of what was itself a repetition of those earlier scenes. The figure of the waves is an element in a series projected backward from the present attempt to give experience form in poetry towards the past moment when the poet took his walk. It is as true to say that the figure of the waves names the musical, rhythmical, rhyming form of the poem itself as that it names the form the experience intrinsically had when it occurred.

In Hardy's poems, and in this one more obviously than in many others, there is always some discrepancy between the rigid stanzaic pattern and the material put into it. Once the pattern is set up it goes on repeating itself from stanza to stanza, coercing whatever it is Hardy wants to say into taking that shape. The past experience is repeated in a new form that has its own intrinsic power of replication. This occurs, for example, whenever the poem is reread and its form takes shape once more in the mind of the reader. What "In Front of the Landscape" communicates is not the "original original" experiences to which it refers and not the repetitions of those in the "original" experience when the speaker took his walk and confronted his tide of visions. What the poem communicates is itself, its own form. The figure of the waves names that form.

The signs of this "present" activity, the craftsmanship involved in the writing of the poem, include the artifice of the difficult stanza pattern and rhyme scheme. These are evidence of present choice and deliberate work to make the words fit. Another sign of poetic work, often present in Hardy's poetry, is a slowing down of the forward rhythmic movement of the poem in the counter-movement of a careful choice, one by one, so it seems, of words or phrases. Many of these seem slightly odd, unexpected, or out of place. The reader, if he is a teacher, may have a subliminal desire to write "dic." in the margin, until he has thought more about the lines and comes to see how right the word or phrase is: "brinily trundled"; "harrowed"; "unreason"; "wryness"; "misprision"; "corporate"; "frilled"; "scantly"; "perambulates." It is a feature of Hardy's poetry that he gets away with or even admirably exploits words which hardly any other poet would dare use at all. Often these words are harsh monosyllables slowing the line down almost to a halt, as word follows word: "Cheeks that were fair in their flush-time, ash now with anguish." Or the words may be polysyllables full of clogged consonants, technical or archaic words, words not in everyone's vocabulary, like "brinily" or "misprision." This slowing-down by word choice is a counterpointed rhythm fighting against the swelling forward wave-like movement. The reader can see the poet feeling his way along the line, choosing word after word carefully, after much thought. He chooses each word not only for its more exact correspondence to the experience in the past he wants the poem to duplicate but for its creation of an integument of signs, there on the page. These will have a coercive power over the reader, as the notation of musical sounds in a score, when played aloud again, will, to borrow a formulation from *Tess of the d'Urbervilles*, "lead" the listener "through sequences of emotion, which [the composer] alone had felt at first" (chapter 13). It is impossible to tell whether these sequences of emotion were intrinsic to the original experience which the poem records or whether they are created by the formal properties of the poem as Hardy has happened to compose it. The reader has access only to the poem. He cannot compare it with anything which it might seem to copy.

The great tide of visions of which the poem speaks is made of scenes, such as the "headland of hoary aspect / Gnawed by the tide," or of objects – for example, "Instruments of strings with the tenderest passion / Vibrant, beside / Lamps long extinguished, robes" – but most of all of persons with whom the poet had once been associated over the various times of his past life. These are, to borrow some fine phrases from "Wessex Heights," "shadows of beings who fellowed with myself of earlier days" (*Complete Poems*, 319). The sequence from musical instruments to lamps and robes continues with the fine irony of "cheeks, eyes with the earth's crust / Now corporate." The poet detaches parts of the bodies of those he has known and lists them as vanished objects like the rest. He thinks of them now as parts of the vast corporate body of the earth. Of that body we will all one day be members. These persons are now apparently all buried in the graveyard which is the goal of his long walk through the Wessex countryside:

> So did beset me scenes, miscalled of the bygone,
> Over the leaze,
> Past the clump, and down to where lay the beheld ones.

It has been suggested by Hermann Lea that the scene of the poem is "Came Down near Culliver Tree," about three miles south of Dorchester. J. O. Bailey has observed that there is a chalk-pit nearby to match the one mentioned in stanza 2 of the poem, as well as many burial tumuli "scattered in all directions from this point."[2] The latter may be referred to in the last lines. Those lines imagine passers-by wondering who this dull perambulating form is who walks where there is nothing to see "save a few tombs." But the phrase "where lay the beheld ones" must refer to a modern burial ground, perhaps the one southward in Weymouth, perhaps the ones northward in Dorchester or in Stinsford. Though all these old associates are now dead, this does not keep them from appearing before the poet as "infinite spectacles," "speechful faces, gazing insistent." These walking ghosts have so much solidity that they are "hindering [him] to discern [his] paced advancement / Lengthening to miles." The ghosts of the old associates apparently do not speak (though in one place he says he can "hear them"), but they have "speechful faces." Their "dumb pleading" is a double reproach. It is a reproach to the speaker for not having appreciated them sufficiently when they were alive and it is a reproach for his having in any case later on betrayed them.

> For, their lost revisiting manifestations
> In their live time
> Much had I slighted, caring not for their purport,
> Seeing behind
> Things more coveted, reckoned the better worth calling
> Sweet, sad, sublime.

It appears to be a law, in this poem, if not necessarily always in Hardy, that what you have in the present as an actual physical presence you do not really have. The fact that something is there and that you possess it makes it seem worthless. It also makes it impossible to understand its "purport." The mind and feelings always look beyond or behind what is possessed now to what is not possessed. Those always seem more desirable, more valuable. What you have you do not have. You do not have it in the sense of neither understanding it nor valuing it. What you have and understand in the sense of "reckoning" it as this or as that, "sweet," "sad," or "sublime," you do not have. Only later on, when they come back "before the intenser stare of the mind," intenser, that is, than the look of his "bypast / Body-borne eyes," intenser than any real stare at what is physically present, only when they come back as avenging ghosts, are they comprehended. Only then are they read, interpreted, deciphered, "with fuller translation than rested upon them / As living kind."

The irony of "In Front of the Landscape" is that the speaker is recalling a walk in which he committed again the crime he deplores. The real landscape is scarcely seen by the walker and not valued by him. His eyes, his attention, his feelings are all intensely focused on what in this case is not behind what is immediately present but in front of it, between him and it. He sees only what is not any longer the desired and as yet unpossessed future but the betrayed past. In either case, however, in either desire or regret, the detachment from what is actually there is almost total. It is as though Hardy goes through the world always out of phase. He dwells in anticipation or in memory. He never lives in other than a false appearance of the present. He always lags behind in his efforts to "translate" the people and places he encounters. This anachronism can never by any means be put back into harmonious chiming. There is always a delay before the feedback, and the feedback always comes too late. While he is occupied in "reckoning" at last the worth and purport of something he once had undervalued, misread, he is already confronting a new scene which his preoccupation is leading him once more to misvalue and misread. He is thereby storing up for himself yet further times in the future when he will suffer again the pangs of retrospective understanding. It will then once more be too late. The effort of retrospection will then once more put swarms of ghosts like an almost impenetrable fog or like an obliterating flood between him and the real scene, the real present. That present he will once more misvalue.

On the one hand, then, the ghosts reproach him for not having understood and valued them when they were alive and bodily present, before his body-borne eyes. On the other hand, they also reproach him for having in any case betrayed them thereafter. The lines stating this are central to the poem. Their difficulty calls for commentary:

O they were speechful faces, gazing insistent,
  Some as with smiles,
Some as with slow-born tears that brinily trundled
  Over the wrecked
Cheeks that were fair in their flush-time, ash now with anguish.
  Harrowed by wiles.

The faces of the phantoms pass him in a beseeching procession, some "as with" smiles, some "as with" tears. The repeated "as with" is odd. Does the poet mean that the ghosts do not really either smile or cry? Or does he mean that he could not quite make out their features? Or does he mean, as perhaps is most probable, that the speech of these "speechful faces, gazing insistent" is the expressiveness of their features, so that it is as if they were speaking to him with their smiles or with their tears? The puzzle is a good example of the grammatical, syntactical, and lexical difficulty of Hardy's poetry. Overwhelmed by the great flood of their abundance, the reader hurries on from poem to poem, moving towards those generalizations which will allow him to encompass the whole. If he is at all a "good" reader, he will nevertheless constantly be slowed down or even stopped by local difficulties. These must be brooded on and meditated over. They must be teased for their just meaning before the reader can proceed even to the next lines, much less to all the other poems.

If the faces of the ghosts are "speechful" because they speak to him "as with" their smiles or their tears, then when the poet says in the next stanza that he can "hear them" he may mean that he reads their legible features as though they were audible sounds, not that the ghosts actually speak aloud. The lines of the smiles and the wrinkles that have been carved into the cheeks of the ghosts by their suffering, "harrowed" by "wiles" in the literal sense of being trenched out as well as in the figurative sense of "worn by fear or anxiety," are deciphered as speaking signs. They are interpreted as "insistent" messages of reproach, "pleading dumbness," beseeching demands for response from the poet whom they haunt. The pervasive image of the waves of waste waters is obliquely present in the image of the tears that "brinily trundled / Over the wrecked / Cheeks." It is as though the faces were battered ships aground in a storm dripping with salt water cascading down from the last wave which has just washed over them. If the poet is overwhelmed by a tide of visions, each separate ghost too swims bathed in the universal medium of the total simultaneous presence of all the scenes, places, objects, and persons from the poet's past. There is a congruence between the form of a book of Hardy's poems, or the whole volume of them taken together in *The Complete Poems*, and the poet's mind as he presents it in "Wessex Heights," or, in a different way, in "In Front of the Landscape." Both book and mind are capacious spaces filled pell-mell in profusion with an incoherent multitude of persons, scenes, and actions all going on at once side by side, without touching and without connection. Each is a detached fragment of a life story missing its context before and after.

If the stanza quoted above contains puzzles which slow down the reader or ought to slow him down, this is even more true of the following stanza:

> Yes, I could see them, feel them, hear them, address them –
> Halo-bedecked –
> And, alas, onwards, shaken by fierce unreason,
> Rigid in hate,
> Smitten by years–long wryness born of misprision,
> Dreaded, suspect.

If the reader can guess what the poet means by saying he can "hear" the ghosts when they do not speak, what is he to make of the claim that the poet can also "feel" the ghosts? A ghost by definition is impalpable, and yet somehow the word seems right for the coercive intimacy, like an urgent touch, with which the phantoms appeal to him and "capture" him in their "pleading dumbness." A formulation by Jacques Derrida in "Télépathie"[3] is strangely apposite here. It is as though, by a species of telepathy, Derrida has written his sentence with this line of Hardy (which he has never read) in mind. He seems to have had a premonition of a critic's need, at some point in the future, to account for the strange presence of "feel them" in Hardy's sequence. This is an example of the theme of Derrida's essay, which I have elsewhere discussed more fully in its relation to Hardy's poetry.[4] "Before 'seeing' or 'hearing'", says Derrida, "touch, put your fingertips there, or [it seems] that seeing and hearing amount to touching at a distance – a very old idea, but it requires the archaic to deal with the archaic."[5]

The poet can see the ghosts, hear them in their pleading dumbness. He can even (therefore) feel them, as though seeing and hearing were touching at a distance, in this case a distance of years, or as if he were doubting Thomas palping the wound in the side of the resurrected "halo-bedecked" Christ, or as if the ghosts were putting an importunate insistent hand on his arm. He can also "address them," presumably to plead with them in justification of his past actions towards them. The four lines which conclude the stanza are fundamentally ambiguous. It is impossible to be sure whether the "onwards" and all that grammatically hangs from it – the series of four participles, "shaken," "smitten," "dreaded," "suspect" – apply to the ghosts, as is most probably the case, or, as would be an equally possible reading of the syntax, whether the "onwards" applies to the poet, the "I" which is the "subject" of the sentence:

> And, alas, onwards, shaken by fierce unreason,
> Rigid in hate,
> Smitten by years-long wryness born of misprision,
> Dreaded, suspect.

This can either mean that the procession of ghosts passes majestically and silently on, unappeased by the poet's appeal, unforgiving, or that the poet himself moves "onwards," as in fact he does, shaken, smitten, and twisted to wryness by the ghosts' misunderstanding of him. Even though the former is more likely, the latter remains hovering as a possibility for the reader (for this reader at least) as he tries to identify the reference of "shaken," "smitten," "dreaded," "suspect." Even if a decision is made about that – if the reader decides, for example, that it must be the ghosts who move onwards – the participles in all their violence remain undecidable in meaning. They oscillate between active and passive possibilities. Are the ghosts "rigid in hate" because they are shaken by the "fierce unreason" of the speaker who has taken them wrongly, twisted them to a "years-long wryness" by his "misprision" of them, or is their refusal to accept the explanation offered by the speaker's address to them a case of "fierce unreason," a taking wrongly of the speaker's treatment of them? It cannot be decided which. The power of the lines is the way they vibrate, affirming both possibilities, and neither unequivocally. Are the ghosts "dreaded" by the speaker, "suspected" by him, because they are so fiercely unreasonable and so bent on taking revenge? They would then take revenge by continuously haunting him, showing "hourly before the intenser stare of the mind / As they were ghosts avenging their slights by my bypast / Body-borne eyes." Or is it the speaker who is "dreaded" and "suspect" in the sense that the ghosts abhor him without reason, unreasonably blaming him for having taken them wrongly?

There is no way to tell, nor is there any way to tell whether the "misprision" in question is the mistaking of the ghosts by the speaker, who took them wrongly in the sense of misprizing them when they were alive, "caring not for their purport," or whether the ghosts are twisted into wryness by *their* misprision of the speaker's attitude towards them. "Misprision" – the word means etymologically "taking wrongly," from late Latin *minusprehendere*, from Latin, *minus*, less, plus *praehendere*, to take. "Misprision" has lately been restored by Harold Bloom to its now archaic meaning of "mistake" by his use of it to name the misinterpretation of the writings of an earlier writer by a later writer who is influenced by that earlier writer. Hardy too uses the word here to name a misreading of one person by another. Misprision is a misinterpretation of the signs presented by the face and features of others, whether fair in their flush-time or marked by lines of care and smitten to wryness. Misprision also has an overtone of "misprizing." Its strict modern meaning is a double one. It means either the misconduct or neglect of duty of a public official, for example in wrongfully appropriating public funds, or "misprision of felony (or treason)." The latter is a term used in common law to define the offence of concealing knowledge of a felony or treason by one who has not participated in it. Both these meanings resonate in Hardy's line. The ghosts may be smitten to wryness by having been misappropriated by the speaker or by others, taken wrongly, or there may be some crime somewhere, some treasonous betrayal, either on their part or on the part of the speaker, which they have wrongly concealed or which they have suffered for because it has been wrongly concealed by others. In any case, there is a lot of guilt around somewhere. It is a guilt born of betrayal of trust. Both the ghosts and the speaker are suffering intensely for it. Exactly what betrayal is in question for each of the ghosts the reader is not told. He knows only that they were once fair and happy and that the speaker "fellowed" with them. Later they were betrayed by him or by others, or thought they were betrayed. They suffered intensely for this, so intensely as to be left, even after death, with a fierce, implacable, unreasonable desire for revenge. No reason is given for these betrayals or for these misprisions. They just happened. By the time the speaker is able to appreciate the "purport" of these persons now dead and enghosted, it is too late. Not only are they dead. They are wholly unforgiving, rigid in hate of him.

The phrase "fierce unreason" may be given a wide application as an accurate description of many aspects of Hardy's poetry. "Unreason": the word suggests an absence of *logos* in all its senses of reason, meaning, word, mind, measure, and ground. The word "fierce" is as important as the word "unreason." It names the psychic and spiritual violence of Hardy's experience and of the experience the poems inflict on the reader. The relation between one person and another in Hardy's poetry, or in this poem at least, is the fierce unreason of a multiple betrayal. This betrayal has no reason and leads to a hatred exceeding reason. The poet himself is the victim of a fierce unreason which makes it impossible for him to remain of one mind long enough to be a single continuous self. At the same time he is unable to escape enough from his earlier selves to avoid being unreasonably persecuted by ghosts remaining in his mind from the acts of those earlier selves. He can be neither continuous with those earlier selves nor discontinuous enough to free himself from himself, and so he suffers from the fierce unreason of this anomaly. What

David Hume describes objectively enough as a lack of substance and consistency in the self,[6] Hardy experiences as intense suffering born of the co-presence of continuity and discontinuity. He has the continuity of an elephant's memory and the discontinuity of a butterfly's inability to remain the same self for longer than the duration of a brief episode in his life. This inability has no reason or is given no reason. It is an unreasonable fact.

Fierce unreason defines well enough, finally, the local lack of reason, in the sense of single determinate meaning, in the verbal texture of Hardy's verse, however straightforward in meaning that verse first appears to be. The unreadable oscillations in meaning I have identified are born of syntactical, grammatical, and lexical ambiguities. They impose on the reader a sense of fierce unreason, the lack of a firm ground in a single meaning, as he struggles to make univocal sense of what Hardy is saying. This local ambiguity is matched on a larger scale by the "unreason" of the poems' inconsistency with one another, if Hardy is right (and he is) in what he repeatedly says, in his prefaces to individual books of poems, of his poems' lack of a coherent philosophy. They cannot be made to hang together, either individually or collectively. The poems too are cases of 'fierce unreason." They respond to the reader's search for a comprehensive logic with a violence of repudiation undoing all his attempts to "translate" them into an order satisfying to the mind.

Hardy's use of the word "translate" must be scrutinized more carefully as a translation to the last step in my interpretation of "In Front of the Landscape." The word appears in the next to last line of the next to last stanza. The phantoms who haunt the intenser stare of the poet's mind, almost blotting out the real landscape behind, now "Show, too, with fuller translation than rested upon them / As living kind." This leads to the last stanza, with its altered rhyme scheme of closure and with its shift to an imagining of what the speaker must look like to others who see him on such walks and of what they must say of him:

> Hence wag the tongues of the passing people, saying
>   In their surmise,
> 'Ah – whose is this dull form that perambulates, seeing nought
>   Round him that looms
> Whithersoever his footsteps turn in his farings,
>   Save a few tombs?'

"In Front of the Landscape" seems in many ways compatible with "Wessex Heights." Both are poems in which the speaker confronts swarms of ghosts from his past. He confronts also his own past selves and experiences the pain of being neither wholly different nor wholly the same, neither wholly continuous nor wholly discontinuous with himself.

In "Wessex Heights," however, the act of physically climbing the heights gives the speaker at least a partial detachment from those past selves and those past relationships. He knows "some liberty" (*Complete Poems*, 320), a liberty like that of being not yet born or already dead and a revisiting ghost haunting others. "In Front of the Landscape," on the contrary, offers no hope of liberation. The poet remains in the lowlands, haunted by implacable avenging phantoms. Neither the poet nor the poem gets anywhere, in spite of the poet's movement across the landscape. They get nowhere but perhaps to a better understanding of where he is. The poet remains in the same situation at the end as he was in the beginning. The poem can end only with a shift to the different perspective of the imagined watchers of his "perambulations." The poem does not record a movement towards liberation. It iterates rather the fact that no liberty is possible.

Something has happened in the poem, however. The poem itself has got written. This act is the covert dramatic action of the poem. This action is a shift from passive suffering to verbal praxis. This is the linguistic moment in this poem. The shift from "experience" to "language" is covertly signalled in the shift from the past to the present tense at the beginning of the penultimate stanza: "Thus do they now show hourly before the intenser / Stare of the mind." The stanzas until then are in the past tense. They record something which occurred to the poet at some time in the past, something he suffered. With the change to the present tense pathos becomes action. This action is within the poem. It is performed by its words. What takes place takes place within the space of the poem. It is translated there, carried over into the pages of a book.

This "translation" is a successful defense. It is an impressive act of will to power over the ghosts. In the poem the ghosts are no longer intense presences which can almost palpably be felt. They are now no more than words. Though, for Hardy, ghosts in their literal form have power to hurt even more than sticks and stones, when they are turned into words, "translated," they will never hurt him. One motivation driving Hardy to write so many poems and to derive such satisfaction from it[7] is that the writing functions as a successful "trope of defence" against all those reproaching and beseeching phantoms from his past. Writing is a "trope" in the literal sense of turning, displacement, or transformation. "Translation" – the word translates *translatio*. The latter is a traditional rhetorical term in Latin, for example in Quintilian's *Institutio Oratorio*. *Translatio* translates the Greek *metaphora*, "metaphor." The linguistic moment in this poem is a triple act of translation: the translation of the phantoms the poet's mind beholds into words; the translation of the phantoms into metaphor, the metaphor of the tide of visions which underlies and pervades all this poem; the translation or transportation of the phantoms into the formal order of the poem. They are transposed not just into words, but into words architecturally or musically ordered. Within this order all those ghosts and the scenes, objects, episodes which are their contexts can exist side by side, just as all Hardy's poems, in spite of their discord, exist side by side in Hardy's *Complete Poems*. This complex act of translation is not, as it first seems, a seeing clearly for the first time these people and their true "purport." It is a metaphorical transformation. It is a misreading or distortion, as all translation, for example from one language to another, necessarily is. In the act of defending himself from the reproach the phantoms make that they have not been seen clearly, that they have been misprized, Hardy commits again the crime of misprision from which he would defend himself. He commits it blatantly, out there in the open, on the page, where all who read may see. Therefore another poem in self-defense must be written. This commits the crime once more, and so yet another is necessary, *ad infinitum*. The poet never has a chance to catch up with his past transgressions. He cannot compensate for them, do justice to his past at last, pay off his debt to himself and to others, and wipe his slate clean. The act of compensation, the plea of innocence in response to the phantoms' recriminations, always turns into another act of self-incrimination.

This failure is also the triumph of the poetry. It is only by this constantly repeated act of misprision that Hardy can successfully defend himself and maintain his integrity. It is the integrity not of a self but of a grammatical function producing ultimately that disharmony of *The Complete Poems* Hardy so insists on in the prefaces. The individual acts of defense, turning perception into language, are more important than their hanging together.

It would appear at first that "In Front of the Landscape" depends on the experience of disjunction between the actual landscape and those mental visions which intervene for the speaker between his eye and the scene, blotting it to feeble mist. The poem, it seems, exemplifies that law of Hardy's experience which says you never have or prize what "is" in the present, but always look before and after, and pine for what is not. The fundamental categories of the poem, it seems, are perception and interpersonal relations. The poem has to do with seeing and not seeing, and with struggles for power, by way of appropriation and misappropriation, between one person and another. The speaker cannot see the landscape because its place has been taken by the phantoms who exercise a coercive power over him, captivating him: "so in their pleading dumbness / Captured me these."

Is this in fact the case? If the full implications of the word "translation" are accepted, the word "misprision" is tipped toward that secondary meaning it can have of mistaking or misreading rather than of simply misappropriating. The speaker's original misprision of the phantoms was a mistaken interpretation of the signs they displayed, their "purport," what they said and what their features showed as legible tokens. The activity the poem first records as having taken place in the past and then, with the shift to the present tense, enacts within itself, is also an activity of "translation." This means it is mistranslation or misreading, a doing violence to the signs he sees. The signs now misread, however, are not merely, or not originally, those internal ones of memory. They are the tombs scattered around the landscape, perhaps initially the many prehistoric tumuli which dot the region where Hardy was walking, but also the graves of the dead friends, lovers, and relatives whose ghosts Hardy sees. He looks across the scene and then walks "Over the leaze, / Past the clump, and down to where lay the beheld ones." The passers-by who see him out walking know that he "sees nought," wherever his footsteps take him, "save a few tombs." The poet transforms those tombs. He translates them into the tide of visions the poem so eloquently names. Far from being detached from the landscape, the speaker's linguistic activity in the poem, like the past crimes of misprision he deplores, is based on taking features of the visual scene, in this case not faces but tombs, as signs, not merely as perceptual objects, as they are for the passers-by. These signs are then translated. This activity transforms the neutral notation of topographical description into what might be called a tropography. This tropography is the mapping of an act of figuration which is both Hardy's crime and his defense.

The poem, words on the page, is the monument or tomb of this act. The linguistic act of "translation" is not a figure for perception. Perception is translation. This means the writing of the poem is not the record of the appearance of the ghosts. The writing is the act which raises the ghosts by turning dead signs into beseeching phantoms. The poem in turn, as the remnant of its writing, becomes dead letters once more waiting for some reader to "translate" it again and to raise again the ghosts which inhabit it. In doing so the reader commits in his turn the crime of misprision which the poem both regrets and commits. In this case too, the linguistic moment has a momentum which leads to its repetition time after time, without hope of ever laying the ghosts once and for all.

Once again, as in passages by Wordsworth I have elsewhere discussed, but also in passages in Hegel and in Baudelaire,[8] among many others, in a tradition already present in the Greek pun on *soma/sema* (body/sign), the relation between a dead body and the mound or tomb above it, or between the corpse and the inscription on the tombstone above it, figures the complex relation between perception and language, or between language and its necessary material substrate – the stone, paper, or modulated air on which it is inscribed. The passers-by see the tombs as tombs, as harmless and insignificant matter. Hardy tells the reader in "In Front of the Landscape" that the robes, cheeks, and eyes of those he once loved are "with the earth's crust / Now corporate," and that others who "had shared in the dramas" are now "clay cadavers." The dead are not just dead. They are turned to earth, incorporated in it, dispersed into the landscape. To see that landscape is to see the dead, or it is to see what they now are, harmless mounds on the earth. The "intenser stare" of Hardy's mind resurrects those clay cadavers. It translates them back into what they were. It then transforms them into a "tide." This activity at first seems to be one of perception ("stare"). It then emerges as in fact an act of writing ("translation"). This act of translation is the writing of the poem itself. The poem is written as it were on or over those mounds, tombs, clay cadavers. The poem is a species of epitaph, an inscription on a tombstone, *sema* over *soma*.

There is more to be said of this act of inscription.[9] It is, as all epitaphs tend to be, also an act of invocation, an apostrophe or prosopopoeia addressing the absent, the dead, and thereby raising the ghosts of the dead. Though prosopopoeia overlaps with catachresis, as is evident from the way so many catachreses are personifications or anthropomorphisms, e. g. face of a mountain, leg of a chair, prosopopoeia differs fundamentally from catachresis in a curious way. Though, as the word prosopopoeia suggests (*prosopon* is "mask" in Greek), personification gives a face to what no longer has one or never had one, it is at the same time an act of effacement or defacement, while catachresis makes things appear by naming them. Catachresis has to do with the phenomenal, the visible, the aesthetic in the Hegelian sense of "shining forth." Prosopopoeia, on the other hand, always buries what it evokes in the apostrophic praise, like Antony speaking over the dead body of Caesar. Prosopopoeia effaces what it gives a face to by making it vanish into the earth and become "a body wholly body,"[10] *soma* without *sema*, or *soma* coming into the open as the material base of *sema*, as no longer overt personification but now effaced catachresis become mere literal name, like a tombstone with the letters worn away or a coin rubbed smooth, "effaced."

Hardy in "In Front of the Landscape" raises the dead from their tombs, where they have become "clay cadavers," their "eyes with the earth's crust / Now corporate." He is confronted and indicted for his betrayals by those "speechful faces gazing insistent," "halo-bedecked." At the same time this drama of personification has been dispersed unostentatiously or in effaced form throughout the whole landscape or in the literal words the poet uses to name the aspects of that landscape. The upland is "Coppice-crowned," as though it were a king's head, the light "strokes" the landscape, and if one of the images from the past which rises to haunt the poet is "the one of the broad brow," the cliffs by the sea are named as "a headland of hoary aspect / gnawed by the tide, / Frilled by the nimb of the morning." "Headland" is not metaphor. It is the "proper" name for this topographical feature, though of course a cliff by the sea is not properly speaking a head. It is another personifying catachresis, and the reader may not even notice, so effaced is the linguistic action, so easy to take for granted, that the lines project into the landscape exactly the same image of a halo-fringed head, in this case that of an old man ("of hoary aspect") that the reader has already encountered in the description of the ghosts the speaker confronts as he advances through his tide of visions. These ghosts are no more than the embodiment or bringing into the open, like a photograph being developed, or an inscription in invisible ink being made to appear, of something already dispersed everywhere in the landscape in the ordinary language anyone could use to name it. To recognize this turns the ghosts back into language or disperses them back into the earth's crust. They are no more than a trick of words, and to see this is to lay the ghosts and to confront mere earth.

Moreover, the two lovers who once stood on the headland "touched by the fringe of an ecstasy / Scantly descried" should have taken warning from the scene around them, for what is going on there is a grotesque horrible Dantesque scene of a halo-nimbed head being gnawed by some remorseless creature, apparently another head, as in Ugolino's gnawing of Ruggieri's nape in *Inferno* XXXII and XXXIII. If the sea can chew, it must have teeth, a mouth, eyes, a face, though the prosopopoeia is evanescent, latent, once more effaced. This horrible drama proleptically figures the relation of mutual pain-giving which all human love, for Hardy, comes to in the end, even love like that between the two guilelessly glad friends who stood there on the headland touched by the fringe of an ectasy. The image of the sea wearing away the land, as one head might gnaw at another, also figures the ultimate engulfment of each distinct shape or form, for example each living human body, by the shapeless matter which will eventually reincorporate it, as a cadaver is consumed, decomposes, and disperses into the earth. The figure, finally, figures the activity it itself manifests in effaced or scarcely manifested form, namely the effacement of the inaugural figures by which man takes possession of nature. These figures vanish into the innocently "literal" language whereby, for example, we call a cliff by the sea a "headland." If "In Front of the Landscape" brings those "dead metaphors" back to life, it also kills them again by exposing their base in baseless habits of language, projecting life where there is none. These habits no one, not even the greatest poet, with his matchless mastery of language, can either fully efface or fully control. He can neither do without that form of translation called prosopopoeia, nor can he safely manipulate it for his own ends.

"In Front of the Landscape" develops a tropographical ratio: as the perception transfiguring the landscape is to that landscape as it is in itself, neutral and harmless earth, so the poem as language is to its material base, the indifferent body which in one way or another is necessary to support any inscription, for example the paper on which Hardy's poems are printed. This ratio is a false or misleading one, since what appears to be the literal base of the metaphorical transposition, "perception," does not, it turns out, exist as such for Hardy at all. Perception is the figure and reading is the literal activity, in more senses than one, "lettering" and "real" at once, of which perception is the figure. Perception for Hardy does not literally exist. It is always already translation. It is an activity positing, reading, misreading, transposing, dead earth as signs. For Hardy, the identity of the literary text is this proliferating act of translation. This act repeats itself before and behind within the poem. It is again repeated whenever you or I or another reads the poem.

Notes

1. Thomas Hardy, *The Complete Poems*, New Wessex Edition, James Gibson, ed. (London, 1976), pp. 303–5.
2. J. O. Bailey, *The Poetry of Thomas Hardy: A Handbook and Commentary* (North Carolina, 1970), pp. 261–2.
3. Jacques Derrida, "Télépathie," *Furor*, 2 (1981), pp. 5–41.
4. In chapter ten of this volume.
5. Derrida, "Télépathie," pp. 15–16, my translation.
6. In "Of Personal Identity," section 6 of Book I, Part IV of *A Treatise of Human Nature* (1739).
7. The poet's second wife noted that her husband was never so happy as when he had finished writing another gloomy poem.
8. In "The Stone and the Shell: Wordsworth's Dream of the Arab," in *Moments Premiers* (Paris, 1973), pp. 125–47. Paul de Man discusses related passages from Hegel and Baudelaire in an essay on Michael Riffaterre, "Hypogram and Inscription," The Resistance to Theory (Minneapolis, 1986), pp. 27–53.
9. I am indebted here to astute comments made orally by Patricia Parker when an earlier version of this essay was presented as a lecture at the University of Toronto.
10. Wallace Stevens, "The Idea of Order at Key West," in *The Collected Poems* (New York, 1954), p. 128.

13

Impossible metaphor

Stevens' "The Red Fern" as example

Two ways of honoring Paul de Man may be distinguished. I mean honoring him in the sense that one speaks of honoring a check, paying it back or paying it off, keeping its value in circulation, making it pass current.

One way to honor de Man is to read him. That this has happened, is happening, or will ever happen does not go without saying. The argumentation of his essays is so intricate and goes so much against the grain of common sense assumptions about language and its relation to empirical reality, including the "self," that it is exceedingly easy, perhaps inevitable, that we should misread him, forget what he says, in one way or another suppress his teaching, even in the act of paying him homage. This happens perhaps most effectively when something he explicitly denies is affirmed as his position. As readers of de Man will know, a recurrent theme in his work is the question of why expert readers, not to speak of ordinary ones, tend to misread the plain sense of texts they discuss. "Hölderlin," affirms de Man, "says exactly the opposite of what Heidegger makes him say."[1] Speaking of Jean Starobinski's interpretation of Rousseau, de Man observes, "How curious that, when a text offers us an opportunity to link a nonlinguistic historical concept such as perfectibility to language, we should refuse to follow the hint. Yet a critic of Starobinski's intelligence and subtlety goes out of his way to avoid the signs that Rousseau has put up and prefers the bland to the suggestive reading, although it requires an interpretative effort to do so. . . . There must be an unsuspected threat hidden in a sentence that one is so anxious to defuse."[2] "Interpretation" is here opposed to reading and may even be implicitly identified with "misreading."

What de Man applies to Heidegger and Starobinski must no doubt apply to us as readers of de Man. Moreover, the reader of de Man may uneasily remember that one of de Man's conclusions about reading is that it is "impossible" if one means by reading the reaching of a single logically consistent interpretation of a given text, an interpretation clearly and exclusively supported by evidence from that text. Any text, for example, can be shown to be "rhetorical," including de Man's own essays, and, as de Man says, "considered as persuasion, rhetoric is performative but when considered as a system of tropes, it deconstructs its own performance. Rhetoric is a *text* in that it allows for two incompatible, mutually self-destructive points of view, and therefore puts an insurmountable obstacle in the way of any reading or understanding" (*AR*, 131). This seems clear enough, but insofar as *Allegories of Reading* or this citation from it is itself a *text*, which it evidently is, what de Man says about the impossibility of reading must also apply to his apparently so lucid statements about the impossibility of reading.

In the light of this double difficulty (a general tendency of even distinguished readers to misread, to suppress even the apparently straightforward sense of declarative sentences, and in addition an intrinsic impossibility of the enterprise of reading in any case), it would be naïve to assume that there is a broad understanding of de Man's work, that that work has been "assimilated" by the community of critics and theoreticians, and that we can go on from there. As de Man himself says, in another context, "one sees from this that the impossibility of reading should not be taken too lightly" (*AR*, 245). One way to honor Paul de Man, then, is to renew the attempt to read him, even in the teeth of the possibility that this may be impossible, since the encounter with that impossibility may be what distinguishes reading from nonreading or from the interpretative imposition of some presupposed pattern of assumptions about the meaning of a given text.

A second way to honor Paul de Man and to help keep his work current, passing from hand to hand, is to attempt to read this or that poem or novel or philosophical text on one's own, or, to return to my initial metaphor, to write one's own checks rather than cashing those of de Man. This assumes of course that one has money of one's own in the bank. To say that one might do one's own readings in the light of Paul de Man's work or with help from his thought is mere foolishness, since each critic in the work of reading is on his or her own, face to face with the text, alone with it, never so alone as at that moment. One thinks, to vary the metaphor quite a bit, or perhaps not all that much, of the narrator of Henry James' "The Aspern Papers" appealing for help in a crisis to the portrait of Jeffrey Aspern: "He seemed to smile at me with friendly mockery, as if he were amused at my case. . . . What an odd expression was in his face! 'Get out of it as you can my dear fellow!'"[3]

One way to understand the isolation of each act of reading, and in addition one further reason for the inevitability of falsifying de Man's work in any report of it or borrowing from it, however scrupulous and careful, is to recognize a curious ironic doubleness in all those general "theoretical" statements about language and reading he makes, for example those about the impossibility of reading I have just cited above. On the one hand, these statements are affirmed with universal apodictic generality, as for example when he says, "The paradigm for all texts consists of a figure (or a system of figures) and its deconstruction" (*AR*, 205). There is no reason to doubt that de Man means what he says here, that "all texts" means all texts whatsoever, in all times and places. On the other hand, all such statements in de Man are made in the course of a specific reading of one text or another. They draw their validity from this context, also whatever comprehensibility they may have, in defiance of de Man's own theory of unreadability. In spite of their apparent universality they mean something else or are even emptied of meaning when they are detached from their original context within the intricate maneuvers of a particular act of reading and appropriated either in any account of "Paul de Man's theory of reading" or as the justification by another critic of a reading of his or her own. There is no help for it. Each of us is alone as a reader and must "get out of it" as he or she can, no doubt by repeating one or another of the inevitable "aberrancies" de Man so indefatigably analyzed.

Take, for example, Wallace Stevens' "The Red Fern," a little poem from *Transport to Summer* not even included by Holly Stevens in *The Palm at the End of the Mind*, nor commented on by Harold Bloom in his comprehensive book on Stevens' poetry. No doubt the extraction of a single poem from the vast shifting panoramic linguistic theater of Stevens' work is another version of that falsification by citation out of context which I have already mentioned apropos of de Man's work. It is an example, that is, of citation as such, since citation is the extraction of a fragment from its home and its insertion in unfamiliar surroundings, where it means something different, if it has meaning at all. All citation is therefore tropological and ironic. No claim of synecdochic similarity, part like whole and bringing that whole virtually along with it, will stand scrutiny. "The Red Fern" is not a valid sample of Stevens' work "as a whole." The part, in this case the extracted citation, is unlike the whole and it becomes even unlike itself when it enters as a far fetched stranger within another house, the discourse of its reader or critic. The question of the entry of the "unfamiliar" into the "familiar" is in fact thematic and named as such in "The Red Fern."

In spite of these preliminary and persistent difficulties "The Red Fern" appears to open itself relatively easily to exegesis. Not only is it bound by many ties of conceptual and figurative terminology to Stevens' other poems, for example, "The Man with the Blue Guitar," "A Primitive Like an Orb," and "The Rock," poems I have elsewhere discussed.[4] The poem is also, in itself, detached from *The Collected Poems* and inserted here, woven of manifold conceptual and figurative interchanges, substitutions, displacements. It gives the reader all sorts of interpretative lines to follow. Here is the poem:

The Red Fern

The large-leaved day grows rapidly
And opens in this familiar spot
Its unfamiliar, difficult fern
Pushing and pushing red after red.

There are doubles of this fern in clouds
Less firm than the paternal flame,
Yet drenched with its identity,
Reflections and off-shoots, mimic-motes

And mist-mites, dangling seconds, grown
Beyond relation to the parent trunk:
The dazzling, bulging, brightest core,
The furiously burning father-fire . . .

Infant, it is enough in life
To speak of what you see. But wait
Until sight wakens the sleepy eye
And pierces the physical fix of things.[5]

This poem itself opens like a red fern, unfolding its leaves from stanza to stanza of proliferating phrases, like mist-mites and dangling seconds. The first stanza is a single sentence stopped at the end. The second sentence unfurls more generously in a string of appositives and ends in the open with the three dots of ellipsis. These are followed by the abrupt new start in the fourth stanza of direct address to the "infant" reader or perhaps to some infant within the poet himself. The title says this is a poem about a red fern, but the reader soon sees that the fern is a figure. Like "A Primitive Like an Orb" and like many other poems by this solar poet "The Red Fern" is a poem about the sun. Or perhaps it would be better to say that it is about the day as governed, centered, and powered by the sun: "The large-leaved day grows rapidly." Unlike some of Stevens' solar poems "The Red Fern" is explicitly about sunrise, the "appearance" of the sun out of its nighttime occultation at dawn. "The Red Fern" joins a long tradition of sunrise poems, for example the great opening lines of Part Two of Goethe's *Faust*, where deafening sound substitutes for blinding sight: *Ungeheures Getöse verkündet das Herannahen der Sonne.* In Stevens' case the substitution is not of sound for sight, but of one "sight" for another, fern for sun. In "The Red Fern," as in "A

Primitive Like an Orb," the unspoken law of the poem is that though the poem has as its goal to name the sun the word *sun* may not be used. It is banished from the dictionary. This convention indicates the impossibility or at least the impropriety of naming the sun in so many words, looking it in the eye, so to speak.

Why is this? Though the sun is the source of all seeing and of all procreative energy, vitality, and growth, for example those of red ferns or of human fathers and mothers, it cannot itself be looked at directly. To look the sun straight in the eye is to be blinded, to see nothing. The sun does not therefore, strictly speaking, "appear" at all when it rises. Though it is the condition of seeing, there is nothing to see where sight arises. One sees nothing there. Since by definition literal naming is possible only of things which are open to the senses, phenomenologically perceptible, especially available to eyesight, and since the "sun" does not ever appear in this way, it is, paradoxically, improper or indeed impossible to name the "sun" in the way the things made visible by the sun may be named. The sun is not one of those things we encounter, see, and know "under the sun." The "sun" can therefore only be named in figure, veiled or misted in metaphor, covered by a word or words which serve as a protection against the danger of blinding. Even the word *sun*, or its equivalents in other languages, is, as Aristotle long ago saw, already a metaphor, not a literal name, since the conditions for literal naming are not fulfilled in this case. These conditions are, for example, made incomplete by the invisibility of the risen sun or by our inability to track the sun even out of the corner of our eye when it has set and is out of sight, beneath the horizon. Any name for the "sun," even the most apparently literal one, *sun*, is a kind of blank place in the syntax of a sentence, a coverup of the fact that there is nothing there for perception to know and then to name. The word *sun* is not even a catachresis, since it is not transferred from some other realm where it has a straightforward literal meaning, as in the case of *face* or *leg* in "leg of a table," "face of a mountain." The word *sun* is, strictly speaking, nonsense, a kind of surd within language, however easily we all, even a great poet like Goethe, use it every day. Stevens' avoidance of the word may therefore be seen as a kind of linguistic scrupulosity or fastidiousness, an unwillingness to use a word which names nothing though it appears to be an ordinary name.

There are, however, two ways to respond to this avoidance in "The Red Fern," two ways to read the poem. Or rather, following a useful distinction proposed by Andrzej Warminski, the poem may be either *interpreted*, that is, misinterpreted, or it may be *read*.[6] The first way, hermeneutic interpretation, assumes that the sun, origin of seeing and knowing, symbol of the transcendent one, the *logos*, is in fact itself visible. Do we not see it rise each day! The problem is to name its unfamiliarity, its diurnal novelty, adequately. Metaphor is the means of doing this, but not by imposing the known on the unknown, rather by the mechanism of the classic Aristotelean proportional metaphor in which all the elements of the metaphorical displacement are seen, therefore open to being known and literally named. Literal naming depends on seeing and on the knowing which follows seeing: "it is enough in life / To speak of what you see." Naming or speaking in fact depends on seeing, since literal language, the base and origin of all metaphorical transfer, is defined as the match of the word with the perception of the thing. We see the sun and we call it "sun." Or rather, seen from this perspective of interpretation, the poem apparently depends on the exchanges among the elements in a chain of such metaphors. As the sun rises with each new day and sheds light everywhere, illuminating the clouds, so tropical red ferns grow rapidly from their genetic nodes and then reproduce themselves on runners or stolons, and so the male organ of generation becomes erect and ejaculates semen. "The Red Fern," on this interpretation, is generated by the play of substitutions among these three realms, each open to perception, knowledge, and naming. Terms from one realm are dispersed, disseminated, carried over, transported, according to the etymological meaning of *metaphor*, to another region in a crisscross of substitutions which can go both ways. If, according to the familiar romantic assertion that poetry "lifts the veil of familiarity from the world," the unfamiliarity of the new sun on the new day is named and kept in the open by calling it a red fern and an erect male member, words from the realm of the sun are borrowed to call that erect penis a "furiously burning father fire." The resemblances and consequent verbal displacements in both directions are objective. They are in the nature of things as they are, things as they are seen and known. This seeing and knowing precedes the names for things and the subsequent shifting of names involved in making metaphors. Such shifting fulfills Aristotle's affirmation that a "command of metaphor" is "the greatest thing by far" in a poet: "it is the mark of genius, for to make good metaphors implies an eye for resemblances."[7] The resemblances are there. The poet of genius has an eye for them. For this reason it is enough in life for the infant poet to speak of what he sees. The word *sun* is a legitimate part of the lexicon, but it has through much use become too familiar, its effigy effaced, like a worn out coin. To call the sun a fern or a phallus corresponds to our sight and knowledge of the sun by affirming what the sun resembles. The basis of the poet's speaking is mimetic. The infant poet is a child of the sun, one of its reflections, mimic motes, and exterior resemblances. The poet is himself a mimetic doubling. The poet's speaking, in turn, say in the form of a poem, is not autonomous creation, nor even in itself the revelation of something invisible, but another form of mimesis. The poem, for example "The Red Fern," is another of the offshoots of the sun. The poem is a resemblance of the sun. It is governed entirely by the prior ontological authority of the sun as substance: visible, knowable, namable.

If, however, we now take a close second look at the poem and *read* it rather than *interpret* it, problems with the clear schematizing of its meaning I have just proposed begin to appear. Three anomalous features of the language of the poem may be identified which forbid reading it according to the logical scheme of a chain of Aristotelean metaphors, forbid reading it, that is, as logocentric, as governed by the *logos*, here apparently represented, in the most traditional of images, by the sun. These anomalous, unlawful, or alogical features of the language of the poem mean that it is in fact a series of impossible metaphors. "Impossible" is here meant as a discrepancy between the language and any possible physical fact. Rather than being grounded in nature, in things as they are, in perception leading to knowledge leading to naming and then to that interchange among such firmly grounded names called *metaphor*, such alogical language indicates the unsettling freedom of language from perception and its ability to pour into the mold of its syntactical and grammatical patterns forms of locution which, in relation to the empirical world, are strictly speaking, nonsense, for example that something should be simultaneously all male and all female. Such impossible metaphors are in fact a regular law of words describing the sun. "The Red Fern" is one of the latest in a long line of resemblances of the sun which includes Plato's parable of the cave as well as those passages in Aristotle to which I have alluded, comes down through Shelley's "The Triumph of Life" to a passage in Nietzsche's *The Birth of Tragedy* to a passage in Proust to Derrida's "La Mythologie blanche," and passes along the way almost innumerable other examples of man's wrestling in words with the sun.[8]

Stevens in a well-known formulation in the *Adagia* asserts that "poetry should resist the intelligence almost successfully."[9] It is perhaps too easy to assume that because it is poetry it is all right for it to be nonsense from a logical or empirical point of view. The reader would err in underestimating the importance in Stevens' poetry of that resistance to the intelligence, that presentation of alogical or impossible locutions, locutions that do not make sense when tested against empirical reality, though he would also no doubt err in underestimating the force of that "almost." Poetry should resist the intelligence *almost* successfully. It may be that the moment when the intelligence resumes mastery over poetry is the moment of a shift from interpretation to reading, that is, the moment of a shift to the intelligence of those linguistic features in a poem which do make sense either tropologically or empirically. Or it may be the other way around. The moment when the intelligence resumes mastery over a poem may be no more than an illusory clarity of the mind gained by suppressing elements which can never be mastered by logic. It depends on whether you consider the experience of the impossibility of reading as a victory or a defeat for the intelligence. As Paul de Man says, in another context, the implications of such an intelligence of the limits of intelligence in relation to language are "far-reaching" (*AR*, 61). Let me try to identify three moments of such alogic in "The Red Fern" and attempt to figure out their implications, working against the strong resistance of the poem, as of Stevens' poetry in general, to the reader's intelligence.

The first alogic is the absence of the word *sun* in the opening sentence of the poem. I have already said something about the conspicuous absence of the word *sun* in this poem about the sun, and of the way this corresponds to the absence of the sun from direct empirical perception. You cannot look the sun in the eye without being blinded and therefore, though it is the source of seeing and speaking, it cannot itself be spoken of in literal language based on direct perception. The sun must be spoken of indirectly, in the shifting into the place where the sun might be, but where there is in fact nothing for perception, nothing to see and nothing to name, of a word borrowed from some realm where seeing and naming are possible. In the first stanza of "The Red Fern" the absence of the sun is signalled by the fact that Stevens says not "The sun rises," but "The large-leaved *day* grows rapidly" (my italics). It can be day or daylight in the absence of the sun, for example on a cloudy day. The word *day*, in its encompassing abstraction, as a name for the whole temporal period we oppose to night, names not the sun but what the sun brings. *Day* is a name for everything under the sun but the sun. The day might be expressed by a vast empty sky stretching from horizon to horizon, a place of light but a place of the absence of any source of light. The fact that there is nothing there where the sun might be is indicated by the alogical shift in Stevens' lines between figuring the day itself, in its totality, as a large-leaved plant of some kind ("The large-leaved day grows rapidly . . ."), and then going on to speak of the day as the locus, milieu, or "spot" within which the invisible and unnamable sun grows as a red fern: "And opens in this familiar spot / Its unfamiliar, difficult fern, / Pushing and pushing red after red." The sentence does not make sense as the description of any empirical phenomenon. It is like Proust's description of the sun on a cloudless day turning its eye elsewhere. It is impossible for the day to be simultaneously a large-leaved plant and at the same time the place within which a red fern opens and grows. As a literal representation of an empirical phenomenon the sentence is impossible, but as the manifestation of a linguistic necessity it is scrupulously accurate. It exposes or expresses the necessity of presupposing a center or *logos* for the exchanges of metaphor, while that center is always absent, a vacancy, not even a negation, since it cannot be said whether or not there is anything there, only that there is nothing there to be perceived and named. Into that vacant place in the syntax is introduced one or another figure, for example the figure of the red fern, but this figure must name simultaneously the presupposed center and something which is derivative from that center. Into the emptiness of a sky vacant of any sun, in the syntactical place of that originating motivation for speech is put the name of something else, for example a red fern, which is one of the children of the sun and owes its life and growth to the sun's warmth and light. The empirical impossibility or absurdity of the sentence brings into the open the necessity of presupposing an originating *logos* in any act of speaking, while at the same time, never by even the most extravagant contortions of language, being able to speak of that source of language except in words which presuppose the very thing the sentence is supposed to interrogate, to try to face clearly, and to name. The sentence uses the invisibility of the sun to reveal a linguistic necessity. Such sentences can never do more than name once more something derived and secondary and put that name in the place of what can never be named because it is the presumed base of language, for example by putting a red fern simultaneously in the place of the sun and in the place of the whole region of day within which the sun rises.

A second alogic in the poem is the impossibility of deciding for certain whether the sun is personified as male or as female. It seems certain that the sun must be male, especially if the reader knows the Pennsylvania Dutch slang meaning of *fern*, links this with "trunk," "furiously burning father fire," and sees the imagery of tumescence and ejaculation in "bulging" and "mimic motes / And mist-mites." On the other hand a shadowy underthought suggests a female rather than a male gender for the sun. The sun "pushing red after red" may be giving birth to all those infants of the sun, including the poet. There is an incompatibility between that phallic image of the sun as trunk and the image of a "dazzling" "brightest core," the sun as a fire which cannot be looked at without blinding the beholder and which therefore is experienced as an absence, as a hole in the sky. It will not be advisable to take too lightly the double gender of the sun, to speak of it as if it were a simple oscillation within perception between *Gestalts*: "Now you see it, now you don't." It is impossible for something to be male and female at once with the full powers of each gender. It does not make sense. Though the androgyne may be possible it has always been a scandal to reasonable habits of classification. If the reader takes that second look at the text, the male gender of the sun can be "seen" to correspond to *interpretation* governed by the presumed referentiality of the words, while the female gender of the sun corresponds to *reading*, that is, to a shift of attention to the language of the poem as such. Rather than being a free oscillation, the movement from male to female gender is a one-way road in which there is no return from reading to interpretation, only a further movement deeper into the intelligence of what resists the intelligence almost successfully.

To see the sun as male, as a father, corresponds to the male child's reassuring (or perhaps not so reassuring) sight of his father's member, in the obscure (not all that obscure) sexual drama of the poem. As might be expected, Stevens imagines this drama in the traditional androcentric way, that is, from the point of view of the male child. As soon as something intrinsically linguistic is expressed in terms of sexual difference, even the gender of nouns or the sex of the reader or protagonist, either one, is no longer indifferent. What it would be like to see and speak of what "The Red Fern" names from the point of view of a female child is being explored by some feminist critics, though not, so far as I know, in terms of this poem as example. In "The Red Fern" the implied perspective is definitely male. It should be remembered that the father's "fern" is not the penis as such but the phallus as head signifier, what the male child may appropriate and control by putting himself in the place of the father, what guarantees the validity of the metaphorical exchanges of naming, speaking of what you see.

A possible female gender for the sun, on the other hand, still thinking of it from the point of the male child, corresponds to reading, not interpretation. In the place where the phallus, head signifier, might be there is nothing, an absence, or nothing perceptible, or something that dazzles and blinds. The Greeks embodied their fear of the sight of female genitals in the story of Baubo, who used self-exposure, lifting her skirt, as a power. In the case of "The Red Fern" if there is nothing or nothing but a dazzling brightness when we try to look the sun in the eye, this means that the metaphorical exchanges involved in speaking are governed and validated by no empirically known chief signifier, though speaking necessarily presupposes such a first signifier at the head of the chain of substitutions. It is then impossible to speak of what you see because the ground or presupposition of all speaking can never be seen. The place where that signifier should be but is not is a syntactical requirement. The place is filled, groundlessly, illegitimately, without authority of seeing, by one or another name brought over from somewhere else, the word *fern*, for example, though the word *sun* would be no more legitimate, since what is in question here is a linguistic necessity, not an empirical fact. The sign that it is a question of signs rather than of extralinguistic reality is, once more, the absurdity of the language when the reader tries to take it as having literal, referential meaning. The poet has not spoken of anything one could see.

After what has been said so far, the final area of alogic in Stevens' language here, that in the last stanza, is easy to "see." If it is enough in life to speak of what you see, on the one hand that would mean never speaking at all, since speech presupposes always some original and originating governor or leading signifier whose referent, it turns out, can never be seen. The infant poet, child of the sun, always remains *infans*, deprived of language by his inability to look the fathering or mothering fire in the eye, so to speak, though that confrontation is necessary to any authoritative speaking. On the other hand, this means that it is enough in life, must be enough, since there is nothing else, to speak of what can be seen in place of what cannot. This means speaking of other children of the sun that rise up in the sun's heat and light and make themselves visible, tropical red ferns, for example, or the father's erect member, though, as we have "seen," when the fern as plant turns into the fern as phallus, it becomes invisible. There is nothing there to see but a dazzling core, core as absence rather than core as central presence, father turned to mother or to Baubo.

This double meaning, nonsense according to referential logic, of the sentence telling the infant poet it is enough in life to speak of what you see is doubled again by the final alogic of the last sentence of all: "But wait / Until sight wakens the sleepy eye / And pierces the physical fix of things." *Sight* here, like *day* in the opening line, is a curiously nonlocatable abstraction, everywhere at once, inside and outside at once. A "sleepy eye," like that childhood partial blindness in one eye called "lazy eye," is an eye which is not using a power of seeing which it has. Sight wakens the sleepy eye as a body becomes conscious, by a wholly internal change. On the other hand, *sight* may be a figure for the illumination of the external world when the sun rises. The eye is sleepy because there is nothing to see, but when light floods the world and is disseminated everywhere, then the fact that there is now something to see wakens the sleepy eye, as light penetrates under the eyelids of a sleeping infant and wakes him. *Sight* is a metonymy for "something there to see," the name of one part of the process substituted for another part which is next to it, or for the general condition of illumination. *Sight* is in this reading a synonym of *day* in line one, that is, it names what the sun brings without ever being visible itself. *Sight* in this sense is a name for the absence of the sun. If it is enough to speak of what you see, this speaking has to wait on seeing, and what can be seen are things under the sun, red ferns, for example, not the sun itself. The ultimate cause of sight can never be seen, just as the chief signifier, generator, guarantee, and legitimizer of all speech, can never be seen and named as such, only seen and named in displaced representatives of it, for example the sun.

Something exceedingly odd happens, however, in the completion of the last sentence in the last line when sight is taken not as an intrinsic property or power of the eye, which may be awake or asleep, but as something done to the eye from the outside, waking its latent power of sight. This oddness is the final alogic of the poem: "But wait / Until sight wakens the sleepy eye / And pierces the physical fix of things." When *sight* is read the first way, this sentence says the awakened eye has a power of penetration, as when one says someone has "piercing eyesight," a power to penetrate nature, lift her veil of familiarity, go beyond the stillness, "the physical fix of things," behind which movement and life are hidden. The fix nature is in forces it to repeat the familiar, the same, as in the stuttering alliteration of "phys" in "fix." The piercing eye of the infant poet is here, as I have said, a male power of penetrating and possessing a female nature which includes even that feminized mothering sun present shadowily behind the furiously burning father fire. On the other hand, if *sight* is taken in the second way, as something done to the sleepy eye of the infant poet by the light, then that "physical fix of things" is also internalized. It is a condition caused by the infant's sleepy way of seeing things as fixed and dead. He is one of those who seeing, see not. For a moment, before the intelligence protests and says the lines cannot be saying that, the words "Until sight wakens the sleepy eye / And pierces . . ." are read as saying "sight," a power coming in from outside, wakens the sleepy eye by piercing it, blinding it, as Oedipus blinded himself as punishment for seeing what he should not have seen, as looking on the goddess naked is punished, and as the sun is a dazzling core, blinding the one who looks it in the eye. The sentence cannot logically say both these things at once, since they cannot both make sense referentially at once, and yet if the sentence is read to the end as opposed to being interpreted according to some hermeneutical principle of assumed coherence and unity, it does, impossibly, say these two things at once, two things which can in no way be reconciled or dialectically sublated. If it is enough in life for the infant poet to speak of what he sees and if he waits until sight pierces his eye, he will be blinded and will have nothing to speak of. Speaking can only be of what cannot be seen. This includes in the end red ferns and ferns in the phallic sense as much as the blinding sun. The poem demonstrates this, though not as something that can be "seen," in the noncorrespondence of its speaking with any conceivable form of seeing.

What happens to the infant poet, finally, happens also to the infant critic when he or she tries to speak of what he or she "sees" in the poem.

Far from inviting a shift from *sight* as seeing, that is, an interpretation of the poem according to its referential logic, to *sight* as insight, some presumed mastery of the language of the poem gained through a shift to reading, the act of reading leads to a double'experience of that blinding by the text which Paul de Man calls its unreadability. An intepretation of the poem based on its presumed referential sense leads to irreducible alogical absurdities. This experience of the impossibility of reading leads to a doubling demonstration of this unreadability in the way the reader's insight into this first unreadability, the one at the level I have called interpretation, is powerless to prevent in the act of deconstruction it performs the repetition of the errors it denounces. The example of that here is my illicit use of the metaphor of blindness and insight, in spite of myself, to name a mastery and failure of mastery over what can in neither sense of the word be "seen" and therefore clearly "spoken of." The second unreadability, then, is the inability of the critic to read and draw lessons from his own act of reading. To put this in another way, in my reading I have of necessity used as the instrument of deconstruction a version of the very thing I have deconstructed, or shown to deconstruct itself in the text, namely acceptance of the myth of the necessity of a head signifier beyond and outside the play of language in order for there to be logical language, for example the language of the critic even in "reading" (as opposed to "interpreting") a poem. I have made use of this myth in one of its most powerful forms, that is, the one depending on sexual differentiation for its figures (the presence of the paternal phallus and the absence of the maternal one). In order to read the poem on this basis I have yielded to the literalization of the figurative, in this case the confusion of the symbolic phallus with the literal penis, as when I have said of the sun, "There is nothing there." Whether it is possible ever to escape from this androcentric or phallogocentric myth through any conceivable act of contesting it is another question. It is a question that for the moment, and perhaps indefinitely, must remain open. Certainly my own procedures here would rather confirm once more that "impossibility of reading" which Paul de Man says should not be taken too lightly.

Notes

1. Paul de Man, *Blindness and Insight*, 2nd ed. (Minneapolis, 1983), pp. 254–5, henceforth *BI* 2.
2. Paul de Man, *Allegories of Reading* (New Haven and London, 1979), p. 144, henceforth *AR*.
3. Henry James, *The Aspern Papers and Other Stories* (Harmondsworth, 1979), pp. 97, 99.

4. In *The Linguistic Moment* (Princeton, 1985) and in chapter fourteen of this volume.

5. Wallace Stevens, *The Collected Poems* (New York, 1954), p. 365, henceforth *CP*.

6. In "Prefatory Postscript: Interpretation and Reading," *Readings in Interpretation: Hölderlin, Hegel, Heidegger* (Minneapolis, 1985).

7. S. H. Butcher, *Aristotle's Theory of Poetry and Fine Art, With a Critical Text and Translation of The Poetics* (New York, 1951), p. 87.

8. The passage in Proust is discussed in a remarkable footnote in Paul de Man's "Reading (Proust)," *AR*, pp. 60–61, and the passage in Nietzsche is read by Andrzej Warminski in the essay cited above.

9. Wallace Stevens, *Opus Posthumous* (New York, 1957), p. 171.

14

When is a Primitive like an Orb?

My strategies of textual analysis in this reading will more or less speak for themselves. Their provenance will be obvious. This essay was originally conceived as a part of *The Linguistic Moment* (Princeton, 1985). Here, as in that book, I am concerned with moments in poems when the medium of poetry becomes an issue. I am especially interested here in the way the line between conceptual and figurative terms becomes blurred in Wallace Stevens' late poem "A Primitive like an Orb."[1] The latent figures in abstract terms are extracted and exposed, while overt figures become, in their turn, the only way in which certain "abstract" insights can be expressed. This interchange is related to the way both abstractions and figures here are catachreses, "improper" terms for an evasive center, "the essential poem at the centre of things" that can never be named directly. My interest in the latter gives my strategy of textual analysis here an extralinguistic, even an ontological or metaphysical, orientation. This orientation is demanded by the poem. I think such a bias is in general in one way or another demanded by works of literature, though it is extremely easy to misunderstand what is meant or called for by this demand.

"Like" Yeats's "Nineteen Hundred and Nineteen," Stevens' "A Primitive like an Orb" presents a serial arrangement of images organized in a circular "as" or "is" structure around an absent center. This center can only be named evasively. Why? This taboo against literal naming and the effort to break this taboo make up, one may say, the chief topic of the poem, the place or commonplace around which the poem rotates. "A Primitive like an Orb" has twelve numbered eight-line stanzas in blank verse. These are almost like the digits arranged around the face of a clock. Within the sequence of the twelve, there are sharp grammatical or thematic breaks after each quarter, or group of three. After each quarter the poem begins again with a new syntactical pattern and a new set of images bound together by "as" or "is." Each new set displaces the one before. If the images are linked by their implicit and problematic equivalence, the motive energy that makes each inadequate and makes each need to be replaced by another is their even more problematic relation of likeness to the absent center. This is figured by the unnamed sun. "Sun" is the one word that may not be uttered or written within this poem. If a "primitive" is "like" an "orb," this is because both primitive and orb are "like" the Ṣ⋈ɋ. A primitive is like an orb. An orb is like a primitive. Neither of those words is the normal "literal" name for what it refers to by a displacement both in its use and in the syntactical slippage of the "like" that follows or precedes it. The sun, that "close, parental magnitude, / At the centre on the horizon, concentrum, grave / And prodigious person, patron of origins" (86–8), emerges gradually in the course of the poem as the apparent literal referent of the chain-linked series of figures making up the poem. But the sun is of course in its turn only a figure for the true "literal" theme of the poem, which is named in the first line: "the essential poem at the centre of things." This obscure phrase is immediately followed by an even more obscure phrase in apposition: "The arias that spiritual fiddlings make" (2). If a primitive is like an orb, the essential poem at the center of things, whatever that means, is like the arias that spiritual fiddlings make, whatever *that* means. The poem moves from enigma to enigma, like a long-legged fly skating on water. It moves in phrases, each of which must be interrogated in detail for its depth of figurative, syntactic, and semantic play.

Saying, for example, as the title does, "a primitive like an orb" differs greatly from saying, "the primitive like the orb," or "the primitive like an orb," or "a primitive like the orb." In Stevens' phrase both primitive and orb are no more than examples of indefinitely large categories of primitives and of orbs, not the original primitive or the original orb. Each of the two words, moreover, opens up within itself an unexpected complexity. An orb may be a solid substance, the fiery paternal orb of the sun, or it may be a hollow 0, a zero, the nothing named at the end of the poem as "the giant of nothingness" (95). This recalls the equation made by Paul Claudel of egg, seed, open mouth, zero – "oeuf, semence, bouche ouverte, zéro" (Claudel and Gide, 91). Moreover, an "orb" may be at the center or it may be the circuit around the center, the orbit or trajectory. One example would be the course of that sun which in this poem is a "concentrum" "at the centre on the horizon" (87). Another example would be the circuit of the horizon itself, that vanishing point in the distance all around the spectator. The word "primitive," on the other hand, is something that in one way or another comes first. A primitive fathers forth a sequence of generations modeled on the father but varying it, making the primitive gradually more complex. A primitive is a "patron of origins" (88). The word "primitive" has technical meanings in linguistics, in algebra, and in anthropology. A primitive is a radical or root word from which ever more complex words have been derived through time. A primitive is an algebraic equation that is the source of a series of increasingly complex derived equations. A primitive is an aboriginal human being who is not yet quite human, containing only virtually, in undeveloped embryo, all the burden of civilized culture.

Both a primitive and an orb have simultaneously temporal and spatial dimensions. It might be more accurate to say that each is a spatial image for time. Each falsifies time, since time cannot be mapped as a space. At the same time, each gives the reader access to time, an intuition or sense of temporality that is impossible without spatial images. Both space and time, in this contradictory inherence of one in the other, rotate around the absent center or expand from it or orbit with it, according to the incoherent implications of the images of orb and primitive. Speech, time, and space come together around the eclipsed sun, the essential poem at the center of things. Of this the poet says that "It is and it / Is not and, therefore, is" (13–14). As soon as it is glimpsed through being named in one of the riddling figures that make up the notes or spiritual fiddlings of Stevens' poem, it vanishes in the revelation, once more, of the inadequacy of any name for the poem at the center. The force of the intuition that something is there lies not in its unveiling but in the recognition that any naming, after a moment, covers it over, according to a general law of apocalyptic language: "In the instant of speech, / The breadth of an accelerando moves / Captives the being, widens – and was there" (14–16). In the next stanza this instant of speech opens "a space grown wide" and reveals "the inevitable blue / Of secluded thunder" (21–2). This blue is an empty sky that nevertheless hides a lightning storm, over the horizon, blinding light occluded. This hidden light is then defined as "an illusion, as it was, / Oh as, always too heavy for the sense / To seize, the obscurest as, the distant was . . ." (22–4). The "is" that is not becomes when it is named or sensed instantly "was" and therefore another simile or another metaphorical equivalent, an "as" adding itself to the constantly proliferating chain structure of displacements making up the poem.

To get the reader within the play of language in "A Primitive like an Orb" I shall juxtapose to it a passage from Jacques Derrida's *De la grammatologie*:

Is it not necessary to think through [*méditer*] this heliocentric concept of speech? As well as the resemblance of the logos to the sun (to the good or to the death that one cannot look at face to face), to the king or to the father (the good or the intelligible sun are compared to the father in the *Republic*, 508 c)? What must writing be in order to threaten this analogical system in its vulnerable and secret center? What must it be in order to signify the *eclipse* of what is *good* and of the *father*? Should one not stop considering writing as the eclipse that comes to surprise and obscure the glory of the word [*la gloire du verbe*]? And if there is some necessity of eclipse, should not the relationship of shadow and light, of writing and speech, itself appear in a different way? (139)[2]

Derrida's language moves from one to another of a set of terms that are implicitly equivalent, each a substitute for the last, a "resemblance" of it, in a series of transformations in which no term is the first or the pivot around which the others turn or the end at which they may stop. The logos equals the sun equals the good equals the death that cannot be looked at in the face equals the king equals the father equals mind equals speech. In this analogical sequence no term is the beginning or the end, because each is only another term. By the fact that it is only a term, a word, it is not *the* word. It is only a derived image in a potentially endless sequence of images, each of which always refers to another image, and so on indefinitely. Each term for that which is the source of terms is a metaphor drawn from that realm which is supposed to have derived from that which it is a term for. Sun, father, king, light, and so on are supposed to be metaphors for the one, the logos, pale material copies of it, analogies or symbols, as one speaks of the Creation as the speech of God – "news of God," in Gerard Manley Hopkins' phrase. The metaphor drawn from what is condemned as secondary is the most appropriate term for that from which it is supposed to be derived. Derrida's argument is that the condemnation of writing works to obscure this fact. It works to keep the analogical system intact by hiding the similarity between writing and speech. Both equally create that from which they claim to be derived, but the autonomy, repeatability, and detachment from any living voice of writing make this so much more evident that it appears to eclipse the sun, to uncover the blackness at the vulnerable and secret center of this whole analogical system.

A similar set of equivalences may be seen operating throughout "A Primitive like an Orb," though the force of the word "similar" must be taken anasemically[3] here too, ana-analogically. Similarity or analogy inevitably implies some central logos in the name of which the examples are analogous, speak with similar voices, but the existence and nature of that central logos are just what is most in question here. In any case, "Primitive like an Orb," like Stevens' work as a whole, is – as much as Plato's dialogues – heliocentric. Stevens' pervasive use of the figure, or concept, or literal objective fact (it is all three) of the trajectory of the sun, its rising, its majestic march across the sky, its setting, is one more example of the heliotropic unity of the occidental repertoire of tropes. Our metaphorology is a photology, since all metaphors are modes of illustration or of bringing to light, even though this light may be spurious or artificial, a lamp and not the sun. This is, to say it again, in each case just the question. Is the light original or is it human-made, a case of poiēsis? Stevens' "A Primitive like an Orb" seemingly chooses the first possibility. The poem presents a theory of poetry as revelation of the giant on the horizon, the poem at the center of things that pre-exists any lesser poem, is its source, its begetter, and yet exists only in the lesser poems. "A Primitive like an Orb" proceeds from one to another of the following images in their metaphorical circulation: center, poem, speech, good, food, light, gold, void (by way of the pun in "gorging" [3, 5]), air, melody, space, time, music, being, primitive, the primitive as aboriginal man, as primitive word, as radical, as primitive formula from which others are derived, as illustration, as source of form, as egg, as seed, as both center and sphere, concentrum and orbit, as world, as husband, as desire, as will, as joy, as self, as father ("The essential poem begets the others" [47]), as circle ("ring" [56]), as whole, as vis, as principle, as primitive source, as nature, as "repose," as magnet or source of magnetic field, as giant, as fire, as following as well as origin, as angel, as power or source of power, as fate ("prodigious" [88]: Latin *prōdigiōsus*, from *prōdigium* 'omen,' 'portent'), as matrix, as abstraction embodied, as illustration, as skeleton, as the total of paintings, prophecies, poems, and love letters, as change.

"A Primitive like an Orb" proceeds through the problematic equivalences affirmed among this astonishing diversity of terms. These equivalences are established by the fundamental syntactical principle of this poem: phrases in apposition. Phrases in apposition, however, are similes without the words "as" or "like." "Like" and "as" appear in the title and in the lines about "the obscurest as." These locutions call attention to metaphor and simile as fundamental instruments of poetic thinking. Metaphor or simile asserts an equivalence between things that are nevertheless not identical. A similar form is taken by sentences that say, "A is B." The series of phrases in apposition is perhaps the dominant form, however, because such a series is held together by the absence or the effacement of the "is" that is nevertheless implied as the basis of their equivalence. That "is" is the "being" that is momentarily captivated, that which is and is not and so is. This potentially endless series of false equivalences, one "obscurest as" after another, rotates by way of the substitution of each new figurative term for the last around the absent center of the nonexistent literal word for which all these terms are figures.

The "obscurest as" organizes the whole poem. Stanzas 7 through 9, for example, the third quadrant of the poem, are one long sentence of phrases in apposition, each replacing the last, only to be instantly replaced in its turn by a new phrase that picks up a bit of debris from the annihilation of the phrase before, the whole turning on a single verb, the little word "is" in the first line. I cite the whole of this extraordinary sentence, so the reader may see here on the page how Stevens feels his way from formulation to formulation, discarding each but trying then another variation of it. The reader should also note the syntactical complexity of the sentence, not only its dependence on the open serial sequence of phrases in apposition and its reliance on the "a" and "an" of the title, as well as on the "the" in its difference from "a" or "an," but also its shifting from one grammatical pattern to another by way of a constant play of "and"s, "or"s, and "of"s. Stevens' work is surely to be defined, in Roman Jakobson's phrase, as an admirable exploitation of the latent "poetry of grammar" ("Poetry"; see also Hammond). It is also an example of what might be called the poetry of punctuation, a poetry of the comma or the absence of the comma (as at the end of stanza 7 here), and of the indefinite postponing of the period. Here is the sentence:

VII

The central poem is the poem of the whole,
The poem of the composition of the whole,
The composition of blue sea and of green,
Of blue light and of green, as lesser poems,
And the miraculous multiplex of lesser poems,
Not merely into a whole, but a poem of
The whole, the essential compact of the parts,
The roundness that pulls tight the final ring

· VIII

And that which in an altitude would soar,
A vis, a principle or, it may be,
The meditation of a principle,
Or else an inherent order active to be
Itself, a nature to its natives all
Beneficence, a repose, utmost repose,
The muscles of a magnet aptly felt,
A giant, on the horizon, glistening,

IX

And in bright excellence adorned, crested
With every prodigal, familiar fire,
And unfamiliar escapades: whirroos
And scintillant sizzlings such as children like,
Vested in the serious folds of majesty,
Moving around and behind, a following,
A source of trumpeting seraphs in the eye,
A source of pleasant outbursts on the ear. (49–72)

"*The* poem of *the* composition of *the* whole" is not quite the same thing as "*the* poem of *the* whole," though their grammatical juxtaposition suggests that the two phrases must or might be two ways to say the same thing. "A poem of a whole" would be something else again, something partial and contingent as against the absolute and exclusive, the distinguished, the right real thing at last. The repetition of the phrase "of the whole" makes the "of" stand out. "Of" in what sense, the reader asks, "of" as "about," or "from," or "participating in"? Is it a poem about the whole, or a poem coming from the whole, or a poem sharing the whole, a "tenacious particle" (92) of it? Does the "of" have the same sense in "composition of blue sea and of green" as in "composition of the whole"? The "of" would seem to go in a different direction in each case, coming from (or going toward) totality in one case ("composition of the whole") and coming from (or going toward) the multiplicity of nature in the other ("composition of blue sea and of green"). The reader must grope his way so from phrase to phrase and from line to line, testing or tasting each on his mental palate to see what is uniquely released by each in its slight difference from the one before.

The stanzas are, moreover, the reader can see, a manifestation of what they talk about. They are a miraculous multiplex of lesser poems. Each phrase is a little burst of aphoristic revelation moving toward an uncovering of the whole or toward an expression of the whole. Or is it more properly "*the* uncovering of the whole, *the* expression of the whole"? Stevens' "the's" are insistent here, at least in the first stanza, though "*the* poem of the whole" in line 1 becomes "a poem of / The whole" in lines 6 and 7. Is the "composition" in question the unveiling of a wholeness already there, the already made composition of the whole, or is the composition of the whole a poetic act of making, or putting parts together in one place to make a whole, as in courses in freshman composition? To put this another way, does the "of" in "poem of the whole," placed ostentatiously in the open at the end of a line ("Not merely into a whole, but a poem of / The whole"), have a constative or a performative force? Is such a poem descriptive of a whole already there, or is it the making of a whole not there before the composition of certain words in a certain order? Or is it the revelation of composition (the already there) through composition (the act of making)?

In any case, the constant slight variation of syntactical and lexical patterns not only makes the basic grammatical armatures of thoughtful discourse stand out ("the A of the B," for example). Such variation also releases so-called abstract words like "whole," "composition," and "poem" from their engagement in the flow or curriculum of argument and makes each stand out alone, free of syntax, as a naked power of signification in relation to that absent and unnamed center, or poem at the center, or central poem. This is particularly evident in the second of the two stanzas quoted above, stanza 8. There is a syntactic slippage between stanza 7 and stanza 8, indicated by the absence of a comma at the end of stanza 7. The wholeness of composition of the central poem, what the poet calls "the essential compact of the parts," which I take it means not just that they are compacted or pressed in together but that they have, as it were, an agreement to belong together and to stay together, is said to be an encircling roundness or outer ring, like a final barrel hoop, or rather it is a force that pulls that outer ring tight and holds the whole together. This roundness or compact, that which makes the whole a whole, at the same time "pulls tight" something, a pervasive energy of unification, which otherwise would fly off ("in an altitude would soar").

The poet experiments with various names for this energy in stanza 8. He moves by way of the "or" from one to another and tests each word for its validity, for the insight it releases. Each new formulation replaces the one before but does not disqualify it, as the poet moves toward the most explicit revelation of the sun as such, though it is still veiled in a personification: "a giant, on the horizon, glistening." The reader is invited to test out the difference between saying it is a "vis" and saying it is a "principle," or between saying it is a "principle" and saying it is "the meditation of a principle" (which may mean the principle meditates or, more likely, that we think of the principle), or between saying it is an "inherent order" and saying it is a "nature to its natives / All beneficence," or between saying it is "repose" and saying it is "utmost repose," or between saying it is repose of either sort, and saying it is the lack of repose defined by the muscular pull of a magnet. Once again the poem performs what it names. It is the meditation of a principle of unity by way of the rotational naming of that principle by various names, "moving around and behind" it, as it moves too, in a slow circling dance of language around the orbiting primitive.

Stanzas 7 through 9 and the poem as a whole resist paraphrase or interpretative commentary, since their implicit double assumption is, first, that no phrase or name or figure is an adequate label for the primitive and, second, that each inadequate phrase or name or figure has its own unique virtue, unveiling and unavailing at once. Each phrase reveals a certain glimpse of the primitive in the moment of its vanishing, as though the words themselves were the eclipse of the sun. To say it otherwise in attempted paraphrase or commentary – mine here, for example – is to say something different, something perhaps with its own virtue. The poem itself demonstrates this through its testing of slight variations on a given formulation, "utmost repose," for example, as against "repose." Interpreters might conceivably add to the poem, add more phrases to the phrases in apposition, but they cannot elucidate it in the sense of bringing some obscure meaning further out in the open by naming it correctly or literally at last. It is this shared linguistic predicament, not some vague right to be "poetic" or "creative," that is meant, or should be meant, when it is said that criticism is a form of literature.

The poem then at the end of stanza 8 moves by way of that latent personification in "muscles of a magnet" to the major prosopopoeia of the sun on the horizon as a glistening giant "vested in the serious folds of majesty" but at the same time adorned in prodigally frivolous fireworks, "whirroos / And scintillant sizzlings such as children like." These serious folds move "around and behind," or is it the giant himself who turns on his axis or moves into invisibility when he sets and appears to move around and behind the rotating earth? The grammar of apposition makes it impossible to be sure which it is, just as it is impossible to tell whether the sun on the horizon is rising or setting. This makes him both origin ("source") and end ("a following"), alpha and omega. The brilliant revelation or shining forth of his rising or setting is a synesthesia of both sound and sight, *son et lumière*, light so bright it is perceived as sound. The sun on the horizon is origin of "trumpeting seraphs in the eye" and at the same time of "pleasant outbursts on the ear," just as in the great sunrising scene at the opening of part 2 of Goethe's *Faust*, "a stupendous clangor proclaims the approach of the sun" (*Ungeheures Getöse verkündet das Herannahen der Sonne* [stage direction after l. 4665]), and the sun rises "ears bedazing, eyes beglaring" (*Auge blinzt und Ohr erstaunet* [l. 4673]).[4]

I have said that the personification of the sun as a giant emerges at the endpoint of the sequence in the long sentence making up stanzas 7 through 9. The relation of prosopopoeia, catachresis, and apostrophe is complex. Here there is no apostrophe. Stevens does not speak to the sun, though in "Chocorua to Its Neighbor," a poem of 1943 that in many ways anticipates "A Primitive like an Orb," the mountain speaks to a neighbor mountain so that the reader overhears speech intended for another, one half of a dialogue between mountains. In "A Primitive like an Orb," Stevens speaks "about" the sun, in more than one sense of that word. The poem is spoken to an audience of thoughtful men and women who share with him (a "him" almost wholly lacking identifiable personality) the revelation effected by the meditative voices of the poem as it shifts from register to register: "But it is, dear sirs, / A difficult apperception, this gorging good . . ." (4–5). It would be a long work to identify and discriminate the mélange of voices, poems, and levels of diction here. Their multiplicity is not consistent with the model of a single speaker addressing univocal speech to a single audience. The lexical material of which this mixture is made includes abstract terms like "composition," "whole," "compact"; explicit figures of speech like that of the "final ring" or that of the magnet or that comparing the sun to a firework of whirroos and scintillant sizzlings such as children like; and finally, the emergent personification, "an abstraction given head" (81), of the sun or central poem as "A giant on the horizon, given arms, / A massive body and long legs, stretched out" (82–3). "A Primitive like an Orb" has been anticipated in this figure by the extraordinary personification of the starlit night as "more than muscular shoulders, arms and chest" in "Chocorua to Its Neighbor": "Upon my top he breathed the pointed dark. / He was not a man yet he was nothing else" (24, 36–7). "Chocorua to Its Neighbor" joins "A Primitive like an Orb" and "The Owl in the Sarcophagus" in presenting one of Stevens' great prosopopoeias in poems about the act of prosopopoeia.

Nietzsche, in "On Truth and Lies in a Nonmoral Sense," includes "anthropomorphisms" along with metaphors and metonymies among the mobile army of catachreses by which humanity first names the "mysterious X" of the world, uncovering it and covering it over again in one linguistic act (83, 84). It may be personification is the most important or most fundamental of these catachreses: that giant person we always meet mirrored in the landscape at the other end of our wrestle to name the world and so confront it as it is. The giant, it may be, is no more than our own face and body reflected in the mirror of the world, constructed bit by bit out of our inveterate habit of calling landscape features "faces," "heads," "necks," or "legs," as in "body of water," "face of the mountain," "headland of a shore," and so on. Or it may be that there really is some monster humanlike creature at the end of that last corridor wound into the center of the labyrinth, that "centre on the horizon" (87). In any case, for Stevens too there is, in this poem and in many others of his late masterworks, the confrontation of a person at the farthest reaches of the imagination's naming power. As Stevens says here, "It is a giant, always, that evolves / To be in scale" (73–4). This says both that size, "bulging" (32) mass, and overwhelming "parental magnitude" (86) are always characteristics of the central poem and that the central poem always has a human form. If the edge or extreme of sensation, where the light of sense goes out – as for example when we try to look the sun in the face or in the eye – is a place of synesthesia, the place of an exchange among the senses, so that the blaze of the sun is heard as trumpeting seraphs, the reaching of that place is also the moment of the manifestation of a person, an angel or a giant. This is true whatever Stevens may say in "Notes toward a Supreme Fiction" about abolishing Phoebus Apollo and seeing the sun "in the idea of it," washed clean of any metaphor or mythological personification: "How clean the sun when seen in its idea, / Washed in the remotest cleanliness of the heaven / That has expelled us and our images" (*Poems* 381). However resolutely the basic prosopopoeias by which we name the world and so see it are effaced, they always return again, for example as a giant face and body in the sun, as in that sunrising scene in Goethe's *Faust*, "Granite portals groan and clatter, / Wheels of Phoebus roll and spatter" (*Felsenthore knarren rasselnd, / Phöbus Räder rollen prasselnd* [ll 4669–70]), or as in Turner's *The Angel Standing in the Sun* or in his *Ulysses and Polyphemus*, with its outline of Apollo, horses, chariot and all, faintly discernible within the blazing orb of the sun, or as in the giant that evolves in that long sentence of stanzas 7 to 9 of Stevens' poem.

What is distinctive about Stevens' tracing of that evolutionary return here is the way he shows the prosopopoeia coming back again not initially or primarily by way of the remaining personifying catachreses in common language ("eye of the sun") but by way of the kinesthetic movement within abstract words like "composition," "compact," "beneficence," or "repose." The etymological metaphors may seem to be safely dead within such words, but Stevens matches Walter Pater in being acutely sensitive to the "elementary particles" in seemingly abstract words, in feeling "the incident, the colour, the physical elements or particles in words like *absorb, consider, extract*" (Pater, "Style" 20). Those physical elements or particles are not things but acts or movements, as in the act of drawing in the "tract" of "extract" and the movement outward of "ex," or as in the act of placing together in "com-position," or of placing back on itself in "re-pose," or in the act of joining together in "com-pact," with an echo from one word to another of the "com-," or the "pos-." The play on "pos-" had been prepared already in the description in the first stanza of the central poem as "disposed and re-disposed / By such slight genii in such pale air" (7–8). Stevens appears to feel these so-called abstract words as subliminal muscular movement in his own body, kinesthetic acts that respond to or project similar movements into the world outside. The giant on the horizon, glistening, emerges gradually through these obscure bodily acts initiated by the play of abstractions, combined and recombined from phrase to phrase, until finally that inherent order or principle of bringing parts together into a whole, both act and rest, vis and repose, is felt as "the muscles of a magnet." Out of those muscles, inner and outer at once, at once metaphor of a metaphor ("muscles of a magnet"), abstraction, and catachresis as prosopopoeia, the massive giant evolves and takes shape out there in the sun on the horizon.

Among the abstractions is, in stanza 11, the word "abstraction" it-self and three accompanying words: "definition," "illustration," and "labelled." These together give Stevens' own analysis of the rhetorical strategy whereby the distinctions between abstract words, metaphors, and personifications break down in the recognition that all are examples of that overlapping area where catachresis and prosopopoeia, in spite of their different orientations, come together in their mutual interference one with the other. Catachresis goes toward revelation, toward shining forth, as of the sun rising or setting in the blaze of its glory. Prosopopoeia goes toward death and occultation, toward invisibility, as the sun is that death which cannot be looked in the face. Prosopopoeia goes toward ode and elegy, as, most evidently, in Stevens' "The Owl in the Sarcophagus." Prosopopoeia is the invocation of the absent, invisible, or entombed, as of the sun when it is below the horizon, has set, or is not yet risen, for example in that extraordinary embodiment of the disembodied, already mentioned, the personification of starlight in "Chocorua to Its Neighbor": "The feeling of him was the feel of day, / And of a day as yet unseen. . . . / He was a shell of dark blue glass, or ice, / Or air collected in a deep essay, / . . . Blue's last transparence as it turned to black" (16–17, 21, 22, 25).

Catachresis that is also prosopopoeia, as so many are, like "muscles" in "muscles of a magnet" here, is at the intersection or crossroads of these two contradictory orientations, where appearance and disappearance come together, at the center on the horizon. That atopical place is also where the lexical distinctions between abstraction, metaphor, and personification break down. Stevens' abstractions are also metaphors, and they are also latent personifications. As the word "abstraction" itself etymologically says, the giant is drawn out and refined or embodied from the abstractions, abs-tracted from them: "Here, then, is an abstraction given head, / A giant on the horizon, given arms / A massive body and long legs" (81–3). This personification, as the poet exactly puts it, is "A definition with an illustration, not / Too exactly labelled" (84–5). The definition is, it may be, the initial abstraction and its permutations ("The central poem is the poem of the whole," and so on). The illustration is the figuration by catachresis that emerges from the abstractions as a bringing to light (as the word "illustration" etymologically means). The labeling is the final bringing together of these fleeting embodiments as the personification of the central poem as a giant. But all three of these forms of language are at once definition, or a giving boundaries and outline, illustration or bringing to light, and labeling or definitive illustrative naming. All these distinctions, though they are necessary if there is to be poetry or commentary on the poetry, fail or vanish at that center of blinding light, the black hole that must not be too exactly labeled or the terms for it lose all validity. They lose even that fleeting, flickering, or flicking validity of alluding by indirection which Stevens celebrates, and they become the reduced and ludicrously inadequate fixity Stevens' speaker has ridiculed a moment before: "As in a signed photograph on a mantelpiece" (76). Such motionless figures are an abjectly self-referential parody of the definition with an illustration, not too exactly labeled. The giant on the horizon can be given no proper name and does not speak or give himself one, as I do when I sign my own photograph. I have said that Stevens' use, here and in many other poems, of the sun's trajectory as basic abstraction, trope, and figure of personified narrative journey aligns him with Western poetic tradition from the Greeks on down. Stevens also joins himself to a tradition going back at least to Aristotle in making the sun a chief example of catachresis. If a proper or literal name depends on the full visibility, out in the sunlight, of what is named, the sun, in Stevens' phrase "must bear no name" (*Poems*, 381), or cannot properly be named, since it is invisible during that part of its orbit when it is hidden or entombed below the horizon. The word "sun" is as much a catachresis as are all the circumlocutions making up Stevens' poem. It is neither through accident nor through arbitrary choice by the poet that the "giant of nothingness," the central poem, the primitive like an orb, turns out to be the sun, nor is it a mere poet's joke that the word is forbidden in this poem.

Even so, the reader of "A Primitive like an Orb," this reader at least, seeks to identify that evasive center, to put a proper name to it, in order to still and to control the dizzying movement from figure to figure that makes up the linguistic texture of the poem. Three possible candidates come to mind for the extralinguistic reference that might, if it were identified, solve the enigma and appease the mind's dissatisfaction as it moves from image to image in this poem and tries to figure out what the poem is "about." (1) The poem may obliquely name some physical referent, some scene or object in the external world that the poem imitates or represents. Once this objective referent is identified, readers than have something to hold to as they make their way through the poem. Such a reading would see the poem as in one way or another a mimetic picture. (2) The poem, on the other hand, may represent some psychic state, for example the mind of the poet, which could be imagined to exist without the poem and which the poem expresses or copies. This would be a familiar theory of poetry as the expression or imitation of psychic states. (3) The poem, finally, may obliquely name some transcendent or spiritual center: God, the idea of the one, being, the "light apart, up-hill" (48) to which the poem refers in stanza 6. This third possibility would be a notion of mimesis like that of Plato, for whom the scale of imitations is governed ultimately by prototypes in the realm of ideas.

These are three versions of a definition of poetry as imitation. "A Primitive like an Orb" systematically baffles all three possible explanations. The poem copies no coherent scene or single definable object. It proceeds rather through a bewildering proliferation of mixed metaphors, each canceling out the one before. There are fragments and bits of scenes all superimposed incoherently: music, cast-iron life and works, essential gold hidden in some treasure crypt, a picnic scene in the woods, a lightning storm in the distance, and so on. Only when the poem reaches finally the giant on the horizon do readers seem to have something definite to think about, but by this time they know that the giant is only another metaphor, not what the poem is "about." The giant too is only another "illustration," a bringing to light by means of an example. The giant is another picture or emblem, that is, something that refers once more to something beyond itself. All the terms in the poem are names for that central invisible and unnamable primitive, the large that all the illustrations are smalls of (85–6), the father poem of which all actual poems are children. The essential poem, as the poem says, begets the others.

As for the second possibility, though it may be comforting to readers to imagine that they are gaining access to the "mind of Stevens" as they read the poem, nevertheless there is no self in the poem, no personal psyche expressing itself to which the words in the poem can easily be referred. The austerity and impersonality of Stevens' poetic voices and their constant shifts of tone are notorious. The notion that poetry is a man speaking to men does not get the interpreter far with "A Primitive like an Orb," nor with such companion poems as "Chocorua to Its Neighbor" or "The Owl in the Sarcophagus." This means not that Stevens' poems are without passionate intensity but that psychological categories or categories of selfhood are of little use in their exegesis. To reduce the poem to an expression of Stevens' "selfhood" or "consciousness" would be to turn it into that "signed photograph on the mantelpiece" (76) which the poem so scorns. It is a mean-minded and futile attempt by "virtue" to cut the giant on the horizon down to size, to "[snip] / Both size and solitude or [think] it does" (74–5).

It would seem, then, that the third possibility must be the answer. All the terms in the poem refer to that evasive spiritual reality, what Stevens elsewhere calls "mere being" (*Opus*, 117). This reality is the shy paramour whom all his poems court, or rather the totality of what may be perceived is the theater of a courtship by the giant on the horizon of nature and the mind as the spouses of that giant. This marriage is admirably named in lines 39–46 of the poem:

. . . It is
As if the central poem became the world,

VI

And the world the central poem, each one the mate
Of the other, as if summer was a spouse,
Espoused each morning, each long afternoon. . . .

Even this third possibility, however, the possibility that the poem is a performative act of revelation, that the words of the poem bring something hidden into the open, is put in question by the poem's linguistic strategy. There is a systematic ambiguity in the images of "A Primitive like an Orb" that makes it like that hermetic egg of which Yeats speaks that continually turns itself inside out without breaking its shell. The ambiguity lies in the uncertainty, in spite of the claim that "the essential poem begets the others," about which is father of which. Is the particular poem only a pale copy of the essential poem, or is it actually part of it, as another phrase in the poem affirms? In the successful poem the central poem becomes the world, which becomes in turn her spouse, "her mirror and her look" (44), the particular poem. The essential poem is both outside the particular poem as the center on the horizon, and at the same time it is the total of all "letters, prophecies, perceptions, clods / Of color" (94–5), therefore incarnated in each creative act. These inscriptions or embodiments are both pale imitations of the central poem, its division, fragmentation, and dispersal, and at the same time they are what constitutes it, in both senses of the word. Taken all together they are the central poem, and at the same time they generate it as the vanishing point they all indicate in the failure of each to be more than part of that whole, a synecdoche of it. This paradox is expressed in another way in "The Man with the Blue Guitar" and in the commentary on that poem in Stevens' letters to Renato Poggioli. The imagination must be a son of the kind able to defeat his father and be that father's "true part," his sex. The son will take the place of the father, not destroy him, but become him. The filial imagination must overcome the distance between the lion in the lute and the lion in the stone until they merge and become one.

As soon as this process of merger is complete, it fails. It fails because poet or reader is left with only a faint simulacrum, an image or an illustration in the pejorative sense, a dead husk, a copy – a "second," in Stevens' terminology. This husk must be destroyed, since it instantly loses all authenticity. As soon as it is proffered it has already become something that was, "an illusion, as it was," like "a signed photograph on the mantelpiece." It is for this reason that the definition with an illustration must not be too exactly labeled. Each definition with an illustration must be immediately rejected as soon as it is presented and must be replaced by the next, in that proliferating series of phrases in apposition which makes up so much of this poem. In its vanishing each image reveals itself as a new name for the void. The giant is "the giant of nothingness" (95), however much he is given attributes of bulging masculine substance and muscular solidity. Only as each image reveals itself to be a copy, another mimetic illustration, can it be adequate to that of which it is an illustration, because both the illustration (the act of bringing to light) and that which it illustrates (the giant) are "ever changing, living in change" (96). The image must partake of the nature of that of which it is an image. Its fictive, hollow, evanescent quality is essential to its adequacy. Since the patron of origins himself (itself?) lives in time and change, he (it?) can only be adequately expressed in temporal images – that is, in images that are and are not and therefore are. The light of this central primitive is not a light apart, uphill. Stevens as much as Yeats rejects a universe of Platonic emanations descending from some early spiritual warmth. Stevens too chooses the whirlpool over the waterfall. He chooses the labyrinth of immanence over any hierarchy depending from the transcendent One.

Stevens, like Yeats or William Carlos Williams, makes strong claims for the power of poetry. These claims in each case remain indeterminate. Is it creation or is it discovery, this invention of the poem? Does the illustration illustrate a light that preexists it, the father fire that begets all the little fires? Or are the little fires parts, particles, of the father fire and therefore essential to it, so that only in a poem does the light come into the open? Or are the little fires in fact identical with the father fire, so that the father fire exists in, and is generated by, only the intercourse of images, the child becoming father to his father? "A Primitive like an Orb" is caught, like all Stevens' mature poems, in the space between these three positions. Each position is the mirage of the others. Each generates the others. Each is impossible without the others. Stevens is not confused or willfully contradictory. He is caught in an inevitable oscillation within language and within the experiences language both imitates and creates, in another version of the same oscillation. It is impossible to have creation without discovery, or discovery, illustration, without creation, without the joy of language when it is the human being who speaks it out of desire. There is no invention (in the sense of discovery) without invention (in the sense of creation). Until the lover, the believer, and the poet speak there is no essential poem. The essential poem exists only in lesser poems. Nevertheless, the essential poem then seems always to have been there all along and to bind together all the lesser poems. It makes them whole or creates out of them the poem of the whole – that is, something that moves, like time, always toward the whole, toward an end it can never reach.

The answer to my initial question about Stevens' poem, "Why can the sun not be named directly here?," is now clear enough. It is as clear as such things can be, as clear as looking the sun in the eye. The word "sun" exists, and the sun is named indirectly in manifold ways in the poem. To reduce the sun to its seeming proper name, however, would mislead the reader into thinking that the "subject" or the "object" of the poem, its controlling head meaning, is the literal, physical sun, whereas the sun, named in riddling condensations and displacements in the poem, is only one link in a chain of such dislocations naming "the essential poem at the centre of things." This essential poem in its turn, as the word "poem" indicates, is something made in the illustrations of it. Poiēsis means "making." The central poem proceeds from those illustrations, though it also exceeds and precedes any illustration.

At the center of the maze or whirlpool of words that makes up Stevens' "A Primitive like an Orb" is an unknown X that cannot be named except in figure. Those names are therefore not figurative substitutions for a literal word labeling an object open to seeing or to theory. They are tropes of something that is neither a word, nor a thought, nor a thing, nor a force – but is not nothing either. It is, in Stevens' precise phrase, "the giant of nothingness," something that is and is not and therefore is. This "giant" is word, thought, thing, force, person, all at once, all and none. It therefore obliterates or disqualifies the oppositions needed to make a comprehensible topology of the figures and concepts in the poem. The poem cannot quite be thought through clearly, though, as my discussion shows, there is much to be said in commentary on it. Nevertheless, the progress of the commentary gradually deprives the interpreter of the clear distinctions between subjective, objective, and linguistic; literal and figurative, on which explication has traditionally depended for its clarities. The interpreter is left with a paradoxical space at once interior and exterior, objective and linguistic, a space of elements organized as rotating rings around a center that cannot be named or identified as such and that is, moreover, not at the center at all but "eccentric," out beyond the periphery, like a thunderstorm over the horizon. "A Primitive like an Orb," in short, "[resists] the intelligence almost successfully," as Stevens says poetry must do (*Opus*, 171).

Notes

1. *Collected Poems*, ll. 440–3. Citations from this poem will henceforth be identified by line numbers only. Other citations from Stevens are identified by page numbers in *Poems* and *Opus Posthumous*.
2. I have used, with slight alteration, the translation by Gayatri Chakravorty Spivak (pp. 91–2).
3. For this word see Abraham, and see Derrida's discussion of Abraham's use of this word ("Fors" pp. 7–82, esp. 11). For an English translation of this essay see Barbara Johnson, "Fors."
4. For the translation, see the Norton Critical Edition (119); for the German text, see the Hamburger Ausgabe (pp. 147, 148).

Works Cited

Abraham, Nicolas, "L'écorce et le noyau," *Critique* 24 (1968), 162–181.

Claudel, Paul, and André Gide, *Correspondance: 1899–1926* (Paris, 1949).

Derrida, Jacques, *De la grammatologie* (Paris, 1967).

Derrida, Jacques, "Fors," pref. to *Cryptonymie: Le verbier de l'homme aux loups*, by Nicolas Abraham and Maria Torok (Paris, 1976), pp. 7–82.

Goethe, Johann Wolfgang von, *Faust*, ed. Cyrus Hamlin, trans. Walter Arndt, Norton Critical Ed. (New York, 1976).

Goethe, Johann Wolfgang von, *Faust*, vol. 3 of *Werke*, Hamburger Ausgabe, 14 vols. (Hambrug, 1972).

Hammond, Mac, "On the Grammar of Wallace Stevens," *The Act of the Mind: Essays on the Poetry of Wallace Stevens*, eds. Roy Harvey Pearce and J. Hillis Miller (Baltimore, 1965), pp. 179–184.

Jakobson, Roman, "Poetry of Grammar and Grammar of Poetry," *Lingua* 21 (1968), 597–609.

Johnson, Barbara, trans. "Fors," by Jacques Derrida, *Georgia Review* 31 (1977), 64–116.

Pater, Walter, "Style," *Appreciations, with an Essay on Style* (London, 1910), pp. 5–38.

Stevens, Wallace, *The Collected Poems* (New York, 1954).

Stevens, Wallace, *Opus Posthumous* (New York, 1957).

15

Prosopopoeia in Hardy and Stevens

In a remarkable essay on the critical theory of Michael Riffaterre,[1] Paul de Man moves towards the conclusion that prosopopoeia, the ascription of a name, a face or a voice to the absent, the inanimate, or the dead, is the fundamental trope of lyric poetry. Prosopopoeia is more essential to poetry, de Man argues, even than metaphor. Without prosopopoeia no poetry, though prosopopoeia is, for him, fictive, without ontological ground. A mountain does not have a face, but though the poet can expunge metaphor from his language, see things "with the hottest fire of sight," as Wallace Stevens says, "without evasion by a single metaphor,"[2] he cannot avoid those personifications that are woven into the integral fabric of our language, like "face of a mountain," "headland," "eye of a storm." This essay explores the consequences of this fact about poetic language through discussion of two poems, Thomas Hardy's "The Pedigree" and Wallace Stevens' "Not Ideas about the Thing but the Thing Itself," along with ancillary passages about prosopopoeia in a pamphlet by Immanuel Kant and in Hardy's book of short stories, *A Group of Noble Dames*.

For Kant, the personification of the moral law as a veiled Isis is merely "an *aesthetic* manner of representing" something beyond all figuration and especially beyond personification. The moral law is not a person. It is permitted to use such personifications as long as we begin with the naked concept and as long as we understand that the personification is a merely sensible, analogical, and aesthetic presentation of something that is unavailable to the senses, not able to be grasped by any trope, and invisible behind the veil of all aesthetic representations.[3]

I mean to argue here, against Kant, that the prosopopoeia is not added to something that has the clarity of philosophical reason and has been already taken back to first principles. The personification of the moral law as a veiled goddess is fundamental, original, there from the beginning. It cannot be erased or suspended by a return to clear, philosophical, reasonable, non-figurative first principles. The demand made on us by the moral law is always made through the veil of personification. The same thing may be said of the claims made on us by lyric poetry and by works of fiction. Prosopopoeia is not adventitious in them but essential.

Paragraphs at the end of the first story in Thomas Hardy's *A Group of Noble Dames* introduce the topic of prosopopoeia. The issue of prosopopoeia is already folded within the frame story. This frame story is introduced only at the end of the first story proper. As Kathy Psomiades observes in a brilliant unpublished essay on *A Group of Noble Dames*, in this case the frame is framed by what it frames. In these paragraphs the frame–story narrator draws a parallel between the bringing to life of the stuffed birds, "deformed butterflies, fossil ox-horns, prehistoric dung-mixens"[4] in the provincial museum where the male members of an antiquarian club tell their stories about dead women, and, on the other hand, the bringing to life of the dead noble dames in the act of story-telling. Both these events are prosopopoeias in the strictest dictionary sense. They give life to the absent, the inanimate, the dead. Here is the passage:

> As the members waited they grew chilly, although it was only autumn, and a fire was lighted, which threw a cheerful shine upon the varnished skulls, urns, penates, tesserae, costumes, coats of mail, weapons, and missals, animated the fossilized ichthyosaurus and iguanodon; while the dead eyes of the stuffed birds – those never-absent familiars in such collections, though murdered to extinction out-of-doors – flashed as they had flashed to the rising sun above the neighbouring moors on the fatal morning when the trigger was pulled which ended their little flight . . . Many, indeed, were the legends and traditions of gentle and noble dames, renowned in times past in that part of England, whose actions and passions were now, but for men's memories, buried under the brief inscription on a tomb or an entry of dates in a dry pedigree. (49–50)

As the firelight animates the stuffed birds and animals in the museum, so the memorial story-telling of *A Group of Noble Dames* brings the dead women back to life, animates them, lets them speak again. What is problematic about this act of personification is most fully developed in the Preface to *A Group of Noble Dames*. It is presented by way of the image of the pedigree. The opening of the Preface of *A Group of Noble Dames* is an extraordinary affirmation of the power of prosopopoeia to raise the dead. This power of resurrection is like falling in love with a statue and giving it a voice, a face, a personality. This is, in fact, what the heroine of "Barbara of the House of Grebe" does. At the same time, however, Hardy at least implicitly recognizes that the act of prosopopoeia is fictive, illusory, mystified, as deluded as falling in love with a statue. The personalities that are raised from the dead were never there as such nor can they in any way be verified to have been there. Here is Hardy's

account of this process. It is the process of "reading" "the pedigrees of
our county families." Such pedigrees are rudimentary, iconic poems.
They mix words and the diagrammatic or ideographic feature of "family
trees."

> The pedigree of our county families, arranged in diagrams on the pages of
> county histories, mostly appear at first sight to be as barren of any touch of
> nature as a table of logarithms. But given a clue – the faintest tradition of
> what went on behind the scenes, and this dryness as of dust may be
> transformed into a palpitating drama. More, the careful comparison of
> dates alone – that of birth with marriage, of marrage with death, of one
> marriage, birth, or death with a kindred marriage, birth, or death – will
> often effect the same transformation, and anybody practised in raising
> images from such genealogies finds himself unconsciously filling into the
> framework the motives, passions, and personal qualities which would
> appear to be the single explanation possible of some extraordinary
> conjunction in times, events, and personages that occasionally marks these
> reticent family records.
>   Out of such pedigrees and supplementary material most of the
> following stories have arisen and taken shape. (vii)

In this extraordinary passage, each story is seen as ,rising like a ghost
from the dry bones and dust of the schematic pedigree on the page. Or
rather, first the personalities arise, spontaneously, "unconsciously," as
Hardy says, as the only possible explanation of a given conjunction of
times, the dry facts of marriage, birth and death. Then the story is
written down. The story is figuratively another pedigree, in the sense
that it is black marks on the page from which the reader raises the
personalities and the story that were originally suggested to Hardy by the
diagrammatic pedigrees, as dead on the page as a table of logarithms.
Hardy does not say that what is raised was what was really there, but that
"the motives, passions, and personal qualities . . . would appear to be
the single explanation possible of some extraordinary conjunction."
What Hardy says is rather like what Sigmund Freud says about
"constructions in analysis."[5] The analyst's construction ("You had a
passion for Frau X," or whatever) is the only possible explanation of the
patient's memories and symptoms, but there is no way whatsoever to
verify that construction. In this sense, it is fictive, like all prosopopoeias,
like, for example, my ascription of an interiority or selfhood like my
own to the faces of those loved ones around me.
    If Hardy's framing in the Preface and in the frame story describes the
fiction of prosopopoeia as the source of the stories, the stories themselves
in *A Group of Noble Dames* are about the devastating effects of the same
process. An example is Barbara's infatuation with a face, which

becomes, after her husband's death, infatuation with his statue. When she is cured of that infatuation by her cruel second husband, her insane laughter is like the laughter of Jocelyn Pierston in the original version of Hardy's *The Well-Beloved*. Both Barbara and Jocelyn suffer the madness of insight into the fact that personification is fictive. It is not that Barbara has loved a statue, but that her first husband was in a sense also a statue. She did not love him. She loved his face and figure and raised a supposititious personality on that iconic basis. The mutilation of the face first of the real husband and then of his statue shows her this fact and leads to her mad laughter. Insight into the power of prosopopoeia is intolerable. No human being can live with it. Barbara, in "Barbara of the House of Grebe," shifts immediately to an infatuation with a displaced substitute for the substitute, that is, with her second husband, who replaces the statue of her first husband, that replaces the first husband himself. Barbara clings to Uplandtowers, her second husband, bears him baby after baby, in a frenzy of sexual bonding. It is no wonder the male club members who hear the physician tell this story conspicuously misunderstand it and make absurd comments on it in the paragraphs that end the story. The listener or reader too cannot look the meaning of this story in the face. We return spontaneously to that ascription of a personality not only to the people around us but even to inanimate things, as in my figure of looking the truth in the face.

I turn now to Hardy's poem, "The Pedigree." This poem has rarely been anthologized or interpreted. It is an example of the many extraordinary poems the reader may find more or less buried in the splendid abundance of Hardy's poetry. "The Pedigree" makes a series of transformative equivalences from stanza to stanza. These are in fact the same set of equivalences on which Hardy's novel, *The Well-Beloved*, is based, or rather, they are the symmetrical narcissistic image of those equivalences. The novel is in the poem as mirror image. Here, first, is the passage from *The Well-Beloved* on which "The Pedigree" might be said to be a commentary, or vice versa. Both texts echo Shelley's fragment, "To the Moon," in which the moon is "ever changing, like a joyless eye / That finds no object worth its constancy":

He was subject to gigantic fantasies still. In spite of himself, the sight of the new moon, as representing one, who, by her so-called inconstancy, acted up to his own idea of a migratory Well-Beloved, made him feel as if his wraith in a changed sex had suddenly looked over the horizon at him. In a crowd secretly, or in solitude boldly, he had often bowed the knee three times to this sisterly divinity on her first appearance monthly, and directed a kiss toward her shining shape.[6]

Here is "The Pedigree." The same motifs are present as in the passage
from *The Well-Beloved*, but in the case of the poem, the meaning emerges
from the superimposition of its successive stanzas.

The Pedigree

I

I bent in the deep of night
Over a pedigree the chronicler gave
As mine; and as I bent there, half-unrobed,
The uncurtained panes of my window-square let in the watery light
Of the moon in its old age:
And green-rheumed clouds were hurrying past where mute and cold
it globed
Like a drifting dolphin's eye seen through a lapping wave.

II

So, scanning my sire-sown tree,
And the hieroglyphs of this spouse tied to that,
With offspring mapped below in lineage,
Till the tangles troubled me,
The branches seemed to twist into a seared and cynic face
Which winked and tokened towards the window like a Mage
Enchanting me to gaze again thereat.

III

It was a mirror now,
And in a long perspective I could trace
Of my begetters, dwindling backward each past each
All with the kindred look
Whose names had since been inked down in their place
On the recorder's book,
Generation and generation of my mien, and build, and brow.

IV

And then did I divine
That every heave and coil and move I made
Within my brain, and in my mood and speech,
Was in the glass portrayed
As long forestalled by their so making it;
The first of them, the primest fuglemen of my line,
Being fogged in far antiqueness past surmise and reason's reach.

V

Said I then, sunk in tone,
'I am merest mimicker and counterfeit! –
Though thinking, *I am I,*
And what I do I do myself alone.'
– The cynic twist of the page thereat unknit
Back to its normal figure, having wrought its purport wry,
The Mage's mirror left the window–square,
And the stained moon and drift retook their places there.

(1916)[7]

The first stanza sets the "literal" scene of the poem. The poet studies his pedigree by moonlight. Already a figure enters the poem, however, as well as an echo before and after of other texts. The image is an ugly one, but powerful. The moon is an old woman with a watery eye, like Yeats's moon, in its old age, variant of Shelley's: "Crazed through much child-bearing / The moon is staggering in the sky."[8] Or rather the moon, for Hardy, *is* the old eye, grotesquely detached from its body, open and yet alien, green–rheumed, mute and cold, a dead eye, closed mysteriously in on itself, keeping its secrets, "like a drifting dolphin's eye seen through a lapping wave." A detached eye is, Freud argues in his reading of Hoffmann's *The Sandman*, the symbol of something else missing, of castration in short, or of the female pudendum.[9] Is this equation at work here? The poet's confrontation of a female moon which turns into his own image in the mirror matches, in any case, the meeting of male Narcissist and sisterly counter-image in Shelley's "To the Moon." It matches also that strange passage in *The Well-Beloved* I have quoted. In the latter, the reader will remember, Jocelyn bows the knee three times to his "sisterly divinity" the moon, seeing in her "his wraith," his double "in a changed sex."

In the second and third stanzas of Hardy's poem, the major figurative transformation takes place. The window turns into a mirror and the pedigree into the face of an enchanter who produces magic visions in that mirror. A scene of necromancy superimposes itself in palimpsest on the "realistic" scene of the first stanza. That realism has already been perturbed by the turning of the moon into an uncannily detached eye, with its disturbing sexual implications.

The change into a scene of magic potentiality goes by way of another figure, the figure of figuration itself. The word "pedigree" comes from the Old French *pie de grue*, crane's foot, called that from the lines in a genealogical tree. The spectacle of a man poring over his lineage, trying to confirm who he is by identifying who he has come from, studying that crane's foot like a soothsayer reading tea-leaves, palms, or bird entrails, must have struck those Old French as more than faintly ludicrous. The lines of genealogical "descent" mapped out on the page are of course a schematic graphing of that descent. They make a spatial figure for a temporal process which does not involve "lines" as such at all. This figure is as arbitrary and artificial, and yet as socially binding, as the tangled network of kinship names itself. In response to an irresistible instinct of sign-making and sign-reading, men have seen those graphed lines in turn as an emblem: as a tree, as a map, or as writing in hieroglyphs, or as a crane's foot, or as a seared and cynic face. What was already a conventional sign is further metamorphosed into another sign, according to that irrepressible tendency in signs, since they are metaphorical in the first place, to proliferate laterally into further metaphors and metaphors of metaphors. The end point of this series of transformations of figure into figure is a prosopopoeia, a face, or rather, it is appropriately an endless series of faces, one behind the other, as though there were no end to the power of personification, no getting behind or beneath this figure to some literal ground.

Hardy's poem depends throughout on the figure of lines. It depends on the inherent tendency in man the sign-making and sign-using animal to take any configuration of lines, natural or artificial, as a hieroglyph, as some kind of signifying token. The poem depends also on the inherent tendency of such hieroglyphs to be multiple, to multiply metaphors. In Hardy's poem the pedigree becomes a tree, becomes a text in "hiero-glyphs," becomes a map, becomes a face. The lines "charactered" on a man's face are, of course, an index to his "character," as "cynic," for ex-ample, or naïve, according to a play on the word and the concept of "char-acter" which is implicit in Hardy's poem, though the word itself does not appear. A "character" is an incised sign, made of crisscrossing lines. It is a hieroglyph, but the ultimate hieroglyph may be a character, a face.

What each man reads in the signs confronting him, characters, hieroglyphs, tree, crane's foot, is his own face in the mirror. This is so because there are no meanings in any configuration of intersecting lines but those man has put into it or has had put into it by his "begetters." Those begetters are sower sires who have begotten him by begetting the languages within which he is inscribed. In the third stanza of "The Pedigree," the window turns into a mirror, and the sisterly image of the moon, the speaker's double in a changed sex, turns into his own face or rather into the faces of all those forebears, "with the kindred look," one behind the other, "dwindling backward each past each." The face in the mirror is *mise en abîme*, as if there were a double mirror, not a single one. The multiple image in the mirror is like that in Charles Addams' cartoon of the man in the barber chair confronting in reflection a receding series of men in barber chairs.

The result of the poet's encounter with all his doubling ancestors, "generation and generation of my mien, and build, and brow," is not, as might perhaps have been expected, the making solid of his selfhood by grounding it in his heritage, as a tree is rooted in the earth, but, characteristically for Hardy, just the opposite. It is the reduction of his every thought and gesture to a hollow repetition. He becomes a mere copy and fake. For Hardy, in this poem at least, authentic selfhood lies only in originality and autonomy. The speaker discovers that when he most seems to have these he least has them. He is the copy of his image in the mirror rather than the source of an image that copies him. It is as though the infinitesimal time lag between original and copy went the other way. It is as though my mirror image were to make a movement or gesture an instant before I do, coercing my every move, even anticipating my thoughts, feelings and speech, things that would seem hidden from mirroring:

> Said I then, sunk in tone,
> 'I am merest mimicker and counterfeit –
> Though thinking, *I am I,*
> *And what I do I do myself alone.*'

For "archaic" or traditional man, scholars such as Mircea Eliade say, an action has validity only if it is a copy of some ancestral archetypal pattern. For Hardy it is the opposite. All his work, including *The Well-Beloved*, finds one of the most disastrous ways in which it is impossible to "undo the done" to be the way I am forced, in spite of myself, to repeat what has already been done before. I am forced to make myself one of a long row. I am nothing if I am a mere copy, and yet as soon as I think or do, whatever I think or do. I am nothing but a mere copy. The image in "The Pedigree' of the "heave and coil and move" within the speaker's brain not only picks up from elsewhere in the poem the figure of tangled lines. It also parallels a grotesque image in the "Forescene" of *The Dynasts*. There the whole universe is a gigantic pulsating brain made of "innumerous coils, / Twining and serpenting round and through. / Also retracting threads like gossamers – / Except in being irresistible."[10]

In "The Pedigree," the "I am I" of God, generating himself in self-reflexive relation to himself, is the model for Hardy's impossible ideal of independent human selfhood. This would be another "I am I," a self-enclosed circuit of reflection, I looking at the other I in the mirror, as Narcissus beheld his image and loved it, making and sustaining himself in self-admiration. In "The Pedigree" this becomes a mocking parody in which the I is a false mimicking copy of that previous I in the mirror. That specular I does not copy me but has "forestalled" me, has paralyzed my every move even before I make it. Rather "they have" forestalled me, since the image in the mirror is doubled and redoubled to infinity, image behind image. They force me to copy them. Moreover, the original image behind the row of images is not single but multiple. It is a multiplicity lost in the fogs of past time, unreachable by guesswork or by logical deduction, "past surmise and reason's reach." The initiating "origin" cannot be grounded in the principle of reason, the *logos*. The row is, rather, groundless. It is abyssed.

Even those grand multiple ever-repeating originals, moreover, were not fathers, potent generators, initiators laying down a line. They were sign-makers, signal-swingers, tokeners. They offered a copied model for others to imitate, according to Hardy's striking use here of one of his odd words: "The first of them, the primest *fuglemen* of my line, / Being fogged in far antiqueness . . ." (my italics). A fugleman, according to the *NED*, is a "soldier especially expert and well drilled, formerly placed in front of a regiment or company as an example or model to others in their exercises." The word comes from the German *Flugelmann*, "leader of the file," from *Flugel*, "wing," plus *Mann*, "man." To fugle is "to do the duty of a fugleman; to act as guide or director; to make signals," or, figuratively, "to give an example of (something) to someone." To fugle is also slang for "to cheat, trick." The example given by the *NED* has a sexual implication. To fugle is to mislead, to seduce: "Who fugell'd the Parson's fine Maid?" (1729). A fugleman is not an originator. He is himself a well-drilled copy who stands at the wing and who passes on to others a pattern, perhaps a deceitful pattern, by the wing-like beating of his arms and legs, making signals. Hardy uses this strange word at least one other time in his work. This is in the extraordinary episode in *The Woodlanders* that describes John South's belief that his life is tied to the great elm tree which stands outside his window: "As the tree waved South waved his head, making it his fugleman with abject obedience."[11]

For Hardy in "The Pedigree," as I have noted, "the first of them" are already multiple, not single. He says "primest fugle*men* of my line" where one might expect fugle*man*. The later always mimics the earlier in a perpetual reversal of time, or in a treading water of time, forbidding any novelty, any autonomy, any new beginning, any "*I am I, / And what I do I do myself alone.*" Whatever I do my fuglemen have already been there first. I can never be more than a follower, the momentary last of the line, never be an initiator, a first. The concept of "archetype," as "The Pedigree" shows Hardy knew, is inherently contradictory. Any type (from the Greek word *tupos*, "informing matrix"), is already divided within itself. It is multiple, and it is an iteration. It is already secondary to any *arché* or origin.

At the end of "The Pedigree" the mirror becomes a window again. Through that window the poet sees the moon again in its drift of clouds.

The poet returns to the situation of Jocelyn when he bows the knee three times to his sisterly divinity the moon. The sorry wisdom the poet learns from his magic mirror is the knowledge Jocelyn tries, unsuccessfully, to avoid acquiring. Jocelyn's half-knowledge, his attempt to avoid being a merest mimicker and counterfeit, inhibits him from joining himself to any of the Avices, so repeating his ancestors. By an inescapable law in Hardy's universe, Jocelyn becomes as much a repetition by doing nothing, by refraining from action or marriage, as he would have if he had plunged into them. For Hardy, either way you have had it. The tangle of hieroglyphic lines marking out an heredity is a double bind.

If "The Pedigree" is a kind of commentary or footnote on *The Well-Beloved*, the novel, on the other hand, may be said to be in the poem, folded into it, waiting to have its implications unfolded along the narrative line of the novel proper. Just as Jocelyn's attempt to ground himself in a relation to an ideal beloved leads ultimately to a form of depersonalization, so the sequence of figures, figure behind figure, in "The Pedigree" leads to the figure of prosopopoeia as apparently the ultimate or grounding figure in the line. Nevertheless, the figure of prosopopoeia, for Hardy, far from being a solid ground for the self, dissolves into a receding series of faces that is ultimately devastatingly destructive for the poet's sense of himself.

I turn now to Wallace Stevens' "Not Ideas about the Thing but the Thing Itself." Here is the poem:

> Not Ideas about the Thing
> but the Thing Itself
>
> At the earliest ending of winter,
> In March, a scrawny cry from outside
> Seemed like a sound in his mind.
>
> He knew that he heard it,
> A bird's cry, at daylight or before,
> In the early March wind.
>
> The sun was rising at six,
> No longer a battered panache above snow . . .
> It would have been outside.
>
> It was not from the vast ventriloquism
> Of sleep's faded papier-mâché . . .
> The sun was coming from outside.
>
> That scrawny cry – It was
> A chorister whose c preceded the choir.
> It was part of the colossal sun,

Surrounded by its choral rings,
Still far away. It was like
A new knowledge of reality.[12]

The title of this poem, one of Stevens' last, is a little strange. It is not a complete sentence, but hangs in the air: "Not Ideas about the Thing but the Thing Itself." The title is a label for the poem, as a painting may be labelled by its title, a title that may be written on the painting itself. In this case, does Stevens' title name the poem? Is the poem itself not ideas about the thing, but the thing itself? And what would that mean? Or does the title name the experience that the poem records? That would give the title a rather different meaning. Or does the title simply mean: "I wish I could have access to, or write a poem that was, not ideas about the thing but the thing itself"? Is the title optative, a kind of wish, or is the title some form of hypothesis? There is no way to know for sure. The poem does not confirm certainly any reading of the title.

The word "thing" is, moreover, a pregnant word here. It is not easy to be sure what Stevens means by "the thing." Does he mean, by "thing," the sun? Is the thing rather the scrawny cry? In what sense is a scrawny cry a thing? Either to call the sun a thing, or to call a scrawny cry a thing, does not seem quite right. The sun is not something that one normally thinks of as a thing. In attempting to pin down the meaning of "thing," the reader might move in the direction of emphasizing the word "it" that occurs over and over in the poem. "It" has a clear referent: the scrawny cry. "He knew that he heard *it* / A bird's cry . . ." (my italics). But the word recurs: "*It* was not from the vast ventriloquism / Of sleep's faded papier-mâché . . . *it* was a chorister . . . *it* was like . . ." (my italics). By the time the reader reaches the end of those "its," the "it" has detached itself from the cry. *It* has become a name for "the thing itself." Stevens is using the word "thing" in its full etymological and historical complexity, as a name for that which is manifested by the rising of the sun, or by the bird's cry, or by the coming of spring, but still remains always hidden, as "it" or "unnamable X."

"Not Ideas about the Thing but the Thing Itself" is, then, a poem about the appearance of something out of hiddenness, out of occultation: the sun; the cry; spring; the earliest ending of winter; the poet waking up out of sleep, coming into consciousness. These are all said to be like one another, metaphors for one another. They were all forms of appearance that are related to the thing itself, whatever *that* is: some kind of "it." A "thing," in the sense of a gathering together, as in a medieval assemblage of people; a "thing" in the sense of some substratum which is hidden and never appears, something that remains outside – these are versions of the thing.

The poem depends, in its lateral dislocations, circling around the thing itself, on synaesthesia: a visual thing is expressed in terms of an audible thing. The bird's cry announces the rising of the sun. There is a lateral metaphor in the poem that says "a chorus," a great crowd of people singing something like a Bach mass, "is like" the appearance of the sun. This displacement of sight to sound in the description of the sunrise reminds me not of Walt Whitman, as it does Harold Bloom, but of Goethe in the great opening of the second part of *Faust* where the sun rises as a loud noise, as a tremendous racket. In the passage in *Faust*, as in the poem by Stevens, there is the same displacement from sight to sound. In both cases this displacement has something to do with the impossibility of naming, in literal language, what is behind the appearance of the sun. You cannot look the sun in the eye, and you cannot name it as such, so it seems, so instead of naming it you name the great chorus. The "chorister whose c preceded the choir" is that little pitch-pipe noise that you hear in an *a cappella* choir, the muted, soft, scrawny "c" you hear before the whole noise begins. That sound is a figure here for the literal bird's cry that announces the appearance of the sun, blinding and deafening, and the earliest approach of spring too. The mixture or displacement of senses is fundamental to this poem because it is a lateral dislocation expressing another dislocation, the displacement from the hidden "thing" or "it" to any manifestation or metaphors of it.

Like so many of Stevens' poems, this one too is fragile, evanescent. It is a poem about thresholds. The poem says in effect that "it" – the cry that has become all these other things – is a new knowledge of reality just at that borderline moment before the sun rises. At that moment alone one learns something about reality. Once the sun has risen above the horizon, and the chorus is singing full-blast, one is in the ordinary world, where one has only ideas about the thing. The thing itself takes place and instantly vanishes only at that point: at the earliest ending of winter.

I come finally to the word "panache" and to prosopopoeia in this poem. A "panache" is a tuft of feathers, as on a helmet. A "panache" is also a rare astronomer's word for a solar protuberance. The word comes from the Italian *panachio*, which is from the Latin *penna*, "a feather." Only secondarily does the word mean flamboyant or flagrant behaviour. When Stevens says that "The sun was rising at six, / No longer a battered panache above snow," he must have been reading the dictionary. Stevens must mean to describe the sun rising as if it were that tuft of feathers on a helmet. This is a latent personification of the sun. The sun is a person, like that giant on the horizon he projects in "A Primitive Like an Orb." The seeing of the sun as a person is another version of that displacement from sight to sound, in the sense that it is both a revelation – something that carries meaning – and at the same time another covering-over. The prosopopoeia is another inadequate figure. It is appropriate here to remember another poem by Stevens, "The Snow Man." If the "battered panache above snow" is a helmet with a tuft of feathers on it, that seems a distant displacement of the famous snow man. Stevens' "thing itself," so powerfully anthropomorphized in this poem, is something like the Kantian *Ding an sich*. For Stevens as for Kant the thing itself is always absent, imperceptible, always outside any perception, any idea, any image, though it is what motivates all perceiving, thinking, and naming. It is what most demands to be perceived, thought, and named, though this is a demand that can never properly be fulfilled. Since the thing itself is always outside any perceiving, thinking, or naming it can only be perceived, thought or named in figures or in negations, as not this or not that, or as no more than like this or like that, in a resemblance that is not an assimilation, nor a use of negatives as part of a dialectical sublation. The scrawny cry "seemed *like* a sound in his mind." "It was *like* / A new knowledge of reality." The sun was "*no longer* a battered panache above snow." "It was *not* from the vast ventriloquism / Of sleep's faded papier-mâché."

Though one cannot say what the "it" or the "thing itself" is, one can know that it is always outside whatever can be said of it. Though the scrawny cry, for example, "seemed like a sound in his mind," it was in fact "from outside." Or, "it would have been outside" (an extremely odd locution: it would have been *if* what? What is the conditional here?). In another line, the poet affirms that "the sun was coming from outside." Outside of what? Presumably outside of everything. Outside the mind. Outside the house. Outside the world, where the sun is when it is invisible, after it has set and before it has risen again. Outside, most of all, language.

The thing itself is outside of everything, outside every perception, thought, or name, whether proper, common, or figurative. It is impossible to call it by name because it is neither sensible (not a thing like other things inside the world) nor intelligible (not inside the mind, not even in the depths of the mind below sleep). It is not a perception, nor a thought, nor a word, but is outside those oppositions or hierarchies between inside and outside (inside the mind as against outside it, and so on). The threshold between all those namable elements and the "it" is before all those oppositions. The "it," therefore, cannot be glimpsed or heard as such. It can only be apprehended in its vanishing in the "sharp flash" at the border that is a kind of abyss between winter and spring ("at the earliest ending of winter"), night and day ("at daylight or before"), between sleep and waking, between mind and things, between the absolute outside and all those insides that divide again into insides and outsides.

The "it," on the outside of these thresholds, is the thing itself, though, as I have said, it is not a thing in the sense that the sun is a thing when we can see it, nor an object of thought, nor able to be named except as what it is *like* or as what it is *not*, including especially and primarily *not like* the human form or face that always intervenes between inside and that absolute outside, between us and it.

Both poems, then, Hardy's and Stevens', are about the necessity of prosopopoeia and at the same time they are, if I dare to use the word, deconstructions of prosopopoeia. Even the most powerful and purest of poets cannot not have prosopopoeia, and yet it is a fictive covering of a non-anthropomorphic "X," what Stevens, in "The Motive for Metaphor," calls "The weight of primary noon, / The ABC of being, / . . . – the sharp flash, / The vital, arrogant, fatal, dominant X."[13] However far back or far out or far in, far far back, out, or in, we go, the human form, face, figure, or rather the words or other signs that ascribe to "the thing itself" a human visage, form, figure, and language are there. Is not prosopopoeia still there, for example, when Stevens calls that X which metaphor allows us to "shrink from" "vital, arrogant, fatal, dominant," as though it were some virile hidalgo or that "giant, on the horizon, glistening" of "A Primitive Like an Orb"?[14]

In "The Pedigree" prosopopoeia is present in the *mise en abîme* of the multiple and multiplying ancestors arising from the dry bones and mathematic design of the poet's pedigree. Those ancestors, the poet says, have programmed me to think and feel according to their paradigms, though my recognizing of this is a depersonalizing of myself. My pedigree and its transmutations into a vision of my begetters, "dwindling backward each past each," show me that "I" am a fictive schemata of signs like the rest.

In "Not Ideas about the Thing but the Thing Itself" one of the "ideas" that irresistibly appears as a way of talking about the "thing" that is always "outside," outside of everything, is the image of the human form, present in "panache" and in that chorister whose c precedes the choir. We cannot not see or hear the it as a person or persons, as a "giant on the horizon" or as a great choir singing, but that seeing or hearing is disqualified by "like" or "not," that is, it is seen or heard as an idea about the thing, not the thing itself. The thing itself cannot be seen, heard, or anthropomorphized. Therefore the poet's wish to have not ideas about the thing but the thing itself can never be fulfilled. It is for this reason, among others, that, as Stevens more than once says, the mind cannot be satisfied, ever.

Notes

1. Paul de Man, "Hypogram and Inscription," *The Resistance to Theory* (Minneapolis, 1986), pp. 27–53.

2. Wallace Stevens, "Credences of Summer," *Collected Poems* (New York, 1954), p. 373.

3. Cited by Jacques Derrida in "Of an Apocalyptic Tone Recently Adopted in Philosophy," *The Oxford Literary Review*, vol. VI (1984) no. 2, p. 20. Translated from Immanuel Kant, "Von einem neuerdings erhobenen vornehmen Ton in der Philosophie" (1796), *Werke*, vol. VI, E. Cassirer, ed. (Berlin, 1923), p. 495. For a fuller citation and discussion of this passage see my *Versions of Pygmalion* (Cambridge, Mass., 1990), pp. 135–7.

4. Thomas Hardy, *A Group of Noble Dames, Writings*, Anniversary Edition, vol. XIII (New York and London, no date), p. 48. Further references to this work will be by page number to this edition.

5. Sigmund Freud, "Constructions in Analysis," *The Complete Psychological Works*, Standard Edition, vol. XXIII (London, 1953), pp. 255–69. For the German original see "Konstruktionen in der Analyse," *Gesammelte Werke*, vol. XVI (London, 1942), pp. 43–56.

6. Thomas Hardy, *The Well-Beloved*, New Wessex Edition (London, 1975), p. 148.

7. Thomas Hardy, *The Complete Poems* (London, 1976), pp. 460–1.

8. W. B. Yeats, "The Crazed Moon," *Collected Poems* (New York, 1958), p. 237.

9. See Sigmund Freud, "The 'Uncanny,'" Standard Edition, vol. XVII, pp. 218–56. For the German original see "Das 'Unheimliche,'" *Gesammelte Werke*, vol. XII, pp. 229–68.

10. Thomas Hardy, *The Dynasts* (London, New York, 1965), pp. 6–7.

11. Thomas Hardy, *The Woodlanders* (London, 1958), p. 97.

12. Wallace Stevens, *Collected Poems*, p. 534.

13. *ibid.*, p. 288.

14. *ibid.*, p. 442.

Index